NEVADA
A JOURNEY OF DISCOVERY

Michael Green

with Susan A. Myers

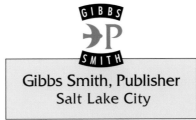

Gibbs Smith, Publisher
Salt Lake City

Published by
Gibbs Smith, Publisher
P.O. Box 667
Layton, Utah 84041
800-748-5439 ext. 148
www.gibbs-smith.com/textbooks

Managing Editor: Susan Allen Myers
Associate Editors: Carrie Gibson, Jennifer Petersen,
Courtney Johnson Thomas, Valerie T. Hatch
Photo Editors: Carrie Gibson, Kris Brunson
Book Designer: Alan Connell
Cover Design: Alan Connell

Cover Photo: © Phil Schofield
Other photos are credited in the back of the book.

Printed and bound in China
ISBN 1-58685-139-x

12 11 10 09 08 07 06   10 9 8 7 6 5 4

ABOUT THE AUTHOR

Dr. Michael Green is a professor of history at the Community College of Southern Nevada, where he teaches United States, Nevada, Civil War, and gaming history. He also teaches for the UNLV History Department and Honors College and teaches a popular video course on Nevada history.

Dr. Green is the author of *Freedom, Union, and Power: Lincoln and His Party During the Civil War*, based on his doctoral dissertation at Columbia University. He was the interviewer and editor for *A Liberal Conscience: Ralph Denton, Nevadan*, University of Nevada Oral History Program, co-author of *A Centennial History of Las Vegas*, to be published for the city centennial in 2005, and the co-editor of the *Nevada Online Encyclopedia for Nevada Humanities*.

In 2005, Dr. Green will become the editor of the *Nevada Historical Society Quarterly*. He is also a columnist for the *Las Vegas Mercury, Las Vegas Senior Life*, and the *Nevada's Washington Watch* newsletter. He has written several museum exhibits, including one for the Clark County Museum.

Dr. Green earned his bachelor's and master's degrees in history at UNLV, where he serves as chair of the Alumni Board of the College of Liberal Arts. He lives in Las Vegas with his wife, Deborah Young, the director of development for UNLV's William F. Harrah College of Hotel Administration, in a home owned by their two cats.

Susan A. Myers is an author and editor and works with historians, reading specialists, authors, editors, and artists to publish quality and engaging history textbooks for elementary and secondary students. She has produced fifteen state history textbooks for schools across the country, including Nevada.

CONTRIBUTORS AND REVIEWERS

Jerome Edwards is an emeritus professor of history at the University of Nevada, Reno. He taught at that institution from 1965 to 2001, and in 2004 was awarded "The Distinguished Faculty Award." He has taught Nevada History since 1976 and is the author of *Pat McCarran, Political Boss of Nevada* (Reno: University of Nevada Press, 1982) and articles on Nevada History. He also wrote *The Foreign Policy of Col. McCormick's Tribune, 1929-1941* (Reno: University of Nevada Press in 1971).

Although retired, he continues teaching Nevada history and other courses.

Michelle Drais Hutchings is a home-grown Nevadan. She earned two bachelor's degrees at Brigham Young University in Utah, then returned to her hometown to teach third grade. While in Nevada she married, started a family, and earned a master's degree in education from Grand Canyon University in Arizona. After teaching elementary school for five years, she moved to the middle school level, where for the past two years she has taught Social Studies and Language Arts in Ely.

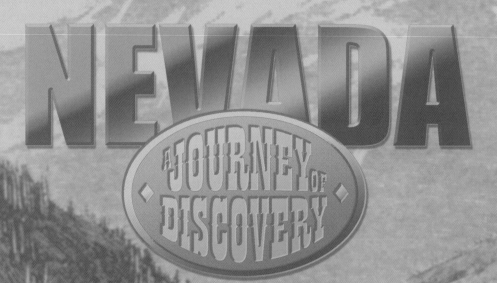

TABLE OF CONTENTS

MAPS, CHARTS, AND GRAPHS

ACTIVITIES AND SKILLS

State Symbols

Bird:
Mountain Bluebird

Nevada's state bird lives in the higher mountains. It eats harmful insects. It sings a short clear song like a robin. School children and the people of Nevada voted as early as 1930 to make it the official state bird, but it didn't happen until 1967.

Tree:

Nevada has two state trees. Both grow on the dry mountains.

Bristlecone Pine

Some people think they are one of the world's oldest living trees. They can survive harsh conditions and survive even when only a few pieces of live bark remain.

Single-Leaf Piñon

This tree smells very good, has short stiff needles, and grows in rocky soil. Native Americans used many parts of the tree. They ate the seeds, used its fibers to make baskets, and made glue from tree gum.

Grass:
Indian Rice Grass

Native Americans once used Indian Rice Grass as a valuable source of food. Today, wildlife and livestock feed on this tough native grass. Indian Rice Grass is found in many regions across the state and can reseed itself even after it has been damaged by fire or animals.

Rock:
Sandstone

Sandstone is found in many natural surroundings and is used to build many beautiful buildings, like Nevada's State Capitol Building. One Las Vegas fifth-grade class suggested sandstone for Nevada's state rock. In June of 1987, the senate bill was signed making sandstone Nevada's official state rock.

Flower:
Sagebrush

Nevada is sometimes called the Sagebrush State. With pale green leaves and yellow flowers in the spring, sagebrush became our state flower in 1917. Farmers tell you that sagebrush is a sign of fertile soil and a great symbol of the American West.

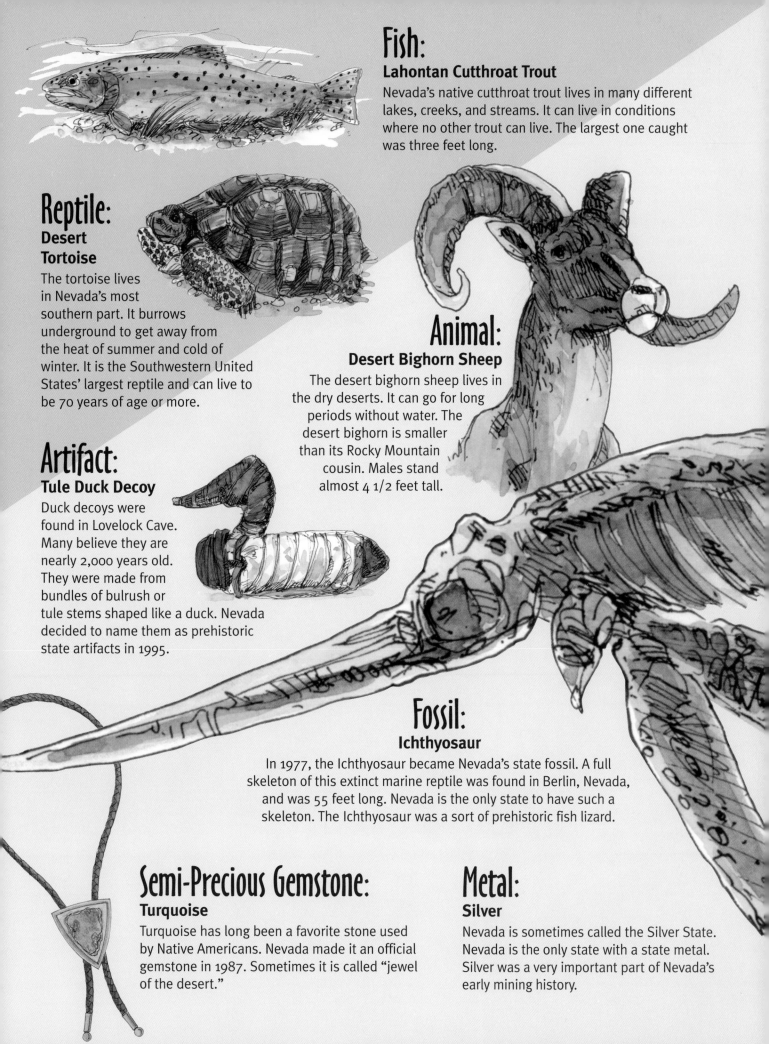

Fish:
Lahontan Cutthroat Trout
Nevada's native cutthroat trout lives in many different lakes, creeks, and streams. It can live in conditions where no other trout can live. The largest one caught was three feet long.

Reptile:
Desert Tortoise
The tortoise lives in Nevada's most southern part. It burrows underground to get away from the heat of summer and cold of winter. It is the Southwestern United States' largest reptile and can live to be 70 years of age or more.

Animal:
Desert Bighorn Sheep
The desert bighorn sheep lives in the dry deserts. It can go for long periods without water. The desert bighorn is smaller than its Rocky Mountain cousin. Males stand almost 4 1/2 feet tall.

Artifact:
Tule Duck Decoy
Duck decoys were found in Lovelock Cave. Many believe they are nearly 2,000 years old. They were made from bundles of bulrush or tule stems shaped like a duck. Nevada decided to name them as prehistoric state artifacts in 1995.

Fossil:
Ichthyosaur
In 1977, the Ichthyosaur became Nevada's state fossil. A full skeleton of this extinct marine reptile was found in Berlin, Nevada, and was 55 feet long. Nevada is the only state to have such a skeleton. The Ichthyosaur was a sort of prehistoric fish lizard.

Semi-Precious Gemstone:
Turquoise
Turquoise has long been a favorite stone used by Native Americans. Nevada made it an official gemstone in 1987. Sometimes it is called "jewel of the desert."

Metal:
Silver
Nevada is sometimes called the Silver State. Nevada is the only state with a state metal. Silver was a very important part of Nevada's early mining history.

PLACES TO LOCATE
Great Basin
Mojave Desert
Pyramid Lake
Walker Lake
Lake Tahoe
Walker River
Muddy River
Virgin River
Colorado River
Owyhee River
Carson River
Humboldt River
Sierra Nevada
Ruby Mountains
Wheeler Peak

WORDS TO UNDERSTAND
adapt
arid
continental drift
elevation
endangered
fault line
geography
geology
igneous rock
invertebrate
metamorphic rock
native
plate tectonics
sediment
sedimentary rock
sink
stalactite
stalagmite

Timeline of Events

600 MYA	500 MYA	400 MYA

Precambrian Era
(85% of the earth's time period)

Paleozoic Era (237–600 million years ago)

Pangaea supercontinent divides.
Shallow seas cover North America.
Trilobites, amphibians, and reptiles live in the seas.

2

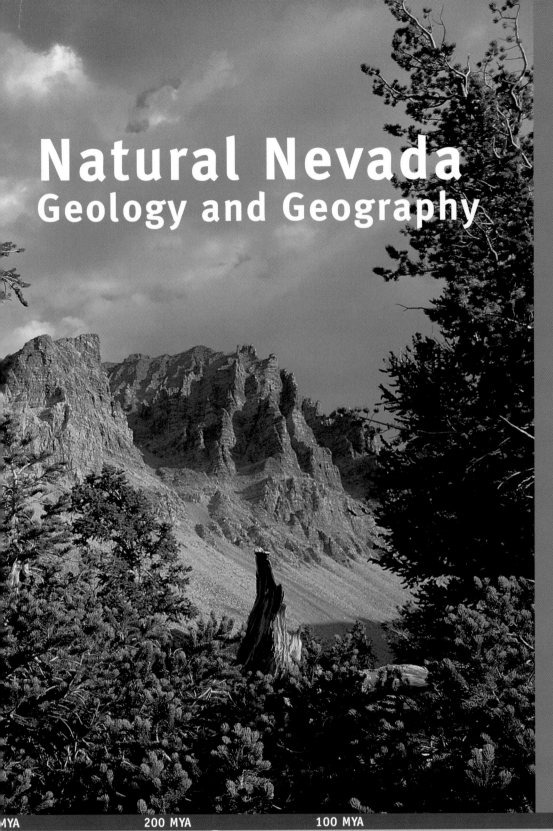

Natural Nevada
Geology and Geography

The bristlecone pine in Great Basin National Park is one of the oldest trees in the state.

Photo by Carolyn Fox

MYA   200 MYA   100 MYA

Mesozoic Era (67–237 million years ago)

Sedimentary rock is formed.
Rocky Mountains begin to take shape.
Volcanic activity creates Valley of Fire, Red Rock Canyon, and the Sierra Nevada.

Cenozoic Era (Today–67 million years ago)

Most of Nevada's major mountains are created then eroded. Volcanoes cover the surface of many Great Basin mountain ranges, making up much of the mountains we see today.

3

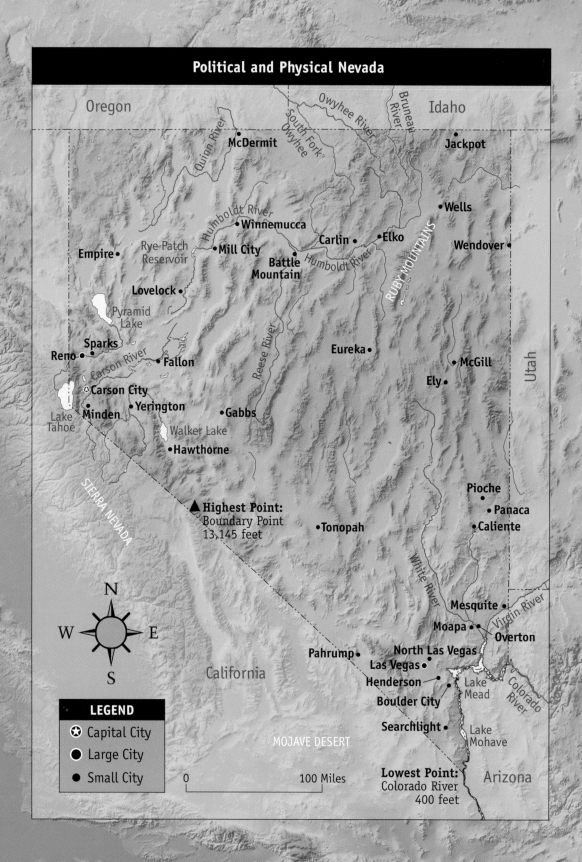

Political and Physical Nevada

Oregon
Idaho

Owyhee River

Bruneau River

Quinn River

South Fork Owyhee

McDermit

Jackpot

Humboldt River

Wells

Winnemucca

Rye Patch Reservoir

Empire

Mill City

Carlin

Elko

Wendover

Battle Mountain

Humboldt River

Lovelock

RUBY MOUNTAINS

Pyramid Lake

Reese River

Sparks

Reno

Carson River

Fallon

Eureka

McGill

Carson City

Ely

Utah

Yerington

Minden

Gabbs

Lake Tahoe

Walker Lake

Hawthorne

SIERRA NEVADA

Pioche

▲ **Highest Point:** Boundary Point 13,145 feet

Panaca

Caliente

Tonopah

White River

N
W   E
S

Mesquite

Virgin River

Moapa

Overton

California

Pahrump

North Las Vegas

Las Vegas

Henderson

Lake Mead

Colorado River

Boulder City

LEGEND
☆ Capital City
⬤ Large City
• Small City

Searchlight

Lake Mohave

MOJAVE DESERT

0   100 Miles

Lowest Point: Colorado River 400 feet

Arizona

A Place Called Nevada

When you think of Nevada, many different images come to mind. Depending on where you live or who you are, you might think of neon-lit casinos and famous entertainers. You might think of mines full of valuable ore and stories of old prospectors, or of snow-capped mountains and dry deserts. Nevada includes all of these and much more.

Different people think differently about our state's features. Some of the titles of books about Nevada have included *The Sagebrush State*, *Desert Challenge*, *A Desert Paradise*, and *The New Western Frontier*. What do these titles tell us about the state? Do you agree or disagree with the titles?

One geographer wrote that Nevada's map looked like "an army of caterpillars crawling toward Mexico." How do you think he came up with that image?

One of Nevada's leading writers said that his native state made him think of:

> Sagebrush that rolled over the vast plateaus and brutal desert mountains like an endless gray sea, ringing the few scattered . . . towns of Nevada so that they were like islands in the sea.

—Robert Laxalt

How the Land Was Formed

Geology is the study of how the earth was formed. Obviously, that is a broad statement—the earth is large and contains different kinds of rock, landforms, and bodies of water. Nevada's geology is incredibly varied. It is a place of high mountains and deep valleys, rolling deserts and life-giving waters.

> Geology is the youngest science. Perhaps this is because it is so imprecise. . . . Chemists solve problems to the sixth decimal place on their computers. Biologists poke and dissect in the laboratory, studying a thin slice of time—the present. Geologists walk around on the little of the earth we see and scratch their heads about the rest.
>
> —G. William Fiero, geologist

A Matter of Time

It is hard to comprehend the long time periods of geology. One geologist explained how to measure time:

> Hold your arms wide apart from your sides. If the beginning of earth time is your right fingertip, then animal life would begin near your right elbow. The Paleozoic clams would be at home from the middle of your left forearm to the beginning of your left index finger. The dinosaurs would cavort along your finger to the last joint. The end of your finger, from last joint to tip, would be the mammal years. And our species? The time people have lived on the earth can be measured by the snip of a fingernail.
>
> —G. William Fiero, geologist

Geologists study rocks, rock layers, land formations, and fossils to learn the history of the land.

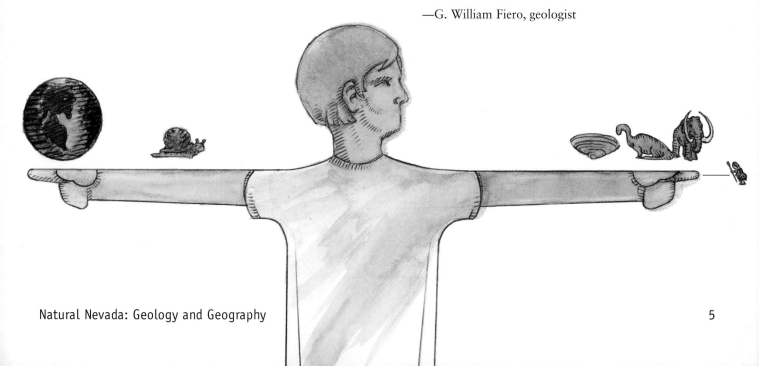

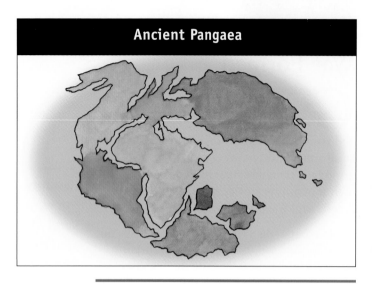

Reveille Range shows mountains formed by volcanic action.

Ancient Pangaea

None of the changes in the earth's surface happened overnight. Scientists think that about 200 million years ago, Nevada and the rest of the North American continent were part of a supercontinent called Pangaea. Pangaea included today's North and South America, Europe, Asia, Africa, and Australia. Over time, underground forces caused the large land masses to drift apart. This is called *continental drift*. As the Atlantic Ocean widened, North America moved to the west.

Plates in Motion

Plate tectonics is the study of how the earth's crust moves. The earth's crust may be made up of around 20 moving plates. These plates carry both the continents and pieces of the ocean floor.

Millions of years ago, some of the plates spread apart, and other plates collided with, or scraped against, each other, forming mountains.

Fault Lines and Earthquakes

Nevada is part of the North American plate and California is part of the Pacific plate. They meet at *fault lines*—dividing points in the earth. These plates are always moving, though we usually don't feel it. At times, however, this movement creates earthquakes.

While California is more famous for them, Nevada also has had plenty of earthquakes. Large earthquakes shook central Nevada in 1954, but quakes have

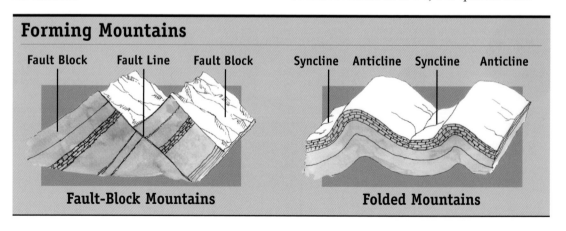

Forming Mountains

Fault Block   Fault Line   Fault Block

Fault-Block Mountains

Syncline   Anticline   Syncline   Anticline

Folded Mountains

What Kind of Rock?

igneous: hardened magma or lava from inside the earth (basalt)

sedimentary: formed by compaction of sediment such as sand or shells (sandstone, limestone, shale)

metamorphic: deeply buried and greatly changed by pressure and heat (slate, quartzite, marble, granite)

gone on for millions of years. They have created at least 160 mountain ranges in Nevada, making up that "army of caterpillars."

Linking the Past to the Present

Has the area where you live been affected by volcanoes, floods, earthquakes, or other geologic activity? Call your state and local emergency preparedness office to see if there are plans to deal with an emergency that could come from any of these natural disasters. Is your family prepared for a disaster?

Ancient Seas and Rock

For millions of years, seas covered parts of our region. Sand drifted in and out with the movement of the water. *Sediment* (loose sand, pebbles, and tiny shells of sea animals) drifted to the bottom of the seas. Over time, the loose sediment was forced together by heat and pressure into layers of sandstone or limestone. As time passed, more layers of sediment added hundreds of feet to the rock.

Mountains and Volcanoes

An age of tremendous volcanic activity took place about 30 million years ago. In the northern Sierra around Lake Tahoe, thick layers of volcanic ash and hardened lava covered the granite rock.

About 10 million years ago, the Sierra began uplifting. The land to the west rose from the ground, and to the east, the land that is now the Carson Valley dropped. Then, over a long, long time, much of the valley filled with sediment.

As soon as mountains rose, wind and water began to erode them. Peaks got lower and sharp edges became smoother. Over time the mountains changed to look more like the peaks you see today.

Nevada's mountains— including Mt. Charleston, the Sierra Nevada, the Ruby Mountains, and Wheeler Peak—are about a million years old.

Minerals From the Ground

Nevada earned its nickname of "the Silver State" with the discovery of the Comstock Lode. It was the first major silver discovery in the United States. Today, however, gold exceeds all other minerals in value.

The minerals we mine today are part of our geologic history. Nevada is rich in minerals. Copper, gold, silver, and other minerals were deposited by volcanic action. How did it happen?

Sandstone and limestone were first deposited as sediment in shallow seas. Then extensive folding, faulting, and other forces formed mountains. Millions of years later, molten rock deep within the earth's crust pushed toward the surface and cooled. The molten rock contained hot mineral solutions that were forced into rock cracks. These minerals are today's silver, gold, and copper.

Nevada also has iron, manganese, tungsten, and mercury deposits in the ground. There is gypsum, limestone, magnetite, and perlite. Nevada's salt is put on icy winter roads.

There are also deposits of oil. Oil comes from ancient deposits of plants and small animals that have been changed by tremendous heat and the weight of earth layers above it. These minerals vary greatly in location, quantity, and usefulness.

When you see large trucks carrying loads of sand, gravel, and cement to building sites, you are witnessing the use of natural building materials from rock.

The rock you see all around you today may have been formed millions of years ago. It may even contain valuable minerals such as copper, gold, or silver!

Something powerful happened here. The wide curved valley and steep valley walls hint at the glacier that once moved slowly downward, carving out the U-shaped canyon. You can see this valley in Lamoille Canyon in the Ruby Mountains.

Prehistoric Animals

Prehistoric animals lived in the water and on the land. The most plentiful Nevada fossils are marine *invertebrates* because Nevada spent thousands of years underwater.

These early creatures are important. Scientists use their remains to learn the age of the rocks in which they are found. Fossils also tell us what kinds of animals and plants once lived in a region, and what the land and climate were like—dry, wet, hot, or very cold. The remains of many ancient animals and plants formed the oil and coal we use today.

You can find a lot of marine fossils in the eastern part of Nevada:

- forams—One-celled animals that look like pieces of wheat or grain imbedded in rocks
- brachiopods—Seashells found in the rocks
- pelecypods—Seashells such as oysters and clams
- gastropods—Snails
- cephalopods—Animals with tentacles, like squid or octopus
- trilobites—Prehistoric animals 2 to 3 inches long

The Ice Age

As the earth cooled, then warmed, over and over again during the Ice Ages, there were more changes to the land. The massive Ice Age glaciers did not cover the warm southern regions of today's United States. However, the extreme cold caused smaller glaciers to form in the high Sierras and other mountain ranges.

As the mountain glaciers slid slowly downward, they carved out long wide valleys. Donner Lake and part of Lake Tahoe were formed this way.

Huge ice dams formed across the Truckee River canyon. When they broke apart, they released walls of water that carried immense boulders downstream. You can see these boulders in the Reno area.

▲ Photo by Jim Stinson

How did volcanoes affect Ice Age glaciers? Heat from the volcanoes helped melt the glaciers on high mountain ranges. Water from melting glaciers rushed downhill and formed large lakes in mountain valleys.

Lake Bonneville

The largest Ice Age lake was Lake Bonneville. It covered much of today's Utah and a small part of Nevada. Today, the Great Salt Lake is a remnant of Lake Bonneville.

Lake Lahontan, another large Ice Age lake, was in Nevada. As the weather warmed even more, the lakes shrank. Today, all that is left of Lahontan are Pyramid and Walker Lakes.

Climate Changes

Geology is also related to climate. Weather patterns have always changed over time. Droughts reduced water levels and increased the temperature, baking the land and causing more water to evaporate. Then, when temperatures fell, glaciers formed at higher elevations. This happened over and over again. Ice Ages came and went. Temperatures got hot, then cooled. Each time this happened, the land changed.

Large Animal Fossils

When the land and climate changed, the kinds of animals changed too. The ancient sea creatures died when the shallow lakes dried up. Land animals took their place.

Nevada is not dinosaur country. The layers of volcanic rock make it hard to find fossils in the western part of the state. However, fossils of large prehistoric mammals—mammoths, sloths, camels, deer, antelope, rhinos, and small horses—have been found.

These early animals are important today. Scientists use their remains to learn the age of the rocks in which they are found. Fossils tell us what kinds of animals and plants once lived in a region, and what the climate was like there—whether it was hot or cold, dry or wet, or if the land was underwater.

▶ Photo by Tom Gamache

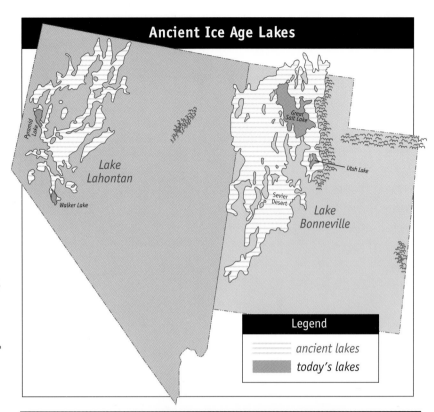

Ancient Ice Age Lakes

Pyramid Lake

Lake Lahontan

Walker Lake

Great Salt Lake

Utah Lake

Sevier Desert

Lake Bonneville

Legend
- ancient lakes
- today's lakes

The Giant Ichthyosaur

The ichthyosaur is our state fossil. It was a giant fish-lizard more than 50 feet long and weighing thousands of pounds. It was as large as today's blue whales. After miners discovered ichthyosaur fossils in central Nevada, the state created a park at the old mining town of Berlin to exhibit them. The remains of about 37 of the animals have been found. Falling ocean tides probably trapped the animals on mudflats that were later buried.

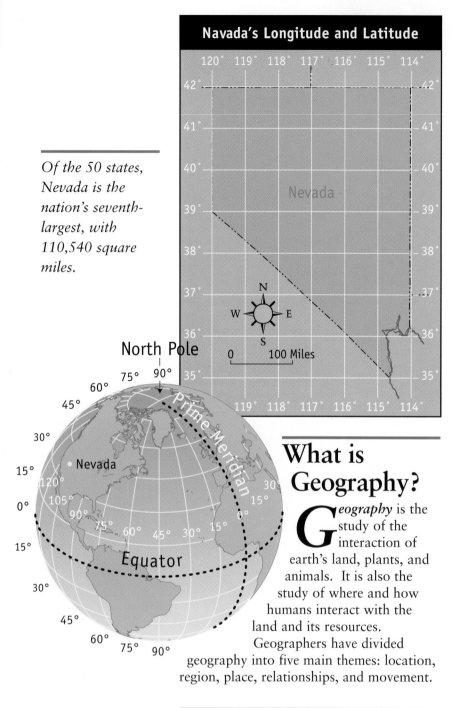

Navada's Longitude and Latitude

Nevada

N
W   E
S

0   100 Miles

North Pole

Of the 50 states, Nevada is the nation's seventh-largest, with 110,540 square miles.

Prime Meridian

Nevada

Equator

Latitude lines run east-west, and longitude lines run north-south.

Latitude lines are numbered north and south of the equator all the way to the North and South Poles. Nevada extends from 35 to 42 degrees north latitude and is closer to the warm equator than to the cold North Pole. This helps explain why Nevada is warmer than places to the north. It also helps explain why the average temperature in northern Nevada is a cool 45 degrees, and in southern Nevada it is a warm 72. Each place has warmer summers and cooler winters.

Longitude lines are also called meridians. The prime meridian runs all the way from the North Pole to the South Pole through Greenwich, England. Longitude lines go from 0 to 180 degrees both east and west. Nevada is at 117 degrees west longitude.

What is Geography?

Geography is the study of the interaction of earth's land, plants, and animals. It is also the study of where and how humans interact with the land and its resources.

Geographers have divided geography into five main themes: location, region, place, relationships, and movement.

Location

You already know Nevada is on the North American continent and in the western part of the United States. You know it is bordered by the large states of California, Oregon, Idaho, Utah, and Arizona.

One of the ways to find Nevada on a globe is by its latitude and longitude.

Regions

A land region is a large land area that has common landforms such as mountains, plains, coastlines, or deserts. A region can also be land in a certain location. Nevada, for example, is a desert region. It is also in the western region of the United States.

Nevada is also part of the Sunbelt. This region includes states stretching from southern California all the way to Florida. The Sunbelt gets its name for obvious reasons—it is sunnier and warmer than in New England or the Pacific Northwest. Many people move to the Sunbelt, so they don't have to deal with cold winters.

The Basin and Range Region

Nevada is part of a very large land region called the Great Basin, or the Basin and Range region. The Great Basin is like a large flat bowl with many small mountain ranges rising up from the desert. The tall Sierra Nevada spreads along the basin's west side, and the majestic Rocky Mountains run along the east side.

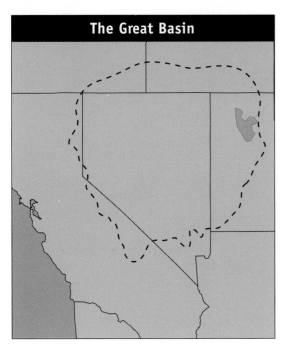

Nevada is part of the Great Basin land region. If you were to draw mountains on the map, where would you put the Sierra Nevada and the Rocky Mountains? They form the sides of the huge land basin. Other mountains are also found throughout the basin region.

Place—Physical and Human Features

All places have both physical features and human features. Physical features are natural and related to the environment—mountains, rivers, and soil, for example. Human features are things we have built and other ways we have changed our environment. Highways, bridges, dams, cities, and plants that are not *native* to the state are all human features. Look out the window. What physical and human features do you see?

Landforms

A landform is a natural feature of the earth's surface. Mountains, basins, and plateaus are all landforms. They are all the result of powerful forces moving inside the earth. Lakes, rivers, islands, peninsulas, and bays are also landforms.

Why Are Mountains Important?

When summer heat melts the snow in the mountains, the water runs in small streams down into the valleys below and supplies water for plants, animals, and people.

People often build towns at the bases of mountains so they can use the mountain water supply. Mountain forests provide lumber. Minerals are often found in the mountains. Mountains provide wonderful places to hike, camp, ski, and enjoy nature.

One man described the Sierra Nevada this way:

> Nothing in nature . . . can present scenery more wild, more rugged, more bold, more grand, more romantic, and beautiful than this mountain scenery. The tall craggy rocks . . . on either side of the deep canyons and gorges . . . The tops of these mountains are carpeted with a heavy coat of green bluegrass. And along the small branches many kinds of wild flowers are to be found.
>
> —James Pritchard, early immigrant

Mountains are very high land formations with large bases and small peaks. A long, wide line of mountains is a mountain range.

Plateaus are high, wide, flat areas many miles across that often end with steep cliffs.

Basins are very large, low, flat areas of land surrounded by mountains or high plateaus. They are shaped like huge bowls. Valleys are much smaller basins between two mountain areas. Most cities, farms, and ranches are in basins and valleys.

11

Great Basin National Park

On those summer days when you yearn to "get away from it all," a trip to a national park may be just what you need. This wild and beautiful land near the Nevada-Utah border is a great place to spend a day or a week walking the mountain trails, fishing for trout in the five lakes and three creeks, or exploring the cool darkness of Lehman Caves. There are four campgrounds where you can listen to coyotes howl at the moon.

Take drinking water with you and wear sturdy hiking boots because the trails are studded with rocks. Be prepared for sudden rainstorms. Watch for rattlesnakes, but leave them alone.

Great Basin National Park

The park, established in 1986, is Nevada's only national park, though there are many state parks and monuments.

Lehman Caves

Sometime in the late 1800s Ab Lehman discovered the mysteries of a large cave with many "rooms," complete with *stalactites* hanging like bumpy icicles from the ceiling, slowly growing a drip at a time. Other formations, called *stalagmites*, had formed upwards as the drips of water deposited minerals ever so slowly. Sometimes, the two had met to form a column. This is still going on today.

Lehman installed ladders and stairs in the caves and started giving tours. Today you can take guided walks in the dark wet caves.

▲ Photo by Larry Prossor

You can watch geology and
nature at work as you explore
Lehman Caves.

Our Hot Dry Climate

The climate is what the weather is like over a long time. In other words, you might have cold or rainy weather one day, a warm breeze another day, and many hot dry days, but the climate would still be a warm dry climate.

Elevation

Southern Nevada's warm climate is partly due to its nearness to the equator. Differences in *elevation* also help explain Nevada's climate. Because it has many high mountains and low deserts, Nevada is a place of extremes.

Usually, the higher a place is above sea level, the cooler it is. This is why you might be very hot while hiking until you get nearer the top of a mountain, where it is cooler. This is also why a hot dry city has snow on the nearby mountaintops.

Rainfall

The average annual rainfall in Nevada is only about 7 inches. But the Sierra Nevada gets more rain. Carson City gets about 11 inches of rain each year, and Reno gets 7.5 inches. People in Las Vegas say they get a little more than 4 inches of rain per year—but it all comes in one day. Flash floods are common.

Desert Water

All people, plants, and animals need water to survive, but nowhere is water so important as in a desert. Here many natural plants survive, but farmers must use irrigation to water crops. People must use natural wells or bring water from rivers in underground pipes to water their lawns and gardens.

Water has been important in deciding how Nevada would be settled. Today, more than 85 percent of Nevadans live in or near either Las Vegas or Reno. One of the main reasons is a major water source near each city. For Reno, it is Lake Tahoe and the Truckee River. For Las Vegas, it used to be underground water. Today, Las Vegas gets most of its water from Lake Mead and the Colorado River.

Drainage Basins

Within a basin, the water from melting mountain snow flows in one main direction to a river, lake, or *sink*.

One northern corner of our state is part of the Columbia River Drainage Basin. The Owyhee River flows into the Snake River,

If there is magic on this earth it lies in water, and nowhere is water so beautiful as in the desert, for nowhere else is it so scarce. In the desert each drop is precious.

—Edward Abbey

▶ Photo by Larry Prossor

The Rainshadow Effect

Nevada is an **arid** state, meaning that it receives little rain. Here is what happens. Far out over the Pacific Ocean, winds pick up moisture from evaporating ocean water. The moist air blows over the coast and continues east.

When the air reaches the Sierra Nevada, it must rise to get over them. As air rises, it cools. Cool air cannot hold as much moisture as warm air does, so the moisture falls to the earth as rain or snow on the mountains. There is little moisture left in the clouds to fall on Nevada.

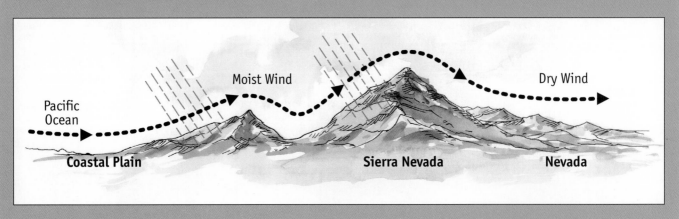

Pacific Ocean · Moist Wind · Dry Wind

Coastal Plain · **Sierra Nevada** · **Nevada**

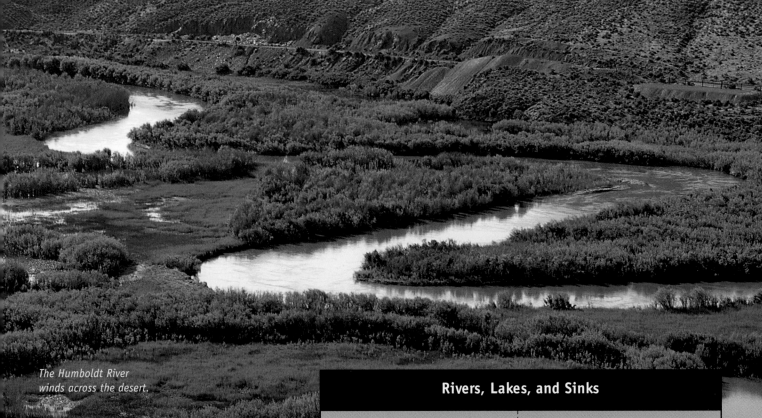

*The Humboldt River
winds across the desert.*

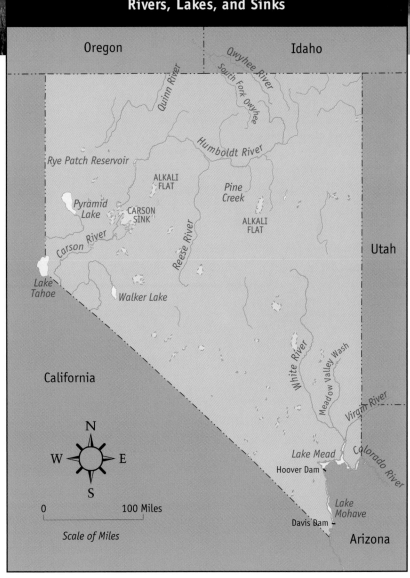

Rivers, Lakes, and Sinks

Oregon   Idaho

Qwyhee River

Quinn River

South Fork Owyhee

Humboldt River

Rye Patch Reservoir

ALKALI
FLAT

Pine
Creek

Pyramid
Lake

CARSON
SINK

Reese River

ALKALI
FLAT

Carson River

Utah

Lake
Tahoe

Walker Lake

White River

Meadow Valley Wash

California

Virgin River

N

Lake Mead

Colorado River

W   E

Hoover Dam

S

0   100 Miles

Lake
Mohave

Davis Dam

Scale of Miles

Arizona

which flows into the Columbia River on its rushing trip to the Pacific Ocean.

The southern tip of Nevada is in the Colorado River Drainage Basin. The muddy Colorado River empties into the Gulf of California.

The Great Basin has many rivers, but none runs out of the basin to the Pacific Ocean. Instead, all of the water flows into lakes or sinks. Sinks get their name because, like your bathroom sink, the water goes down a drain.

The Humboldt River, for example, trickles across Nevada until it drips into the Humboldt Sink. The Carson River drains into the Carson Sink. The Walker River runs into Walker Lake. The Truckee River flows into Pyramid Lake.

All of this may seem less important today because we have roads that lead us across the Great Basin. When the early explorers arrived in the Great Basin, however, they expected the rivers to lead them west to California. Instead, they found too much heat and too few rivers. There were no rivers they could follow all the way to California.

Natural Nevada: Geology and Geography

Lakes Made by Dams

One author wrote that the Colorado River is an "outlaw" because it often came quickly and flooded towns and farms, destroying everything in its path. Dams were needed to control the river.

Hoover Dam was built across the Colorado River, and the water backed up behind the dam and filled in valleys, burying everything. As the water rose higher and higher, Lake Mead was formed. Lake Mohave was formed the same way when Davis Dam was built. Find these dams on the map on page 15.

Today, these lakes are favorite recreational areas in our dry state. Water rushing through the dams' generators produce electricity. The water can be released in a steady flow to avoid floods downstream. You will learn more about dams in another chapter of this book.

Deserts

The Colorado River flows through the heart of the Mojave Desert. Anyone who has traveled through the southwestern United States knows the scene—Joshua trees, cactus, sparse water, red sandstone, lizards and snakes hiding in the shade of boulders, and heat—plenty of heat.

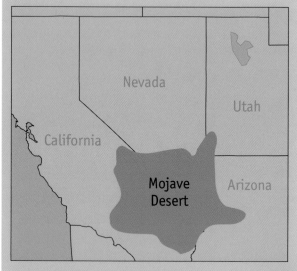

The Mojave Desert

If you travel Interstate 15 from Las Vegas to San Bernardino, California, you will experience part of the Mojave Desert. The Mojave Desert is large—about a quarter of the size of the state of Nevada. Clark County is part of this desert. The desert's climate is hotter and drier than other parts of the Great Basin.

The Mojave Desert is important to understanding Nevada's history. Early explorers and settlers, traveling through the desert on horses or on foot, had a terrible time surviving the heat and lack of water and food.

▲ Photo by Jim Stinson

As glaciers retreated from the Sierra Nevada at the end of the Ice Age, part of the Mojave region was wet, with lakes filled with fish. About 10,000 years ago the ancestors of the Shoshone and Paiute lived along the lakes and in the nearby mountains. Over a long time, the climate became arid and the lakes dried up. Today, only small animals and plants such as the yucca thrive in the desert.

Nevada: A Journey of Discovery

Sagebrush needs little water. Aspen and pine grow in higher, wetter elevations.

Adapting to the Desert

Where you live affects what you do and how you do it. If you are reading this book in Las Vegas, chances are you have little need for a parka. In Elko, winter blizzards may keep you indoors. If you live in Carson City or Reno, you might go to Lake Tahoe for summer fun or winter skiing.

Adjusting your lifestyle to the environment is called *adaptation*. Our desert environment has had a great effect on population growth in different places. While the number of people living in Las Vegas has grown for a variety of reasons, the invention of air-conditioning has a lot to do with it. Early settlers had no desire to spend summers beneath the broiling desert sun.

Desert Plants

Because the climate and rainfall vary in Nevada, so does plant life. Pine, fir, aspen, and juniper trees are abundant in the wetter mountain regions.

Nevada has two state trees. One, the pinyon pine, is common in Nevada because it can grow almost anywhere. The other, the bristlecone pine, received this honor because

it is among the oldest living plants on the planet. Some bristlecone pines in Nevada are thousands of years old.

Other plants grow in the desert. Sagebrush, the state flower, grows throughout Nevada due to a shallow root system that spreads out to absorb water. That means it can grow in dry areas and take full advantage of however much rain and snow there is. In the spring and summer, the gray-green bush produces yellow flowers and a strong aroma and may grow as high as 12 feet.

The shadscale, greasewood, and yellow-flowered rabbit brush grow well in Nevada for the same reasons—a shallow root system and little need for water.

Trees need more water, so they are rare in the desert. Instead, people in southern Nevada are more likely to see shrubs, mesquite, or various kinds of cactus. The Joshua tree grows in the Mojave Desert.

For a few weeks each spring, the desert is alive with wildflowers such as the Indian paintbrush, the blue lupine, and the prickly poppy. Indian rice grass, the state grass, also grows throughout Nevada.

One of Nevada's nicknames is "The Sagebrush State."

Natural Nevada: Geology and Geography

Wild Horses

Federal and state laws protect Nevada's wild horses. A hundred years ago, two million wild horses roamed the West. Today, fewer than 50,000 remain, and about half of them are in Nevada. The federal government and ranchers agree that the horses eat too much of the grass needed to feed cattle and sheep. But Congress passed a law to protect wild horses as "living symbols of the historic and pioneer spirit of the West."

The Bureau of Land Management (BLM) and the State of Nevada have preservation and adoption programs to help save these animals. Each year, the BLM offers about 8,000 wild horses and 500 or more wild burros for adoption. You must pay a fee to adopt an animal and have enough land so it has room to roam. You can find out more information at www.adoptahorse.blm.gov or call 1-866-4mustangs.

Animals

Our state animal, the desert bighorn sheep, lives in the mountains. They eat grass and the fruit of small plants. Once there were many of these animals, but their numbers have declined.

The government has passed laws and set aside land to protect wild animals, but the competition for food continues for bighorn sheep, mountain lions, bears, antelope, elk, and thousands of mule deer. They are all searching for food. Grizzly bears and wolves don't live naturally in Nevada anymore.

Most of Nevada's animals are smaller, including muskrat, porcupine, coyote, red fox, or skunk. Snakes and lizards are very common. Squirrels, chipmunks, gophers, rats, and mice scamper along the ground in great numbers.

Protected Animals

Some animals are *endangered*. This means their species is in danger of disappearing from the earth. It is against the law to harm or kill any of them. Others are in less danger, but are still protected by laws. Sometimes changes in climate affect the fate of these animals. More often, unfortunately, people are the threat—simply because we have moved onto land the animals once used.

One protected animal is the desert tortoise. It lives in the Mojave Desert and other deserts. Government studies found the tortoises to be endangered due to changes in their habitat. In most cases, humans meant no harm to the tortoise, but they built homes and cities on tortoise habitats. Other people drove off-road vehicles through the desert. Better enforcement of the protection laws has helped increase the desert tortoise population. So have programs that allow residents to adopt the tortoises and keep them in their yards where they can be safe.

Birds

Hundreds of types of birds soar above Nevada. The mountain bluebird, our state bird, lives mainly in higher, cooler elevations, but sometimes it flies to the valley in winter when the mountains are covered in snow. Males are bright blue; females are less colorful.

Eagles, hawks, and falcons hover over the highlands in wintertime, and various sparrows, the burrowing owl, the house finch, and the sage grouse cruise above the sagebrush. One of the largest nesting colonies of white pelicans lives at Pyramid Lake, while the chukar partridge, the skittering quail, the vulture, and the raven provide a quest for bird-watchers.

Fish

Some larger birds eat fish, and in Nevada they have many kinds to choose from. Lake Tahoe's Mackinaw trout weighs up to 30 pounds. Two species are rare and have been considered endangered. One is the cui-ui (pronounced kwee-wee), a favorite of Native Americans living near Pyramid Lake.

Another native fish, the devil's hole pupfish, became the center of a lawsuit. Nearby farmers wanted to pump water from their wells, but that would reduce the water in the spring and threaten the fish. Roger Foley, a federal judge and lifelong Nevadan, ruled against the farmers, who then put out a bumper sticker: "Kill the Pupfish—and Foley too!" Both the fish and the judge survived, although the water level dropped even without the pumping.

Nevada may have few lakes, but fish abound in them. The state fish, the Lahontan cutthroat trout, weighing up to 65 pounds, swims in several lakes. Its popularity as a food and a large trophy fish has endangered its survival. The most important fish for sport and food is the rainbow trout, most often found in the Truckee River. Suckers, carps, minnows, and catfish also live in the state's streams, rivers, and lakes.

Birds on the Ground

Not all birds fly above us. The roadrunner is a one-foot-tall, black-and-white bird that prefers walking and running to flying. It eats insects, lizards, and snakes. It is correctly named because it runs along desert roads, but it does not look like the bird you see in the cartoons. It doesn't even go "beep beep." Like any other small desert animal, it has to be careful of coyotes.

Beware of Rattlesnakes!

Desert animals—and you—have to be careful around one of the more common animals found on the desert and valley floors—the rattlesnake. The rattlesnake has diamond-shaped marks on its back and may grow 4 feet long. It tries to stay out of the desert sun and hunt at night—but not always. The rattler gets its name because it rattles its tail when it finds a victim. Its fangs inject small rodents, lizards, and rabbits with deadly poison.

What do you do if you think you have been bitten by a rattler? Look for fang marks and a very nasty bruise. There will be pain, swelling, nausea, weakness, and a rubbery taste in your mouth.

To keep the venom from spreading quickly, keep the bitten area lower than your heart. Avoid using ice, tying off tightly, or trying to suck the venom out of the wound. Go to the nearest medical office for help. Less than 1 percent of rattlesnake bites are fatal.

Tourists, business people, and students flock to Reno, a glittering city at the foot of the Sierra Nevada.

Who Are We?

Many people from around the world come to Nevada—some to visit and others to live. Nevada has a lot to offer. It is the fastest-growing state.

Two urban areas, Las Vegas and Reno, are home to well over 85 percent of Nevada's residents. Las Vegas, with the suburbs of Henderson and North Las Vegas, was the nation's fastest-growing city in 2004. This also reflects geography. Both Las Vegas and Reno were founded because of a water supply. This is especially important in the arid west.

A variety of jobs has attracted many people to live here. Tourism, the building boom, and mining attract many workers. While agriculture is an important industry, hay, potatoes, and dairy farms are less crucial to the economy than ranches, where sheep and cattle roam the vast land. Hotels, casinos, restaurants, mines, ranches, and farms need supplies ranging from food to equipment. Making and shipping these supplies provides jobs.

Our geography has created what is known as a service economy. People move to Las Vegas to work in jobs related to keeping visitors happy, while Reno takes advantage of low taxes on the sale of goods and depends more on sales and storage. Neither city depends on heavy industry.

What do you think?

Our large cities are growing rapidly.
- Why do you think cities such as Las Vegas and Reno have grown so much while other parts of Nevada have stayed much the same or have even gone down in population?
- How have geographical factors affected where people start cities and where they choose to live?
- Why did your family come to Nevada?

Nevada, Our Home

For several years the public radio station in Las Vegas, KNPR, aired a weekly feature, "Making Nevada Home" about why people moved here.

A Las Vegas Chamber of Commerce group began a campaign called "My Hometown" to remind people who are asked where they are from to say, "Las Vegas."

Why would there have to be such efforts?

Chapter 1 Review

What Do You Remember?

1. How has the climate affected the development of Nevada?
2. What fossils are common to Nevada? Where are they most likely to be found?
3. Why are ancient animals important today?
4. How have earthquakes and volcanoes affected Nevada?
5. Describe three things about the Great Basin.
6. Name some of the regions that Nevada is part of.
7. What are some of the things that affect Nevada's climate?
8. List three plants and three animals that are native to Nevada.
9. Give some examples of Nevada animals that are protected by law. Why are they protected?
10. How have the people in the state adapted to their environment?
11. What are some reasons people move to Nevada?

Geography Tie-In

1. From memory, draw a map of Nevada. Then label the surrounding states. Add Las Vegas, Carson City, Reno, Elko, and your town or city if you live somewhere else. Add the Humboldt and Colorado Rivers. Trace the Colorado River all the way to the Gulf of California.
2. On a globe, trace Nevada's longitude and latitude all around the world. Now find the longitude and latitude for places where your friends and family live, where your ancestors came from, and other places you are interested in.

Activity

Write About Nevada

Now it's your turn. Write your own description of the state. Use descriptive words to give life to your writing. If you prefer, write a poem or song about Nevada and share it with the class or with a friend.

PEOPLE TO KNOW
Dat-So-La-Lee
Mark Harrington
Georgia and Sydney
  Wheeler
Sarah Winnemucca

PLACES TO LOCATE
Las Vegas
Fallon
Lovelock
Winnemucca
Lake Tahoe
Lake Mead
Muddy River
Virgin River
Spirit Cave
Lovelock Cave
Gypsum Cave
Tule Springs

WORDS TO UNDERSTAND
archaeologist
atlatl
decade
decay
dialect
drought
figurine
fluted
irrigation
medicinal
petroglyph
pictograph
primary source
radioactive
radiocarbon dating
scholar
secondary source
subtle

Native People

Timeline of Events

10,000 B.C.	8,000 B.C.	6,000 B.C.	500 B.C.	0

8,000 B.C.
Hunter-Gatherers live
in North America.

A.D. 500
The Anasazi begin
trading and using bows
and arrows to hunt.

10,000 B.C.
Paleo-Indians live
in North America.

5,000 B.C.
Paiutes may have first
arrived in Great Basin.
Rock art appears.

300 B.C.–200 B.C.
The Anasazi begin
living on the Muddy
and Virgin Rivers.

22

Many groups of people with many different lifestyles lived in North and South America after the Ice Age. Large prehistoric animals still roamed the land. For thousands of years, family groups moved in and out of the place we now call Nevada. They were our first explorers, hunters, farmers, miners, artists, teachers, students, and religious leaders.

When the first explorers came to the Great Basin, there were five main groups of native people living here. The largest group was the Southern Paiute. In this photo, Southern Paiute women sit in front of their wickiups in 1877.

A.D. 1100
The Anasazi build a huge house that looks like a fort.

1925
Mark Harrington begins archaeological studies at Pueblo Grande de Nevada.

1994
Spirit Cave Man is dated at 9,400 years old.

A.D. 500   A.D. 1000   A.D. 1500   A.D. 1930   A.D. 1950   A.D. 1970   A.D. 1990

A.D. 1150–1200
Paiutes replace the Anasazi as the major native group in southern Nevada.

1933
Harrington digs at Tule Springs.

1940
Spirit Cave Man is discovered in a cave near Fallon.

1949
Radiocarbon dating is discovered.

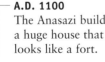

23

It is important to remember that this model of Spirit Cave Man is one idea of how he looked.

reconstruction

● Spirit Cave

Archaeologists thought the remains were about 2,000 years old. The remains were kept for *decades* in the Nevada State Museum in Carson City.

Later, using *radiocarbon dating*, another group of scientists examined Spirit Cave Man. They figured the skeleton was at least 9,400 years old. They were even able to determine that he probably suffered from bad teeth and lower back pain.

The difference in 2,000 and 9,400 years may seem to be a lot of years, but there is more to it than that. Spirit Cave Man's age changed what *scholars* thought about the time when people first came to North America and where they might have come from. What has not changed is the long, important role that Native Americans have played in Nevada from the earliest times to the present.

Discovery at Spirit Cave

Georgia and Sydney Wheeler were working for the Nevada State Parks Commission. They were *archaeologists*—people who study the artifacts left by people who lived long ago. The Wheelers looked in about two dozen caves near Fallon. Finally, in Spirit Cave, they found something of great worth to science—a skeleton wrapped in matting and a rabbit-skin blanket, with moccasins on its feet.

A local doctor looked at the body and concluded that it was an adult male.

[My wife started] to dig near the rear wall while I explored the inner room. The first foot revealed no evidence of [people], just dry, windblown sand. Under this she laid bare a portion of what had been a large mat, very finely twined.... When completely uncovered, this was found to be wrapped around a few human bones, all that remained of some early Nevada inhabitant.

–Sydney M. Wheeler, about the discovery at Spirit Cave

[We] had very few workers that worked with us because you couldn't have people come in there and just shovel because we did things carefully with trowels and brushes . . . you could find [something important] like when we found the mummy.

–Georgia Wheeler

Claiming Ancient Bones

Digging up human remains causes many problems. According to a 1990 federal law, if the remains of Native Americans are found, a tribe can regain the body and bury it—if the tribe can show its own connection to the body. The Fallon Paiute Shoshone Reservation claimed Spirit Cave Man. But scientists said that his age and features made any links to their tribe unlikely.

What do you think?

Why would the government pass a law giving Native Americans the right to claim a skeleton or mummy? Do you think scientists should be able to keep and study skeletons or mummies? Why or why not?

NORTH POLE

ARCTIC OCEAN

NORTH AMERICA

ASIA

SIBERIA

ALASKA

BERING SEA

PACIFIC OCEAN

This image shows how people may have come from the north at the end of the last Ice Age and traveled across North America.

Early Arrivals

Alaska and Siberia seem to have little to do with Nevada, but many scientists think that thousands of years ago the first people walked over a land bridge in that part of the world and traveled south.

Between 12,000 and 20,000 years ago, it was much colder than it is today. Huge glaciers across the northern parts of the globe held more frozen water than they do today. This lowered the level of the oceans by about 300 feet. It was the time of the Ice Ages.

With the lower water level of the oceans, the land between Alaska and Siberia probably was dry. People could walk from one continent to the other. About 10,000 to 12,000 years ago, people reached what we now call Nevada.

There are other ideas about how the first people came. Some people think groups may have come in boats from other places and then walked across part of North and South America. According to some Indian legends, the people were put in the desert lands by their Creator and have always lived here.

Radiocarbon Dating

When you think about the making of atomic bombs, you don't think of how they might help people understand those who lived thousands of years ago. But the study of splitting atoms to make bombs led to radiocarbon dating.

Atoms are *radioactive*, but they change over time into material that is not radioactive. They also start to *decay*—just as all animal and plant remains decay.

Scientists figured out that other kinds of natural radioactivity occur in the atmosphere. One of them is Carbon-14. When lifeforms no longer absorb Carbon-14, they, like atoms, start to decay. A scientist thought that the amount of Carbon-14 decay found in a dead plant or animal might explain how long it had been dead. Then scientists might know when a plant or animal lived.

Scientists have also learned that the amount of Carbon-14 in the air has varied through time. This affects the results. Still, radiocarbon dating gives us better information than we had before.

By 1994, scientists using radiocarbon dating were more accurately tracing the ages of older lifeforms.

Prehistory

The period of time when early people lived here is called "prehistory" because the people left no written history. Archaeologists have to base their ideas mainly on artifacts—the tools and other things that people make and leave behind.

Artifacts give us clues about the tools and weapons the people used, the clothes they wore, and even the food they ate. Scientists, tourists, and hikers have found artifacts in many places of Nevada. Since artifacts have often been found in caves, we know that people lived at least part of the time in the cool dark caves and buried their dead in the shelter of the rock walls.

Carved stone spear points have been found in many places in Nevada.

The first Paiutes may have arrived about this time.

Paleo-Indians

We call the first people Paleo-Indians. We don't know what the people called themselves.

At the time of the Paleo-Indians several species of very large animals roamed the land. Mark Harrington, an archaeologist, said about the prehistoric sloth and camel bones found at Gypsum Cave in Nevada, "We can say that man met these creatures face to face."

The Paleo-Indians made *fluted* points of stone and attached them to the ends of long spears. The men plunged the spears into the animals.

Hunting deer, bighorn sheep, ducks, and other game birds kept the Paleo-Indians alive. Among the artifacts found at Lovelock Cave are duck decoys the people floated on the lake to attract real ducks.

The Indian families also gathered seeds, nuts, and other plants for food. What did they use to carry the food and meat? They may have used bags made of animal skins.

They also cut tall reeds from the lakes and used them to make baskets for carrying and storing food and other things.

The Hunter-Gatherers

About 10,000 years ago, the climate again changed. Another warming trend took place. The amount of rainfall decreased, reducing the number of animals and plants. The large prehistoric animals that lived during the Ice Age were gone.

The people had to adapt once more, and they did. Evidence suggests they began living on shorelines near lakes and in grasslands and woodlands, and that they moved as the seasons changed.

They collected wild plants, hunted the smaller game, and fished—another example of adapting to the environment. We call these people Hunter-Gatherers. They used a stick spear-thrower, called an *atlatl*, to strike smaller faster animals.

At first, people made spears that had a spear point tied onto a stick. Later, people invented a tool called an atlatl. *A hunter could throw a spear harder and faster with the* atlatl.

Geography Tie-In

Trace the route people may have walked from Asia to what we now call Nevada. Granting that the land may have changed, use a map that shows today's rivers and lakes and plan a route that kept the people close to fresh water as they headed south. Why has water always been important to people?

Several years ago, a Las Vegas radio station announced a contest that resulted in hundreds of people searching Mormon Fort, Nevada's oldest building, in Las Vegas. They were looking for a rock with the radio station's call letters on it. It was worth thousands of dollars to whoever found it. The visitors began digging up artifacts at the fort and tossing them aside. Park rangers urgently called the radio station and asked them to announce that the rock was not hidden at Mormon Fort and to stop searching there.

Have you ever touched something ancient? Why is it important to turn over artifacts to museums? Why should we handle these parts of history carefully?

New Arrivals, New Adaptations

About 7,000 years ago, the lives of early people in the Great Basin again began to change in important ways. Archaeologists see *subtle* changes in some of the tools that were used. They also think that hunting may have increased. They base this idea partly on rock art. The art from this time period shows more examples of bighorn sheep that were a source of food.

The people who lived in Nevada from 2,000 to 7,000 years ago made even better use of natural resources than earlier groups. They made baskets, nets, and sandals from stems and leaves of plants. Their stone tools, scrapers, sticks, and clubs show they were far better at making things than the people before them were. They also used stones to grind nuts and seeds. There is evidence of cooking fires.

Finally, this group of cave-dwelling Hunter-Gatherers disappeared from history. What happened is unclear. When ancient Lake Lahontan began to dry up, many kinds of wild animals left. The people may have left then too.

Squawbush and saltbrush sticks wrapped in twisted string were once a snare or trap to catch small animals.

Nature provided seeds, nuts, and roots for food.

Bighorn sheep provided food for men, women, and children.

Rock Art

Hikers view rock art at Petroglyph Canyon, Valley of Fire State Park. You can find rock art in about 100 places around Nevada.

**Valley of Fire ●
State Park**

Rock art is one of the most important sources of information about prehistoric people—and one of the hardest to understand. Drawings in ancient ruins around the world have many meanings. There could be religious meaning to rock art, or it could have been for decoration. Perhaps ancient people, just like today, enjoyed carving and painting.

There are two kinds of rock art—*petroglyphs*, which are cut into the surface, and *pictographs*, which are drawn or painted on the rock. Nevada's rock art ranges from what looks like a tic-tac-toe game to drawings of men, animals, and designs. Small statues or *figurines* have also been found. A "monster" with a rattlesnake tail and fish fins was found in Lovelock Cave.

Nevada's first rock art dates back as far as 7,000 years. The people produced rock art until about 700 years ago—not long after the arrival of Nevada's present-day Native Americans.

Rock art with deer, antelope, and sheep have been found in areas near springs where the animals lived. Since some of the rock art is near hiding places where hunters might lie in wait for their prey, they might have been notices that the wild animals were nearby. The hunters needed to surprise the animals with a swift spear or go home hungry.

For us, then, rock art is a mystery that gives us much to think about as we try to understand prehistoric people.

Linking the Past to the Present

Today it is against the law to take any artifacts from a site where ancient people once lived. It is also against the law to harm rock art or ruins of buildings.

In a cave near the Utah-Nevada border, some of the area's earliest petroglyphs have been discovered. In 2003, two teens admitted to breaking through protective iron gates and using charcoal to draw over the original rock art. State workers had to try to carefully remove the graffiti without damaging the prehistoric drawings.

Nevada: A Journey of Discovery

What do you see in these petroglyphs on Atlatl Rock in Valley of Fire State Park?

The Old Ones

Anasazi is a Native American term for "old one." The Anasazi did not use that term to describe themselves. The Anasazi were a very large group of people who lived in today's Nevada, Utah, Arizona, Colorado, and New Mexico. In Nevada, they lived mainly in the Muddy and Virgin River Valleys near today's Las Vegas. Historians refer to them as the Virgin Anasazi.

They came to the Great Basin about 2,000 years ago, around the time that Julius Caesar ruled the Roman Empire.

Some Anasazi remained Hunter-Gatherers who moved from place to place searching for food, but most made their homes close enough to water to be able to spend more of their time in one area. They dug *irrigation* ditches to supply water to their crops of corn and beans.

Homes

One group built a large community, known today as Pueblo Grande de Nevada or the Lost City. Some of the families there lived in pit houses, built partly underground. These houses ranged from 9 to 20 feet wide, and 2 to 6 feet into the ground. The people entered by climbing down a ladder through a hole in the roof.

Other Anasazi families built stone and adobe pueblos that looked like apartments stacked on top of each other. The thick walls kept the homes cool in the hot desert sun. The people climbed up wooden ladders to get to the upper apartment rooms. They gathered on the roofs to talk, work, and cook. In the summer they probably slept outdoors on the roofs.

The communities were busy places. Just like people today, the Anasazi worked during the day to supply their need for food and clothing. Women raised children and took care of the older people. Children and teenagers helped with the work and learned skills from their parents and grandparents. The people hunted, planted gardens, and even had dogs.

Trading Regions

The Virgin Anasazi traded with other groups. They made baskets, pottery, and jewelry for trade. Shell beads from southern California have been found at Gypsum Cave, which means the people probably traveled long distances to trade with people in faraway places. The split-twig figurines were found in a cave in Utah.

Mining

The people were also miners, but not for gold and silver. They mined salt to make their food taste better and to keep meat from spoiling. They mined turquoise to use in the jewelry they wore and traded with others. They mined minerals and used them to make beads and pottery. They may have found copper.

These split-twig figures were found in a cave near the Nevada-Utah border. Were they toys for children? Were they crafted by a man or a woman who liked to make things? Today, no one knows.

Pit houses were built partly down in the ground. They were cool during the hot summer and provided shelter during winter.

Part of Pueblo Grande de Nevada (Lost City) was rebuilt so visitors today can see how the Anasazi lived long ago.

The Lost City

During the building of Hoover Dam, archaeologists spent long days digging for artifacts at Pueblo Grande. They knew that when the dam was built, the waters of Lake Mead would make the Lost City truly lost. They made models of its buildings and saved everything they could. Much of what they found is now in the Lost City Museum in Overton.

Adobe ruins at the Lost City dig were uncovered by archaeologists in 1926.

What do you think?

How is it possible to balance modern needs for roads, buildings, dams, and reservoirs with preservation of historical sites? Do you think it is important to preserve historical sites? Why or why not?

In the spring of 1938, Lake Mead crept closer and closer to the rebuilt Lost City.

The Anasazi made holes in a large boulder to use as a mass *metate*, or grinding stone. A person poured dried corn or grain into the holes and then pushed down across the grain with another stone called a *mano*. The modern hat and gloves show the size of the holes. Try to imagine a group of children your age talking together as they worked with the stones. What would they talk about?

When Were They Here?

Historians divide the time the Anasazi spent in Nevada into four eras, based on how they learned and changed over time:

- **300 B.C.–A.D. 500** At about the same time as the Roman Empire existed in Europe, the Anasazi made pit houses on the Muddy and Virgin Rivers. They wove baskets and used stones to make knives and scrapers.
- **500–700** They traded for pottery, built pit houses, stored food in bins, and used a bow and arrow for hunting.
- **700–1100** They grew corn, beans, and squash, and dug irrigation systems to water them. They mined salt and turquoise. They hunted small game animals and gathered pine nuts.
- **1100–1150** They had pet dogs and raised turkeys. They raised beans and squash for food and cotton for clothing.

Where Did They Go?

Sometime around the year 1150, the Anasazi disappeared. This is one of the great mysteries of history. Could there have been a *drought* that forced the men and women to take their children and find another place to live and grow crops? Could disease have killed enough of them to make the others want to leave? Could they have been taken as prisoners or killed in war?

We do know the Paiute were here about that time, but they were historically a peaceful people, so it seems unlikely that they drove out the Anasazi. For whatever reason, the Paiute remained, but the Anasazi left.

The largest Anasazi group, at Chaco Canyon in New Mexico, also disappeared about the same time. The Nevada Anasazi may have joined other Anasazi in northern Arizona, or mingled with the Paiute until they became part of that group.

What do you think?

From what you have read, talk with your class about the theories of why the Anasazi left. Which theories make more sense to you? Why?

The Paiute Lived Beside the Anasazi

As with the Anasazi, Paiute history has received a lot of attention. Once thought to have arrived at the end of the Anasazi era, historians now think it is clear that the Paiute lived beside and among the "old ones." Modern Paiutes have provided written records and oral history about their ancestors that prove this idea.

While the Anasazi did a lot of farming, the Paiute were mostly Hunter-Gatherers. They used snares and nets to catch rabbits and bows and arrows to kill larger animals. They got pine nuts by striking tree branches with a pole and gathering pinecones as they fell. They took nuts from the pinecones and ground them between two rocks to make a kind of flour they made into cakes.

The Paiute used a unique system of communication. A small elite group of High Chiefs spoke a special language called Real Speech. They sent runners from group to group to deliver the private messages and gather information.

What do you think?

The prehistoric groups got food in different ways. What is the difference between "obtaining" food and "producing" food? What might be the advantages and disadvantages of each?

This Anasazi sandal is made from yucca fibers. The yucca plant also provided fibers for clothing and rope.

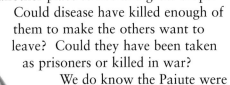

Anasazi pottery was often painted with red and black geometric designs. This pot was found in northern Arizona.

Mark Harrington
1882–1971

Mark Harrington spent only a few years in Nevada, but he discovered a lot about several thousand years of Nevada life.

Harrington was born in Michigan. As a child, he became interested in Native American culture and loved stories about Indian life. As a teenager, he moved to New York City and worked for a museum as a trainee in archaeology. His job was to gather artifacts to fill the Museum of the American Indian there. The artifacts included some from Lovelock Cave in Nevada. Young Harrington traveled across the country to the cave to find more artifacts, and he did. He found duck decoys, which proved that the native people who had lived near the ancient Lake Lahontan had hunted and fished.

In the 1920s Harrington and several others again came to Nevada and explored the Muddy River region. They found the 100-room house and other buildings they called the Pueblo Grande de Nevada. They uncovered Anasazi baskets, farming tools, and other items before Harrington returned to New York.

When he came west once more, Harrington found time to explore more Nevada Indian sites. In Moapa Valley, along the Muddy River, he found 77 ruins of ancient homes. The next year he went to Gypsum Cave in the mountains east of Las Vegas. There he uncovered atlatls and evidence of a giant ground sloth.

Another time, Harrington dug around Tule Springs near Las Vegas. He also took charge of the digging around the Pueblo Grande de Nevada and removed everything he could before Lake Mead washed over it forever. He and his men removed 17 pueblos. They finished as the water began rising around their feet.

In just a few years, Harrington had saved a lot of Nevada's prehistory. He found sites and artifacts that are still studied today. However, modern archaeologists are correcting a lot of what Harrington thought. He lacked the modern equipment to figure out the ages of artifacts and bones. Thanks to Harrington, we know more about who lived here before us. Thanks to more advanced science, we know more about them than he did.

Mark Harrington wrote this about his life's work:

To follow the trail of a forgotten people, to play detective upon the doings of a man who has been dead 10,000 years or so is a thrilling pastime to an explorer. . . . But when the trail leads into a rich virgin field never disturbed by the spade of the relic hunter [the tools of an archaeologist], then your sunburned desert rat of an archaeologist thinks he has discovered a real paradise.

Mark Harrington is the man in the center. Behind him are Zuni men from New Mexico, and in front of him is Willis Evans, a Pitt River Indian. The other two men next to Harrington were involved with the Lost City dig.

Study the photo closely to see how the old Indian clothing, hairstyles, and jewelry have been mixed with the new ways since Indian-white interaction.

Activity

Primary Sources Reveal History

History is not only about what happened in the ancient past; it is about what happened last month and last year.

A historian is a person who studies the past. When we study history, it helps to think like a historian. Ask yourself these questions as you read: **What** happened? **Who** took part in it? **Why** did it happen? **When** did it happen?

Let's start with the first question: What happened? To determine what really happened in the past, you need evidence. There are two types of sources you can go to—primary sources and secondary sources.

Primary sources are records made

▲ Photo by Chuck Place

Washo baskets were tightly woven to hold water and food. Are they a primary or a secondary source? What can you learn about people's lives from the baskets they made?

by people who were there at the time. Primary means "first" or a first-hand account. An Anasazi basket is a primary source. A newspaper can be a primary source when it reports current news. A photograph is a primary source. Is a painting a primary source? Why or why not?

Now you can probably guess what a *secondary source* is. It is something written or made by someone who was not there at the time. A book written at a later time after the event happened is a secondary source. So is a painting done long after the event. They are second-hand accounts.

On a separate piece of paper, number from 1 to 10 and put a P (for primary source) or an S (for secondary source) for each item.

1. A film about the Paleo-Indians.
2. A painting showing the Hunter-Gatherers hunting bighorn sheep.
3. The mummy found in Spirit Cave.
4. A photograph of the mummy found in Spirit Cave.
5. A story about the life of Spirit Cave Man.
6. A rock painting made 4,000 years ago.
7. A sandal found in the Lost City.
8. An Anasazi basket.
9. A 1920 newspaper article about Mark Harrington's discoveries.
10. Mark Harrington's diary.

You will see many primary and secondary sources in this book. To learn all you can about the sources, ask these questions:

- Who was the author, artist, or photographer?
- When and where was it written or made?
- What kinds of information does the document provide? What doesn't it provide?

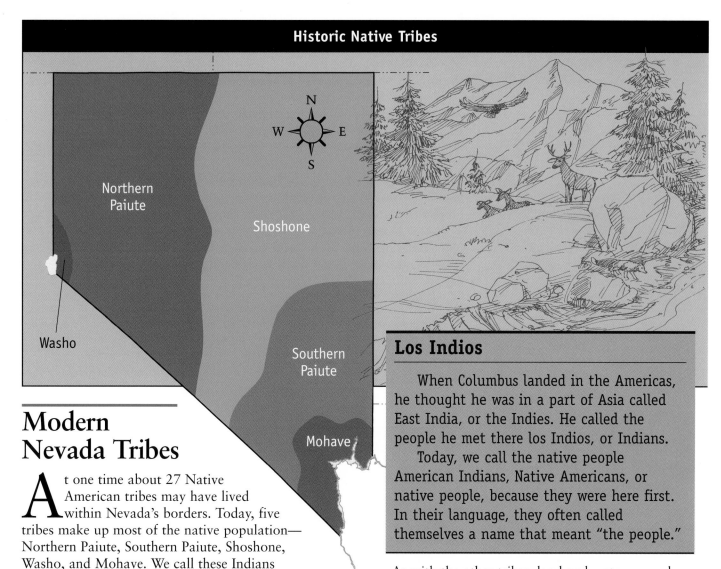

Washo

Northern Paiute

Shoshone

Southern Paiute

Mohave

Modern Nevada Tribes

At one time about 27 Native American tribes may have lived within Nevada's borders. Today, five tribes make up most of the native population—Northern Paiute, Southern Paiute, Shoshone, Washo, and Mohave. We call these Indians "Historic Indians" because explorers and pioneers wrote about the Indians they met and lived near. In other words, we have some written history about the tribes even though the native people did not have their own written history.

Each group has its own history and customs, though they have a great deal in common. Some groups live in warmer places. Some of the tribes are larger than others. Some of the languages are closely related and others are not.

Today, Native Americans live all over the state, though there are still Indian reservations and places where tribal groups live in communities. You will read more about reservations in a later chapter.

The Washo

The smallest group lived near the Sierra Nevada and Lake Tahoe in Nevada and California. The California Indians affected Washo culture. Both have similar artifacts and basket designs, and both groups ate acorns and pine nuts.

Los Indios

When Columbus landed in the Americas, he thought he was in a part of Asia called East India, or the Indies. He called the people he met there los Indios, or Indians.

Today, we call the native people American Indians, Native Americans, or native people, because they were here first. In their language, they often called themselves a name that meant "the people."

As with the other tribes, land and water were always important. Beautiful Lake Tahoe was a crucial part of Washo life. The people often camped in the meadows near the lake and fished in the many streams feeding into it. They guarded their fishing grounds carefully, allowing other Indians to remain only one night. The people smoked the fish and traded it with other tribes. At the end of the fishing season they moved to the hills to gather pine nuts.

Lake Tahoe was a sacred place. It is sacred to us yet, even though it is so different today from what it was in our people's time, before the white people came. . . . Hopefully the people who are here now will have respect and take care of it.

—A tribal elder speaking to tourists

Washo baskets are considered today to be some of the finest examples of native art anywhere in the world. They were a perfectly symmetrical shape, tightly woven, and could even hold water. You can see the baskets on page 34 and read about the women who made them on page 43.

NEVADA
P O R T R A I T

Dat-So-La-Lee
mid-1800s–1925

Dat-So-La-Lee is often thought of as the most famous basket weaver in the world. She was born into the Washo tribe and was given a name that meant "Young Willow." As a young girl, she started learning the fine art of cutting different kinds of willows and reeds, putting them in mud to get a darker color, cutting and shaping them, and weaving them into useful and artistic baskets.

She grew up, married several times, and worked washing clothes for others. Her life changed when she and her husband met Abe and Amy Cohn, who recognized the artistic qualities of the baskets and helped her sell them for good prices. The Cohns provided food and a place to stay so she could quit her other work and spend the next 30 years making baskets.

Today, museums all over the Southwest exhibit the baskets made by Dat-So-La-Lee as a tribute to her fine workmanship and artistic talent.

At the Carson City gravesite of this famous Native American are the words, "Myriads of stars shine over the graves of our ancestors."

Northern Paiute

Northern Paiute territory stretched from Walker Lake to Winnemucca. The Paiute people also lived in California, Oregon, and Idaho. There is more than one correct way to spell the name of this tribe. You will often see both "Piute" and "Paiute."

They often named their bands according to where they were and what they ate. The "jackrabbit eaters" lived north of Pyramid Lake where rabbits were plentiful. To the east lived the "ground squirrel eaters," and to the south lived the "cattail eaters."

While the Northern Paiute had no real chiefs, they relied on a "rabbit boss." He was in charge when they spread their nets to catch rabbits. The rabbits were eaten and their fur made into warm winter robes.

Many Northern Paiute girls were named for the wildflowers that bloomed in the hills. Each spring brought the "Festival of Flowers." Girls wore wreaths and crowns made from the flowers for which they were named.

> Oh, with what eagerness we girls used to watch every spring for the time when we could meet with our hearts' delight, the young men. . . . We would all go to see if the flowers we were named for were yet in bloom, for almost all the girls were named for flowers. . . . I, Sarah Winnemucca, am a shell-flower. . . . I am so beautiful! Who will come and dance with me while I am so beautiful?
>
> —Sarah Winnemucca

Taking Photographs of Indians

When the art of using cameras to take photographs was invented, a few photographers came west to take pictures of the American Indians. The photographs were shown to people in the eastern United States and were sometimes used to entice settlers to come west.

Photographers often gave the Indians elaborate costumes to wear so the photos would look more exciting to people in the East. The clothes also made photographs more "proper," since native people wore little clothing in summer months. Could it be possible that the photographer wanted the children in this photograph to dress this way just for the picture? Or do these clothes look authentic, showing the influence of white settlers who brought cotton clothes? If the Indians were not represented accurately, what may that tell us about other photographs of native people during this period?

NEVADA
PORTRAIT

Sarah Winnemucca
1844?–1891

Sarah Winnemucca was a Paiute who grew up at a time when white people were exploring and settling the West and changing Indian life forever. She wrote:

I was a very small child when the first white people came into our country . . . . My grandfather was chief of the entire Piute nation, and was camped near Humboldt Lake, when a party traveling . . . from California was seen coming. When the news was brought to my grandfather, he asked what they looked like. When told that they had hair on their faces, and were white, he jumped up and clasped his hands together and cried aloud, "My white brothers! My long-looked-for white brothers have come at last!"

Sarah's grandfather welcomed the white people because family stories had said that white brothers would come someday. Her grandfather took her to California when she was six, and there she first met white people. She was frightened to meet the strangers but liked their beds, chairs, and tables. Furniture was new to her.

At age 13, Sarah and her sister went to Mormon Station, Nevada's first white settlement in Carson Valley, to work as household help. From talking with settlers and traders there she learned English and Spanish to add to the three Indian *dialects* she already spoke.

At age 16, the two sisters followed their grandfather's wish that they go to school, so they traveled to California and attended a convent school for girls. They left less than a month later due to complaints by the parents of white students.

While working as an interpreter for the Bureau of Indian Affairs, Sarah married a white soldier. Later, they divorced, and she married an Indian husband, but he did not treat her well and she left again.

For the rest of her life, Sarah Winnemucca worked for her people. She opened schools for Indian children in Washington State and in Nevada. She became a national figure in the fight for Native American rights, giving over 400 speeches, many of them on the East Coast.

Sarah had a hard life trying to walk between the Indian and white cultures. She showed much courage in speaking out as a woman and as an Indian in a time when white men made the rules. You can read more about this famous woman on page 110.

Centennial Series

Just like today, the blazing sun could be very uncomfortable to stand under, so the people built shady roofs of branches. This photo was taken in 1907 near Las Vegas.

The Southern Paiute

The Northern and Southern Paiutes shared much of the same culture and language but lived in different regions. The Southern Paiute lived in southern Nevada and in nearby California, Utah, and Arizona.

The people lived and moved in family groups of parents and children, aunts, uncles, cousins, and grandparents. Usually, each group included a headman who was one of the older males. He gave advice based on what he had learned during a long life.

The families worked together to fish, hunt, and gather food. They ground wild sweet mesquite beans into flour to make cakes. They planted more gardens than most other Nevada Indians, including not only corn, beans, and squash, but flowers and *medicinal* plants.

When the early white fur trappers and explorers visited the Southern Paiutes, they wrote these words in their diaries:

I fell in with a nation of Indians who call themselves Pa Utches (those Indians . . . wear rabbit skin robes) who raise some little corn and pumpkins. . . . the country is nearly [void] of game . . . except a few hares.

—Jedediah Smith, 1826

Many of these Indians had long sticks, hooked at the end, which they used in hauling out lizards and other small animals from their holes. During the day they occasionally roasted and ate lizards at our fires.

—John C. Frémont,
along the Muddy River

I [got] from one of them a bow, made from the single horn of the big horn sheep, covered on the outside with deer sinew.

—Solomon Carvalho

A Paiute Creation Story

The Paiute have their own story of their creation. In the land between the Rockies and the Sierra Nevada lived beautiful giants, one of whom gave birth to a disfigured child.

When all of the giants in the group treated the child badly, the Great Spirit made the land hot and barren with fire and lightning. He allowed enemies to conquer the giants.

Of the two giants who survived, one was named Paiute and the other was his wife. Their skin was baked a brownish color, and they had to live forever in the hot desert.

But the coyote was curious and kept looking anyway. Each time he looked, some of the Newe escaped the basket.

Like the Northern Paiute, the Shoshone named smaller bands according to what they ate. They had bands named for the buffalo berry in Big Smokey Valley, redtop grass in Pine Valley, rice grass in Ione Valley, and rye grass in Ruby Valley.

Families were close. Relatives got together for harvests, festivals and games, and for hunting antelope and rabbit.

The Mohave

The Mohave spent most of their time in small farming villages along the Colorado River in today's Arizona, southern Nevada, and southern California. For about 800 years the Mohave grew corn, melons, beans, and pumpkins.

They were very good at making baskets and taught the skill to people of other tribes.

The Mohave were strong and athletic. Young men were known among other tribes as strong runners who could run long distances. War was a way of life, and they were known for being better fighters than other Nevada Indians. They often had to defend their prized land next to the Colorado River. The people made rafts of thick reeds and used them to travel on the river. Other groups also wanted the river for water and transportation.

Like the other tribes, they had no real chiefs, although some men became leaders when they earned the respect of the others.

This photo was arranged by a photographer in a studio. It shows off a young Shoshone mother and her baby.

The Western Shoshone

The Western Shoshone call themselves *Newe*. They once lived over more than half of the state. A tribal legend says that the Newe covered so much territory because of the coyote. Long ago, two native women told the coyote to carry a large basket with him as he traveled the Great Basin but not to look inside.

Shoshone Legend

This legend tells why people have five fingers on their hands:

Once upon a time, a fox and a lizard had a quarrel. The fox said man should have four fingers, just as he had. The lizard said man should have five fingers, just like he had. The fox became angry and chased the lizard. The lizard ran into a bush, and the fox set fire to it. . . . At last the lizard ran into a crack in a rock and was safe. The lizard won the quarrel, and that is why man has five fingers, just like a lizard.

◀ Photo by John Dittli

Nevada: A Journey of Discovery

The Coming of the White Man

Few tribes had any form of government or power structure until another group of men—the white explorers and settlers—arrived and wanted to talk to Indian leaders. The native way of life was about to change.

Far away from Nevada, the British and French began settling colonies along the East Coast early in the 1600s. At first, relations between the Native Americans and new settlers were friendly—the settlers at Jamestown in Virginia would have starved to death without the corn the Woodland Indians gave them. In Massachusetts, Samoset and Squanto helped the Pilgrims survive their first year at Plymouth by providing food and advice in living off the land.

The Fur Trade

In the East and the Midwest fur trappers and traders from Europe brought things the native people wanted. The Indians traded furs for glass beads, metal cooking pots and knives, woven cotton cloth, and guns. Many Indians changed their native lifestyle and spent all their time trapping animals so they could trade the fur for the European goods.

Some colonists, however, did not treat Native Americans well, and the native people paid dearly for it. When white settlers thought of the Indians as "savages" to be killed, or "lost souls" who must give up their native lifestyle and convert to Christianity, relations grew tense. After more and more colonists arrived, they pushed the native people farther west.

During the Revolutionary War, some Indian groups took the British side, hoping this would protect their lands from more settlement by the colonists.

Often Indian groups adopted white ways. They liked the trade items white people brought, but the Indian men fought back when they were driven from their lands or they saw their traditions threatened.

During this same time period in Nevada, the European settlers had yet to arrive. Here the Indian groups were living much as they had for hundreds of years. But when whites did arrive, life for the native people changed forever.

> I was a very small child when the first white people came into our country. They came like a lion, yes, like a roaring lion. . . .
>
> —Sarah Winnemucca

What do you think?

Compare Sarah Winnemucca's analogy of the coming of the white men being like a roaring lion (above) to how her grandfather felt about the white people traveling across Nevada (page 38).

Paiute wicki-ups like these were summer shelters that provided shade and a place to sleep.

Everyday Lifestyles

The culture of different groups of native people was alike in many ways, though very different in other ways. In the past, the people of the tribes lived in groups or bands of about 50 to 100 people, including an extended family or several families.

They had no official power structure, but some members were treated as more important than others. Nevada Indians usually tried to live peacefully with outsiders and with one another. They were not warlike, which meant that tribes from Arizona and Utah sometimes took advantage of them. The following text will give you a better idea of how the native people of all tribes lived.

Spiritual Traditions

The native people had many spiritual beliefs. The sun, moon, rivers, lakes, and mountains were symbols of the spirits. Ceremonies, including dances and music, had spiritual significance.

A shaman was in charge of rituals and ceremonies. He was supposed to communicate with the spirits who would help in the hunt. He was also a healer and spiritual leader.

Moving With the Seasons

Many of the native people moved from place to place according to the seasons. In the fall, northern tribes headed for the mountains where pine nuts were ready to harvest. In spring, summer, and winter, they usually lived down in the valleys near rivers, lakes, and marshes.

Clothing

The people dressed to fit the seasons, warm or cold. During the summer, men wore a breechcloth of animal skins, and women wore a soft leather skirt. Babies and young children often wore nothing. In the winter, the Washo and other groups wore buckskin shirts and rabbit-skin blankets. They also used the inner bark of sagebrush for shoes and other clothing. Both men and women sometimes wore necklaces and earrings made of bird bones, deer hooves, and seashells.

Homes

Nevada's historic Indian groups lived in temporary shelters called wicki-ups. The people built them with a frame of saplings or branches and wove other branches and grasses into the walls. In winter, animal skins covered the outside of the shelter. The people might dig a circle 2 or 3 feet down into the ground and build up from there, or just build up from the level ground. Sometimes grasses and reeds were tied together to create a drainage system, just as your roof might have gutters so rain or snow runs off it.

For winter warmth, there was a fire pit in the center of the wicki-up and a hole in the top for smoke to escape. The people cooked outside over a fire.

Some of the Southern Paiute lived in tepees with animal skin coverings. The tepees could be taken down and moved when the people moved.

Meeting on the trail, the people rarely said, "Hello." Instead, they would say, "Uduta hada," meaning, "It's hot."

Food

Like the prehistoric people, the family groups hunted wild animals and caught grasshoppers, crickets, and lizards. They would not eat dogs, snakes, or certain birds, however. They gathered wild raspberries, chokeberries, elderberries, seeds, and nuts. Not only did they feast on raw pine nuts, they roasted them, ground them into flour, and made cakes with them. They held festivals to celebrate the harvest, complete with singing and dancing.

Beautiful Baskets

The Washo were probably the best basket-makers. Some of their older baskets can be seen in museums today. You can see some examples on page 34. Other groups also made beautiful baskets and used them to carry seeds, food, and water, and for cooking. To cook in a basket, a woman heated rocks in a fire, then put the hot rocks in a basket with water and food. The hot rocks heated the water that cooked the food.

The people usually gathered the willows, reeds, and grasses in large bundles, then they sat in the shade of a tree or wicki-up and spent many hours weaving baskets. The basket-makers put a lot of effort into the artistic designs on their baskets. Skills were passed from generation to generation.

Grinding stones ground nuts, seed, grain, and corn into meal or flour.

Pine Nuts: Food for Survival

Hunter-Gatherers and modern Indian groups stored hundreds of pounds of pine nuts to eat during the winter.

After the people collected seeds and nuts, they put them on a slab of stone called a *metate*. They held another stone, called a *mano*, and rubbed it back and forth to grind the seeds into flour.

Then they put the flour into a grass basket, added water to make mush, and cooked it. They could not put the basket right on a campfire, so they put hot stones from the campfire into the basket.

"A basket is a song made visible. . . ."

—Meg Brady

A white ranch woman, Helen Stewart, made a hobby of collecting Indian baskets. You will read more about her in a later chapter. Each basket took the basket-maker many hours to weave. All were made from local reeds and grasses.

Celebrations and Games

Life was not all work. There were ceremonies and celebrations of dancing and feasting. Adults, teenagers, and children played games, including forms of football and field hockey. One type of game linked Nevada's past and present—they liked to gamble. The Washo bet on games, gambling with baskets, feathers, jewelry, and other possessions. One of the games involved guessing who was holding animal bones in his hand.

Oral Traditions and Legends

Just as we have family stories, so did Native Americans. They did not have a written language, but passed down stories from generation to generation. Elders told stories to their children and grandchildren over and over so the stories would always be remembered.

Indian legends were a way for the people to explain the happenings and history of the world. They reflected the tribes' beliefs about such things as the creation of the earth, about god or gods, and how men and women interacted with them. Most Indian legends contain natural elements such as animals, land, water, and the sun, moon, and stars.

The Washo told the story of the good wolf god and the bad coyote god. The coyote god made life so bad that the Washo were starving. Finally, the wolf god created pine trees to feed them. Because the Washo were too weak to reach the pinecones on the tall trees, the wolf made the pinyon smaller than other pine trees so the Washo could reach them.

Linking the Past to the Present

Did you get any of your beliefs and knowledge from hearing stories from your parents or grandparents?

Activity

You Choose

Choose one of these projects to help you learn more about the native people of Nevada:

1. With family members, make a list of what events and activities in your life are recorded through documents, photographs, or video. Make a list of those events and activities that you have heard about but that are not documented. Try to find evidence that they happened.

2. Record the stories of an older Native American as he or she was growing up to learn about Indian life in another time.

3. In a library, find books or newspaper microfilm about Indian life 100 years ago and compare it to what you read in this chapter.

4. Research the creation stories of Native Americans who live in other states and compare them with the Paiute legend on page 39.

5. Make a list of the foods the Native Americans ate. Go to a grocery store or health food store and see if you can find any of these items today.

6. Use the Internet to research for more information about Nevada's Native Americans. Choose from these websites or find others:

http://library.wncc.nevada.edu/usefulwebsites/native%20americans.htm
http://www.xeri.com/Moapa/moapa-facts.htm
http://www.nevada-history.org/

Chapter 2 Review

What Do You Remember?

1. What was the significance of Spirit Cave Man?
2. How and from where do scientists think people first came to Nevada?
3. What do artifacts tell us about the Paleo-Indians?
4. Describe at least one prehistoric artifact and tell how it was used.
5. How did the Anasazi interact with other groups in faraway places?
6. Compare the four eras of Nevada's Anasazi people and list some ways the lifestyles were alike and how they were different.
7. What are some possible reasons why the Anasazi left Nevada?
8. How did Mark Harrington contribute to our knowledge of ancient peoples?
9. What are Nevada's five major modern Native American groups?
10. Choose one of the five modern tribes and tell at least two things about their lifestyle.
11. Why are legends important?
12. How were legends passed down to the next generation?

Technology Tie-In

Technology is the combination of tools, skills, and knowledge that people use to meet their basic needs and wants.

- Give two examples of the tools, skills, and knowledge that Native Americans used for fishing or hunting.
- Give two examples of the tools, skills, and knowledge your family uses to get food.
- Who do you think had an easier time getting food—an Indian family of the past or your family today?

Geography Tie-In

On a half piece of posterboard, make a map showing Nevada's five modern Native American tribes. Illustrate your poster by drawing in some natural land features such as mountains, lakes, and plants. The maps in Chapter 1 will help you. You may want to glue on some real dirt, plant leaves or stems, etc. Add drawings, photographs, or postcards to illustrate your poster.

Exploring the West

Timeline of Events

1492 Christopher Columbus finds the New World.

1607 English colonists arrive at Jamestown, Virginia.

1776 Declaration of Independence is signed in the 13 colonies.

1776 Fathers Dominguez and Escalante explore part of the West.

1519 Hernando de Cortés conquers the Aztec empire.

1540 Francisco Coronado begins exploration of the Southwest.

1769 Spanish priests start opening missions in New Spain.

1776 Father Francisco Garces explores near the southern tip of Nevada.

1804–1806 Lewis and Clark explore from Missouri to the Pacific Ocean.

1500   1600   1770   1800

Chapter 3

WORDS TO UNDERSTAND

appease
conquistador
controversial
convert
dispute
ethnocentricity
eventually
imperial
intolerance
lamentable
memorable
popular sovereignty
rendezvous
renowned
reputation
retaliation
skirmish
toll road
treacherous
vicinity

"The Booshway" © *by John Clymer*

1810
The Mexican Revolution begins, eventually driving Spanish rulers out of Mexico.

1824
Hudson's Bay Company opens Fort Vancouver.

1825
Peter Skene Ogden is the first white man in Nevada.

First emigrant parties cross Nevada.

1846
Donner party travels across Utah and Nevada.

1841

1848
Gold rush begins in California.

1849
Pioneers name Death Valley.

1810   **1820**   **1830**   **1840**   **1850**

1812–1815
U.S. and Great Britain fight the War of 1812.

1826
Jedediah Smith becomes the first American in Clark County.

1833
Joseph Walker crosses Nevada to Yosemite Valley.

1843
John C. Frémont leads a mapmaking expedition into Nevada.

1846–1848
Mexican-American War

1850
Compromise of 1850 makes Nevada part of two new territories.

Columbus and the New World

In 1492, Spain wanted raw materials so it could make more goods to sell. It also wanted more markets in which to sell them. The king and queen of Spain felt it was important to spread their Catholic religion to people in Asia. They agreed to finance an Italian, Christopher Columbus, and his crew to explore a western water route to Asia. Before that time, traders had traveled to Asia mostly by land—a long, dangerous route. Robbers along the way had often stolen trade goods.

Columbus sailed west, landing not at islands of Asia called the Indies, but at other islands off the coast of Florida. Thinking he had reached the Indies, Columbus named the island "San Salvadore," which meant "Blessed Savior" in Spanish. He called the native people "Indians."

The discovery *eventually* made Spain an *imperial* power—a nation that owned or controlled territory and people on other continents.

The Americas are named for another Italian explorer, Amerigo Vespucci, who reached the New World about five years after Columbus.

What do you think?

Before Spain agreed to finance Columbus's trip, Columbus had asked England, but they refused. How do you think the development of the Americas might have changed if England had hired Columbus instead of Spain?

The Conquistadores

A few years after Columbus, Hernando de Cortés sailed to Central America and conquered the Aztec empire, putting them under the rule of Spain. He also found millions of dollars worth of gold.

Later, Viceroy Antonio de Mendoza of New Spain fell for a myth. Rumors spread of the existence of cities made of gold called the Seven Cities of Cíbola. Mendoza wanted to build up his empire and his power, and taking the gold would be a way to do both. He appointed a young nobleman, Francisco Coronado, to lead a large expedition to find the golden cities and return to Mexico City with as much wealth as they could carry.

Coronado's group included over 200 men on horses followed by more than 60 soldiers carrying swords, spears, and shields. About 1,000 Indians with weapons were next in line, and finally Indian and black slaves to look after thousands of cattle, sheep, and goats they took along to provide food.

Of course, Coronado never found the Seven Cities. He spent two long, hard years exploring what became the southwestern United States. He found native people, deserts, mountains, and plains but no gold. His failure was a blow to Spain. Spanish leaders decided not to send out any more exploring parties.

Spanish explorers like Coronado were called **conquistadores**. *They conquered native people and their lands for Spain.*

Other European Explorers

While Spain seemed to lose interest in exploring, the French explored parts of America that are now Canada and the Midwest. Great Britain also gradually began staking its claim. Sir Francis Drake circled the globe for England, sailing to South America and bringing home millions in gold that Spain never knew about. Years later, a group of London investors founded Jamestown in what became known as Virginia. It became the first English colony in America.

Chesapeake Bay

Jamestown

The threat of British and French ownership inspired the Spanish to do more with their land claims in America, with important effects on the West.

Spain Builds Missions

Spanish leaders wanted to control their empire, stop other powers from moving in, and spread Christianity. At the same time, Spain did not want to spend a lot of money or send colonists to New Spain, as they called the land in America. They found a solution that revealed the best and the worst of their character. Spain began building missions to be run by Catholic priests.

Spanish soldiers helped build the missions of adobe and wood, gathered natives to come to the missions, and then left the priests to do their duty. Priests taught the Indians religion and a trade, such as farming. Spanish leaders hoped that when the Indians *converted* to the new religion, they would return to their villages to farm and convert other Indians to their faith—and to Spanish loyalty. Some native people came to the missions on their own, but others were forced to live and work there.

Did the mission system work? Yes and no. The Spanish empire survived for many years. Some Indians were converted, spoke Spanish, and followed Spanish customs. Many devoted priests came across the ocean and lived a meager existence working with the native people. Some died in the cause. But evidence suggests that some natives dropped their new faith once they left the mission. How much these conversions did to aid the Spanish empire is not known.

An Indian guide points out Utah Lake to Father Escalante.

Dominguez and Escalante

The date July 4, 1776 is *memorable* in American history as the day the Declaration of Independence was approved in the 13 colonies, far away in the East. That month an event in the Southwest also had long-lasting effects.

An exploring party of 12 men, led by Fathers Dominguez and Escalante, left Santa Fe seeking a route to Monterey, California. They wanted a trail that could be used to send letters, supplies, and soldiers back and forth from the two Spanish outposts.

The men, their pack animals, and horses left Santa Fe in the heat of July. They traveled all summer through dry country and then turned west into what is now Utah. Ute Indians, including an 11-year-old scout, guided them for several weeks until at last they overlooked a wide valley and Utah Lake. They did not think they could find a way to cross the desert before winter began, so they returned to Santa Fe.

The San Buenaventura River Myth

The diaries of the men described a large river. Knowing little about geography and geology, they were unaware that they were in the Great Basin, not California. They drew maps showing the rivers running into the Pacific Ocean. The myth of the San Buenaventura River, as they called it, spread. Future explorers would nearly die of thirst and starvation looking for it. Following Utah's rivers never would have led the explorers to the Pacific.

Linking the Past to the Present

Before you criticize Dominguez and Escalante for dreaming up a river, think of the astronauts who go into space today. Could you accurately map an unknown place?

Dominguez-Escalante Route, 1776

Nevada

Great Salt Lake

Utah Lake

Utah

San Francisco

Monterey

California

Colorado

Santa Fe

Albuquerque

Arizona

New Mexico

San Diego

N W E S

Nevada: A Journey of Discovery

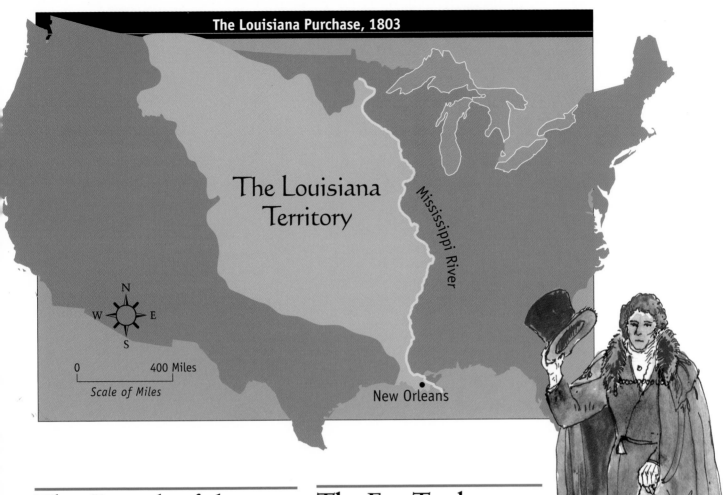

The Louisiana
Territory

Mississippi River

N
W E
S

0   400 Miles

Scale of Miles

New Orleans

*Top hats made of beaver
felt were very popular in
Europe and America.*

The Growth of the United States

The United States grew after the Declaration of Independence. That growth, like so many national events, affected Nevada.

French officials sold to the United States the Louisiana Territory, including the important seaport of New Orleans. President Jefferson asked two men to explore the land. Meriwether Lewis and army officer William Clark led an expedition of 28 "good hunters, stout, healthy, unmarried men . . . capable of bearing bodily fatigue." York, Clark's black slave, was part of the group.

Leaving from a small town near St. Louis, the group worked their way to the Pacific Ocean. They brought back knowledge of plants, animals, native peoples, and natural landmarks that helped future explorers and immigrants. Their adventures excited a young nation already looking west.

The Fur Trade

Fashionable American and European men wore a coat and a top hat when they went out in public. The top hats were made of felt. The best felt came from soft beaver fur. Businessmen understood that if they could find more fur, they could make larger profits.

The quest for fur took French, British, and American traders and trappers to many parts of Canada and the American frontier. The British opened Hudson's Bay Company at Fort Vancouver in what is now the state of Washington. William Ashley, an American, later started the Rocky Mountain Fur Company, sending expeditions of mountain men, as the trappers were called, from St. Louis into the Rockies.

The two leading fur traders in our history were Jedediah Smith, an American, and Peter Skene Ogden, a Canadian who worked for Hudson's Bay Company. Both blazed trails through Nevada.

Exploring the West

51

NEVADA
PORTRAIT

Jedediah Smith's Trials and Trails
1799 – 1831

Fur trappers usually traveled in groups since they were never sure whether the Native Americans they met would be hostile to them. They were businessmen, working hard to make money and get ahead in life.

Jedediah Smith was born in upstate New York, a devout Methodist whose family regularly studied the Bible. As a fur trader, Smith always carried his Bible into the wilderness.

Smith entered the fur trade as one of the first trappers with the Rocky Mountain Fur Company. He quickly established a *reputation* as being careful, intelligent, hard-working, and fearless. He kept records and won the confidence of the trappers who went with him.

In South Dakota on his way west, Smith ended up in a battle with a grizzly bear that ripped off part of his scalp and his ear. One of his men sewed it back on for him.

O you must try to stich up some way or other said he, then I put in my needle stiching it through . . . as nice as I could.

—James Clyman

Smith was different from other trappers. At the rendezvous, while other trappers celebrated loudly, Smith often sat quietly reading. The others often asked him to hold onto their money to keep them from gambling away all that they had earned. They respected Smith, even though he refused to join the crowd.

Into Nevada

Smith and 14 others crossed Utah into Nevada on horses and rode south to the Colorado River. He described the Mohave Indians attacking him and his men near the river in 1827:

. . . in every other direction the Indians were closing in upon us,

The Rendezvous

William Ashley invented the *rendezvous*. He thought it would work better than having a fort where his men would have to return to sell furs and get supplies. Instead, they could agree to meet somewhere in the *vicinity* of where they had been trapping. The men, dressed in buckskin, sold a year's worth of pelts, bartered for supplies, and celebrated among friends.

Jim Beckwourth, another trapper, described the behavior at the mountain man rendezvous:

Rendezvous was painted by William Henry Jackson, a great painter of the West. Notice the trappers' interaction with the American Indians.

"Mirth, songs, dancing, shouting, trading, running, jumping, singing, racing, target-shooting, yarns, frolic, with all sorts of extravagances that white men or Indians could invent, were freely indulged in. The unpacking of the—medicine water—contributed not a little to the heightening of our festivities."

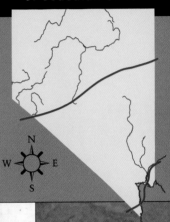

Travel Routes of Jedediah Smith

and the time seemed fast approaching in which we were to come to that contest which must, in spite of courage and all that man could do, terminate in our destruction. It was a fearful time. . . . I directed two good marksmen to fire, they did so and two Indians fell. . . . Upon this the Indians ran off . . . and we were released from the apprehension of immediate death.

Smith's party made their way across the deathly Mojave Desert to a mission near today's Los Angeles, where Mexican officials, unhappy that the men had entered their country without approval, kept them in jail for two long months. Smith left a dozen men to trap beaver in California while he and two others crossed the Sierra Nevada back into Nevada.

They crossed Nevada and Utah deserts in the heat of May and June, carrying furs to the rendezvous near Bear Lake. They nearly starved and died of thirst but made it to the Fourth of July celebration at the rendezvous. Smith wrote in his diary in 1827: "My arrival caused a considerable bustle in camp, for myself and party had been given up as lost. A small cannon brought up from St. Louis was loaded and fired for a salute."

Jedediah and his group then returned to California to pick up the rest of his men. On the way, an Indian attack killed several of the trappers.

An Early Death

By age 30, Smith had done well enough to retire from fur trapping. But wandering was in his blood. He worked as a scout for other trappers. Then, as fate would have it in the wild country, Jedediah came upon some Indians who had had problems with other white men. They killed Smith, who was only 32 years old.

Intolerant Ideas

Future trappers and immigrants followed in Smith's path—and, unfortunately, some of his thinking. While Smith got along well with the Catholic priests at the missions, he was intolerant of their religion. He also felt Indians attacked him for no reason and that they were uncivilized. Other trappers heard plenty from him about Indians and Mexicans, agreeing with him that the land was too valuable to be left in their hands. In this way, Smith was a man of his times. Most Americans then looked down on people of different races and religions.

"Three young men . . . have the first year made a gain of Twenty Thousand Dollars. . . . What a contrast between these young men and myself. They have been only six years in the country, . . ."

— Peter Skene Ogden, writing about Jedediah Smith and his partners

Other Trappers

Captain Walker rides ahead of his Indian wife in this painting by Alfred J. Miller. Native Americans often gave trappers shelter and food, especially in the winter. Many trappers married the native women and had children.

Peter Skene Ogden

Peter Skene Ogden beat Jedediah Smith into Nevada—but just barely. Ogden worked for the Hudson's Bay Company. He led a group of trappers into Nevada from the north and finally came upon a river. Since they did not know about the river, they called it the Unknown River. It was referred to after that as Ogden's River, but future generations knew it as the Humboldt. He wrote: "I will venture to say in no part of the country have I found beaver more abundant than in this river. . . . The trappers now with me average 125 beaver per man and are truly well pleased with their success."

Ogden and his men trapped until winter neared, then headed for Utah.

He led another group of trappers to Nevada later that year, following his earlier route to the Humboldt Sink. After more trapping, the group returned to the Hudson's Bay post at Walla Walla, Washington.

Like Jedediah Smith, Ogden left a legacy of firsts. He was the first non-Indian to see the Humboldt River. Seeing it convinced him, as Smith had learned, that the San Buenaventura River to the Pacific must be a myth. Fortunately for Ogden, he came to a happier end than Smith. He eventually retired from trapping and lived out his days in the Oregon area with his Native American wife.

Joseph Walker: Secret Agent?

One more expedition significantly affected Nevada. U.S. Army Captain Benjamin Bonneville asked the government for a leave—a common request in the early 1800s

Nevada: A Journey of Discovery

army. Bonneville claimed to want to trap for fur in the Rockies. Since that area had been well-traveled, Bonneville knew most of the fur had been found.

He may have had something else in mind. He ordered his chief scout, Joseph Walker, to explore the Salt Lake area. Walker wound up in California, and the evidence suggests he and his party knew ahead of time that this was the plan. Whether he was a federal spy checking out Mexican territory for the U.S. government or just seeking fur, Walker affected Nevada.

Walker and his party trapped along the Humboldt, where they came upon a band of Paiutes and started shooting. Those who survived targeted Walker and other whites for years to come. A member of Walker's party wrote this about the battle:

> We closed in on them and fired, leaving 39 dead on the field—which was nearly the half—the remainder were overwhelmed with dismay—running into the high grass in every direction, howling in the most **lamentable** manner.

Walker's actions caused trouble for future explorers and immigrants who did nothing to antagonize the Indians, yet found them unfriendly. His party crossed the Sierra and became the first non-natives in the Yosemite Valley. The next year, they crossed back into Nevada at a pass named for Walker and rejoined Captain Bonneville in Utah.

Walker had led the first group of whites on a round trip from Salt Lake to the Pacific via the Humboldt and established several shorter trails.

What do you think?

What perceptions of Indians may have prompted Walker and his men to act as they did? Did the Paiutes react the way you would expect? What examples of **retaliation** do you hear about in the news today?

Jim Beckwourth

James Beckwourth was a mountain man who had to overcome more than just wilderness, loneliness, and danger. He was a free African American in a time of slavery. Despite the racism of his time, he became a **renowned** fur trapper and scout.

Beckwourth was born in Virginia. His mother was a black slave and his father was a white slaveowner. When James was a teenager, his father moved him to Missouri.

In his early twenties, Beckwourth joined William Ashley's Rocky Mountain Fur Company. He worked for Ashley and other companies for more than a decade, joining parties led by such prominent fur trappers as Jedediah Smith and Jim Bridger. Ashley once said, "That Beckwourth is surely one of the most singular men I ever met."

Beckwourth had an unusually good relationship with the Native Americans. He briefly operated a trading post with Blackfeet Indians and spent several years with the Crow to help Ashley's company work out trade agreements. He married a Crow woman. From then on, he often dressed like the Crows.

After his fur trading career, Beckwourth worked in scouting, trading, and the military. When he moved on to California, he arrived just in time to prospect during the gold rush.

As a miner, his trapping and scouting days came in handy. Aware of the immigrants having trouble crossing the Sierra Nevada, he discovered a pass that now bears his name. Later he was hired to build a **toll road** across his pass. When it was completed, he guided weary immigrants across the pass.

Beckwourth later dictated his life's story to a writer. Some say he embellished various events, stretching the truth to make the stories more interesting.

The trapper's life came to an unusual end. The U.S. government asked him to help make peace with the Crow Indians, who had once adopted him into their tribe and named him a chief. He died on that mission, reportedly from being served poisoned food. The Crow **allegedly** reasoned that if he could not be their chief, they would kill him so his spirit would be with them always. Whether or not that is true, his spirit and determination helped change the West.

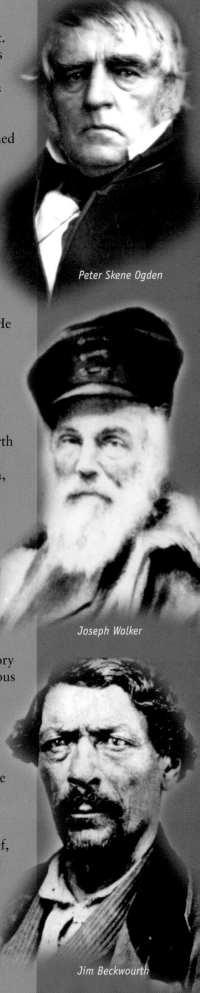

Peter Skene Ogden

Joseph Walker

Jim Beckwourth

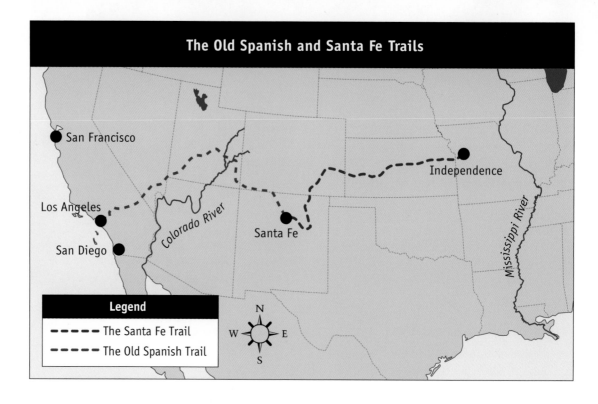

San Francisco

Los Angeles

San Diego

Colorado River

Santa Fe

Independence

Mississippi River

Legend

- - - - - The Santa Fe Trail

- - - - - The Old Spanish Trail

N
W   E
S

The Santa Fe and Old Spanish Trails

Just as the American and Canadian trappers were looking for economic opportunities, so were traders in New Mexico. They were right in the heart of a network of trails. In the early 1820s, traders established the Santa Fe Trail to that city, starting at Independence, Missouri. Most of the early trade involved Missouri mules and Mexican gold, but the Santa Fe Trail also was crucial to the growth of the fur trade.

Those at the western end of the trail also started looking even farther west. One of these traders, Antonio Armijo, hoped to find a route from the Santa Fe area to southern California. He had Mexican *serapes*, and Los Angeles traders had sheep and horses. Trading, he felt, was in order.

Passing by Las Vegas

While the springs of Las Vegas were an attractive stopping place on the trail, the things that made it desirable also made it **treacherous**. Its hot springs and grass appealed not only to travelers but also to horse thieves raiding California ranches. Settlers and traders on the trail preferred to avoid the kind of people who stole horses, so they often settled for the even drier climate to the south.

Linking the Past to the Present

Today, Las Vegas often is called "sin city" because of the gambling there. The lawless image of Las Vegas, however, goes back to the very beginning, when horse-stealing was rampant. Mountain men and Native Americans raided horses from southern California ranches to sell in other places. More than 1,000 stolen horses galloped through the Las Vegas valley.

Manifest Destiny

From news accounts and letters, people in the East heard about California. The area from the Rockies to the Pacific Ocean still belonged to Mexico then. Excited by reports of its rich lands, many looked westward to dream, and sometimes to pack up and follow those dreams.

Through their stories and maps, fur trappers guided those who crossed the mountains and deserts to California. The trappers affected the future in another way. Their attitude encouraged Americans to feel superior to the Mexicans and Indians. *Ethnocentricity*—believing your culture is superior to everyone else's—has been a powerful force in history. The fur trappers contributed to an idea of superiority called Manifest Destiny.

In the East, editor John O'Sullivan wrote, "It is the manifest destiny of the United States to spread across the continent." He meant that North America, from the Atlantic to the Pacific, including Canada and Mexico, should be in the hands of the United States.

The place we now call Nevada was a stopping-off point on the way to California. Americans wanted California, and they were willing to fight a war to get it.

What do you think ?

Do you see examples of ethnocentricity today? How do you feel about it? What do you do about it?

The Bartleson–Bidwell Party

Americans wanted to move west even though the region from the Rocky Mountains to the Pacific Ocean still belonged to Mexico. Former fur trappers and government explorers often served as scouts and guides, leading the newcomers along the trails.

The first group was the Bartleson-Bidwell party. John Bidwell, a teacher, helped put together a group of volunteers to go to California. Only a few people went with him. As they prepared to go, another group, led by John Bartleson, joined them, and they set out for California.

They had little knowledge and no maps of the route west. Fortunately, they joined three priests who were being guided by a fur trapper, "Broken Hand" Fitzpatrick. He guided them as far as the Great Salt Lake. From that point on, the party was on its own and immediately ran into trouble.

West of the Great Salt Lake the land was very dry and covered with salt and sand. Water was scarce. Wagons broke down in the sand.

Some of the men went on ahead, while John Bidwell stayed with the rest of the party as they traveled along the Humboldt River until it disappeared into the ground. The wagons still had to cross 40 miles of desert before reaching rivers near the Sierras. They were bitterly disappointed and knew they would have to empty their wagons of some of their furniture. Their oxen could not pull the heavy wagons all that way without water to drink.

At last they reached the Sierras, but they had to leave their wagons behind because they were too heavy to get up the mountains. The entire journey took six months. The group became the first emigrant party to cross the Great Basin into California. They arrived in November, missing the heavy winter snow that would mean death to the Donner party a few years later.

> We first looked at the high, steep and rough mountain road, then at the wagons, and then at the mules, and lastly we looked at one another, but twas no use looking; the work had to be done.
>
> —Emigrant John Hawkins Clark on crossing the Sierra Nevada

Other Americans learned about the West Coast from news accounts and letters. Excited by reports of its rich lands and mild climate, they crossed Nevada and settled in California and Oregon.

"Our ignorance of the route was complete. We knew that California lay west, and that was the extent of our knowledge."

—John Bidwell

NEVADA
P O R T R A I T

John C. Frémont
1813 – 1890

John C. Frémont, sent west by the U.S. government, mapped and named landmarks that others had only described. The written report of his travels became a best-seller that mirrored the views of earlier explorers—they thought this land of beauty and adventure should belong to Americans, not to Mexicans and Indians.

As a young man, Frémont joined the army, went on a mapmaking expedition, then worked in Washington, D.C. There he fell in love with one of the city's most intelligent young women, Jessie Benton. Her father was a senator from Missouri who helped Frémont join a group of government mapmakers who explored the West.

Nevada just happened to be in Frémont's path to California, but his importance to this state is great. He came west four times, making more accurate maps of the Oregon Trail, Nevada, and other places from Utah to California. Perhaps even more important, he attracted interest in the West.

On one trip, Frémont and his party wound up at a large lake. A rock in the middle reminded him of the Great Pyramids in Egypt, so he called it Pyramid Lake. He followed the Truckee River (which he named for an Indian chief) and the Carson River (which he named for his scout, Kit Carson). The explorers went on to California, headed south, and picked up the Old Spanish Trail for the return trip. When they reached the watery and grassy oasis in the desert, Frémont called it by the Spanish name for "the meadows"—Las Vegas.

In their later lives, John and Jessie Frémont and their daughter pose near a giant redwood in California.

Returning to the East, Frémont and Jessie wrote and published his accounts. For the first time, the public learned of a huge western land region with no outlet to the ocean. Frémont called the region the Great Basin. That disposed of the San Buenaventura River myth once and for all.

On the Way To California

The 40-mile desert was often traveled by night because of the great heat. Starvation stalked every mile. A survey made along the trail in 1850 showed: over 1,000 dead mules, almost 5,000 dead horses, 3,750 dead cattle, and 953 human graves.

The area from Utah's Salt Lake to the Sierra earned a reputation for danger. Emigrants to Oregon and California followed the Humboldt's trickling waters. At the river's end, they still had to ride or walk across a 40-mile desert before reaching water at Truckee Meadows.

The earliest emigrants were not coming to live in Nevada—it was too dry. They were going through Nevada to get to the fertile land in California. Emigrants traveled in wagon trains made up of several families traveling together. Either teams of oxen or mules pulled the wagons. Oxen were stronger but slower than mules. Either way, travel was slow. On a good day, the wagons made 10 to 14 miles.

Stories of unfriendly Indians were often blown out of proportion. Most of the Indians along the trail were friendly and even traded with the pioneers. There were, however, many reports of horses and cattle being taken.

Disease could be another problem for emigrants. Cholera, smallpox, and measles killed many travelers on the trails just as they did in the cities. One woman wrote in her diary:

> We passed a new made grave today . . . a man from Ohio. We also met a man that was going back he had buried his Wife this morning. She died from the effects of measles. . . . We passed another grave today which was made this morning. The board stated that he died of cholera.

The intense summer heat was a real problem in the deserts. Wind and blowing dust caused many pioneers to regret their decision to come west. In some parts of the trail, especially in Nevada, the Humboldt River was the main source of water, but it did not always run very full. The water was often muddy and foul tasting.

When emigrants saw the Forty-Mile Desert at the western end of the Humboldt River stretching in front of them, they were bitterly disappointed. Some had to throw out furniture in order to lighten the load so their animals could make it across the sand.

During winter, the bitter cold in the mountains made travel just as hard. For pioneers going to California, the rugged Sierra Nevada was the last obstacle. Wagons sometimes had to be taken apart so they could be lowered down the high mountains.

Death Valley Trail

A group of 107 wagons led by Lewis Manly followed the Old Spanish Trail across the southern tip of Nevada. Part of the pioneers, including several families with young children, decided to split off this trail in search of a shortcut. In 1849, they traveled slowly through the Mojave Desert, where they nearly perished. Manly and another man made a 200-mile trek to a California ranch to get food and made it back in time to save the starving group. They struggled out of the region and gave Death Valley its name.

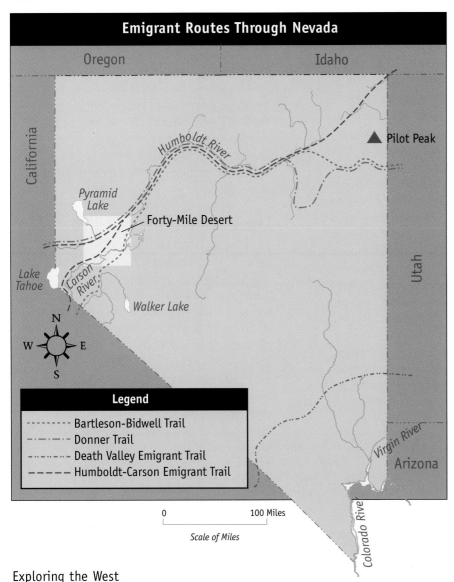

Emigrant Routes Through Nevada

Oregon

Idaho

California

Humboldt River

▲ Pilot Peak

Pyramid Lake

Forty-Mile Desert

Lake Tahoe

Carson River

Utah

Walker Lake

N
W   E
S

Legend
- - - - - Bartleson-Bidwell Trail
- · - · - Donner Trail
- ·· - ·· Death Valley Emigrant Trail
- — — — Humboldt-Carson Emigrant Trail

Arizona

Virgin River

Colorado River

0   100 Miles

Scale of Miles

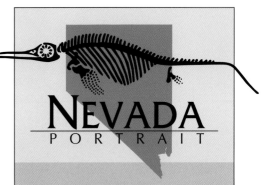

NEVADA
PORTRAIT

Kit Carson
1809 – 1868

Christopher "Kit" Carson's name is all over Nevada. The state capital, Carson City, and Carson River are named for him. He is a legend among mountain men.

Carson left home when he was 16 to work as a trapper and a guide. He could neither read nor write, which may have hurt his chances of becoming a leader when Smith and Ogden were more educated. But Carson compensated for this by learning about the West so well that many fur traders and emigrants wanted his services as a guide.

On the deck of a steamer on the Missouri River, young Kit Carson met John C. Frémont, who wrote of him, "He was a man of medium height, broad-shouldered and deep-chested, with a clear steady blue eye and frank speech and address; quiet and unassuming. . . ." Frémont hired Carson to help guide him through the West.

By joining Frémont's parties, Carson was on his way to fame. He was portrayed in Frémont's accounts as a tough, knowledgeable mountain man who understood trails and the people who traveled them.

Exploring the West

A wide valley and bright sunshine welcomed the pioneers to the Great Basin. Salt Lake Valley was painted by William Henry Jackson.

The Mormons used no guides except Brigham Young's copy of Frémont's report, which he read before leaving Illinois.

Mistaken Migration— The Donner Party

One group paid dearly for its determination to go to California. Three emigrant parties left Missouri in the spring, but the Donner party fell behind. In a hurry, they took a cutoff suggested by Lansford Hastings, who had published a book on how best to reach California. Hastings proved far less knowledgeable than he claimed to be.

The Donner party crossed the desert west of the Great Salt Lake then traveled across Nevada and reached the Sierra foothills. Winter was near. When they tried to cross the mountains, heavy snows made the trail impossible to follow. They were trapped. Almost half of the 87 people, including men, women, and children, died. Some of the survivors may have eaten the human flesh of the dead to survive.

The Reed family were part of the Donner party. Virginia Reed was 12 years old at the time and wrote this after she was rescued:

> We had nothing to eat but ox hides. O Mary I would cry and wish I had what you all wasted . . . we had to kill littel cash the dog and eat him we ate his entrails and feet and hide and evry thing about him.

A Religious Migration

Among the pioneers who came west, one group stands out for why they came and how they survived. The members of The Church of Jesus Christ of Latter-day Saints (LDS), often called Mormons, thrived in the desert valleys of the Rocky Mountains. Most emigrants sought wealth, adventure, and Indians to convert. The Mormons, however, came in search of religious freedom, independence, and safety.

The Birth of a New Church

Just as Jedediah Smith came from an area of religious revivals in New York, so did LDS Church founder Joseph Smith (no relation to Jedediah). Right from the start, the Mormons suffered *intolerance* for differing from Protestant sects and for their claims that a new book of scripture, The Book of Mormon, was, along with the Bible, another witness to Jesus Christ. As more and more converts joined the group, their large voting power angered local residents. Several times they were driven out of different states by angry mobs.

Brigham Young Takes Over

At the death of Joseph Smith, stocky, red-headed Brigham Young, a dedicated supporter of Smith, took over leadership of the church. Young reasoned that Mormons faced opposition, even violence, wherever they went. The answer was to go far away from other people and live on their own.

During the middle of a record-breaking cold winter, Young led about 3,000 people and 500 wagons across the frozen Mississippi River out of Illinois and headed west. They were joined by thousands more that spring and summer. For over a year they made camps in many places across Iowa and Nebraska. Many groups finally crossed the Rocky Mountains into Utah. As Brigham Young looked over the desert valley that July day in 1847, the Salt Lake shimmering in the distance, he said, "This is the right place."

They named the area Deseret (des er ET), a word from the Book of Mormon that means "honeybee," a symbol of industry. The pioneers worked hard to make a home in the West. Almost as soon as they were settled in the Salt Lake Valley, Brigham Young sent groups to start new farming towns all around the West, including Nevada.

The Mexican Cession

Before the Mormons came to Utah, U.S. President James Polk wanted to add three areas to the United States—Oregon, California, and Texas.

Texas had long been *controversial*. Americans began settling this large piece of northern Mexico in the 1820s. By the 1830s, they wanted to break from Mexico. Texas won independence and was a separate nation by 1836. Then, in 1845, the U.S. Senate voted to annex Texas to the United States, and it became a state.

Polk wanted to expand the boundaries of the United States even more. In the northwest, *negotiations* resulted in adding what became the states of Oregon and Washington. Now Polk had his eyes on the biggest prize of all.

The Mexican-American War

Adding sunny California, which belonged to Mexican people whose national religion was Catholic, was far harder than acquiring Oregon, whose people were mostly white Protestant like the rest of the country.

Eventually the solution to winning California was tied up with Texas. The United States and Mexico disagreed on the state's southern boundary. Polk sent troops into the *disputed* area and a *skirmish* broke out. Claiming, "American blood has been shed on American soil," Polk asked Congress to declare war on Mexico.

The Mexican-American War was a success for the United States. Its soldiers swept through the Southwest, suffering few deaths as they beat the Mexican army.

The United States and Mexico signed the Treaty of Guadalupe-Hidalgo. Mexico got $15 million. The United States got 500,000 square miles of land that included most of the West. All pioneers who had left the United States and settled on Mexican land were now back in the United States.

What mattered far more to Americans was that they now owned California. They had no idea just how profitable that would be.

What do you think?

What if the United States had never fought the Mexican-American War? Do you think the United States would own California, Nevada, and the rest of the West today?

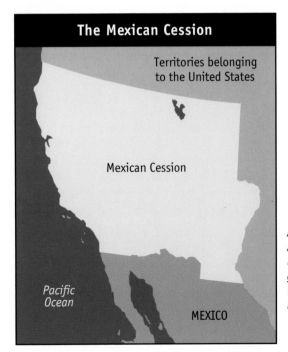

The Mexican Cession

Territories belonging to the United States

Mexican Cession

Pacific Ocean

MEXICO

Polk sent messengers to the Mexican government with an offer. For $40 million, the United States would buy California. Mexico was insulted.

"I had California and the fine bay of San Francisco as much in view as Oregon."

— James K. Polk, on his plans to acquire California

After the Mexican-American War the United States had grown to include the West almost as we know it today.

Many years after the California gold rush, artists painted their ideas of the people and the event. What can you learn about the gold rush from this painting? What can you learn about the time period?

GOLD GOLD GOLD!

Nine days before California became part of the United States, James Marshall was helping dig a sawmill at property owned by Swiss immigrant John Sutter on the American River near Sacramento. He found yellow specks in the dirt. The news worked its way back east. By 1849, the gold rush was underway.

California's Population Grows

During the gold rush, thousands of gold-seekers rushed to California. Many came to dig or pan for gold, but others saw they could make money without getting dirty. They opened stores, saloons, schools, churches, rooming houses—everything you find in a typical city.

Gold seekers, usually single men, could travel one of three main routes to California: sail around the tip of South America; sail to Panama, walk across the malaria-infested jungle to the Pacific, then catch a ship headed north to California; or go overland. The first two ways took too long for most gold seekers.

That left the overland route, which included traveling across Nevada along the Humboldt River. Thousands, traveling in groups or families, crossed the desert between Salt Lake City and the Sierra Nevada. Some who went to California later came back across the mountains to dig in Nevada.

The gold rush proved important to Nevada's growth. In every future mining rush, the people imitated what had

been done in California. They formed a mining district and appointed a recorder to keep track of the claims. A town grew near the mine to provide goods and services to the miners.

How Nevada Became Part of Two Territories

The arrival of so many gold seekers created a problem. A territory could become a state when its population reached 60,000. California had swept past that mark.

If California became a state, it would be a free state, breaking the 15-15 deadlock between slave and free states in the U.S. Senate. This would give the free states a voting advantage. Thus, southern slaveowners and their representatives in Congress had no desire to make California a state.

The result was the Compromise of 1850. The compromise was a way to settle the disagreements over slavery. Far away from Nevada in Washington, D.C., Congress and the president sought to *appease* both the North and the South by giving each region something it wanted:

- People in the North were required by law to return runaway slaves.

- California became a free state.

- Two new territories were formed, and each territory could vote on whether or not it wanted to allow slavery. This was called *popular sovereignty*, or voting by the local people.

The New Mexico Territory consisted of present-day New Mexico, Arizona, and today's Clark County, Nevada. It never did vote on the slavery issue.

The Utah Territory included today's Utah and the rest of Nevada. Utah surprised Congress by allowing slavery, even though it was never widely practiced.

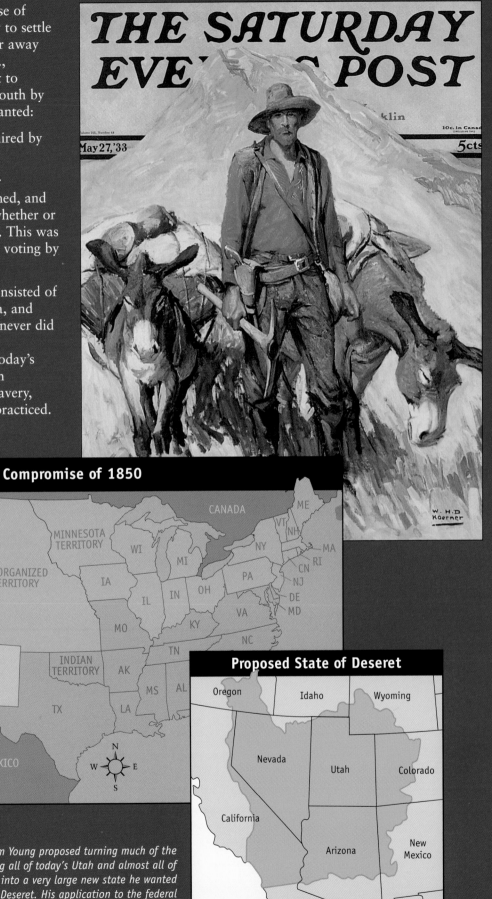

Compromise of 1850

OREGON TERRITORY

MINNESOTA TERRITORY

CANADA

ME

VT
NH

WI

NY

MA

MI

CN
RI

UNORGANIZED TERRITORY

PA

NJ

UTAH TERRITORY

IA

IL

IN

OH

DE
MD

CA

VA

MO

KY

Pacific Ocean

NEW MEXICO TERRITORY

INDIAN TERRITORY

TN

NC

AK

MS

AL

TX

LA

Legend
- Free state or territory
- Slave state or territory
- Territory open to slavery

MEXICO

N
W E
S

Proposed State of Deseret

Oregon

Idaho

Wyoming

Nevada

Utah

Colorado

California

Arizona

New Mexico

In Utah, Brigham Young proposed turning much of the West, including all of today's Utah and almost all of today's Nevada, into a very large new state he wanted to call Deseret. His application to the federal government in Washington was denied.

Exploring the West

Chapter 3 Review

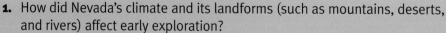

What Do You Remember?

1. Why did Spain send Columbus and future explorers to the New World?

2. What effect did these men have on the Native American population?

3. What national and international events affected Nevada in this period?

4. Why did Spain use the mission system? How did it function?

5. Why were the missions important to the West, including present-day Nevada?

6. Compare Jedediah Smith and Peter Skene Ogden. How were their motivations alike and different? What did they accomplish?

7. What was Joseph Walker's significance to Nevada and its development?

8. What was John C. Frémont's significance to Nevada and the West?

9. What were some of the reasons immigrant parties came to the West?

10. Why did the United States want to own Texas, Oregon, and California? How were these areas alike? How were they different?

11. What problems did adding new territories create for the United States? What was the attempt to solve these problems?

Geography Tie-In

1. How did Nevada's climate and its landforms (such as mountains, deserts, and rivers) affect early exploration?

2. On the maps on page 53 and 59, trace the expeditions of the following people or groups: Jedediah Smith, the Bartleson-Bidwell party, the Donner party, and the Mormons. Find where they started and where they finished. What were the main rivers they followed? Why would they follow rivers?

3. Walk from your home or school to a safe nearby location, like a friend's home or a store. Take along a notebook and draw a map of where you go, including landmarks such as buildings, parks, or other places. How difficult is map-making? Would you say your map is accurate enough for someone to follow? Compare this experience with an explorer who made maps of hundreds of miles of unfamiliar land.

Activity

Gold Strike Prices, 1848

One traveler reported that at the 40-Mile Desert from the Humboldt to the Truckee Meadows, water sold for $1 a gallon! Other prices were:

Eastern newspapers............$1 each	coffee..........................$5 a pound
loaf of bread ....50-75 cents	butcher knives..................$30 each
Kentucky whiskey..............$30 a quart	blankets......................$40 each
apples.......................$1-5 each	boots $100
eggs ....$50 a dozen	hotel rooms....................$1,000 per month

How do these prices compare with today? Look in newspaper ads or in stores to find out. Keep in mind that at the time, normal prices in pioneer farming towns were much lower than they are today.

Activity

Mountain Man Slang

Like other groups and people, the trappers developed some slang words, which they used among themselves. Slang words are words that are deliberately used in place of standard terms. Match the slang words to their meanings.

Slang Terms	Meanings
buffler •	• Rocky Mountains
cache •	• buffalo
critter •	• hiding place for furs
fixins •	• animal
pill •	• bullet
give 'em a teach •	• teach them a lesson
make beaver •	• an even trade
para swap •	• sack of things
possible sack •	• the way things happened
Shining Mountains •	• food
the way the stick floats •	• things needed in the trapping business
vittles •	• make money

Activity

Research a Timeline

Review the timeline on pages 46-47 and choose one event to learn more about. Locate the event in the chapter, use at least two different sources to get information, and then write a paper about it. Or, write a script and act out the event with your class.

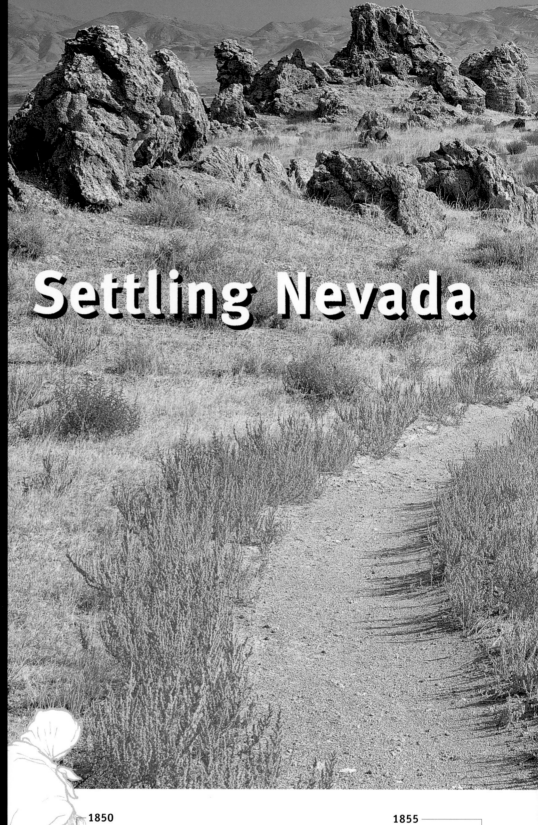

Settling Nevada

Timeline of Events

1850
California, Utah Territory, and New Mexico Territory are created.

1855
LDS Church starts a mission in Las Vegas.

1855
Judges are appointed for Carson County.

1850 — 1852 — 1854

1850
Mormons open a trading post in Carson Valley.

1851
John Reese and other pioneers expand Mormon Station.

1854
Carson County is created as part of the Utah Territory. Its people petition for creation of a separate territory.

Chapter 4

WORDS TO UNDERSTAND
annex
assay
controversy
delegate
distinct
grist mill
legislature
mar
petition
propose
refine
reign
secede
specimen
stringent
subsidy
technology
transcontinental

The emigrant trail along the historic Humboldt River route was hot and dry. Things got worse when Humboldt water sank into the desert. The weary travelers still faced 40 miles of desert before reaching another source of water.

Photo by Jeff Gnass

1859
Gold is discovered in Carson County.

1859
"Rush to Washoe" silver and gold rush begins.

1861
U.S. Congress creates the Nevada Territory.

1863
Leaders write a proposed state constitution.

1864
October 31, Lincoln signs a proclamation creating the State of Nevada.

1858

1860

1862

1864

1857
Las Vegas missionaries move back to Utah.

1857
"Mormon War" Federal troops head for Utah.

1860
White settlers battle Northern Paiutes in the Pyramid Lake War.

1861
James Nye is appointed first territorial governor.

Gold was found at Sutter's Mill in California, and eager miners headed west to get their share of the riches.

Stopping Off for Profit

When gold was discovered in California, it caused a stir across the nation. People swarmed to the West. Some men from Salt Lake City, loaded down with camping gear, mining tools, and food, crossed Nevada on their way to California. They were the first non-Indians to stay for any length of time in what is now Nevada.

One of them, Abner Blackburn, was headed to California when he camped at Gold Canyon and did some prospecting. He found the first known gold discovery in what is now Nevada. Two years later, more than 200 miners were working at the mouth of the canyon and some wintered and stayed on in what is now Dayton, Nevada. A permanent trading post first known as Hall's Station opened there in 1852. As a result, Dayton residents claim their town was Nevada's first settlement. They also claim Dayton as having the first dance party in Nevada, the first marriage, the first divorce, the first non-Native American child born, and the first Chinatown. It was a housing area for Chinese workers.

Settling Carson Valley

Another place, Genoa, also claims to be first. In 1850, Captain Joseph DeMont, Hampton Beatie, and others in their party stopped at the Sierra Nevada foothills when they realized that gold seekers would need supplies along the route to California. Since no major supply points existed that far west, they built a log trading post that came to be called Mormon Station. They brought in flour, bacon, beans, and other goods from California and sold or traded them to travelers. As winter came, DeMont and Beatie returned to Salt Lake City and others went to California, but the building stayed and so did the opportunity for riches.

When Hampton Beatie returned to Salt Lake City he worked at a general store run by John and Enoch Reese. Beatie told his bosses about the Carson Valley trading post. John Reese saw an opportunity. In the spring he took 10 wagons full of supplies

• **Dayton**
• **Mormon Station**

Genoa Fort was formerly Mormon Station. Mormon Station was the first permanent non-Indian settlement in Nevada.

and seeds for planting and headed west. Besides hoping to earn a living, Reese hoped to settle Carson Valley for Utah and for the Mormons.

One man wrote the following about the beginning of Mormon Station:

> I arrived at that station . . . and stayed there to rest one day. I sold a good American horse to the man who kept the trading post for thirty pounds of flour and fifteen dollars. . . .
>
> There were two or three women and some children at the place. . . . They had quite a band of fat cattle and cows which they brought from Salt Lake; some of the fattest beef I ever saw hung from the limbs of a big pine tree. . . . there was one store where they kept for sale flour, beans, tea, coffee, sugar, dried peaches, sardines, tobacco, miners' clothing, overalls, shirts, etc. There was also a grocery where they sold whiskey, bread, cigars and tobacco.

Reese's business was a success, and this inspired others to follow in his footsteps. More settlers, most of them miners came to Carson Valley and nearby Eagle Valley and explored Gold Canyon. They planted the seeds from which the Comstock mining rush, and Nevada, would grow.

Activity

Nevada's First Settlement?
Both Dayton and Genoa have claimed to be Nevada's first settlement. Search the Internet for evidence to support either claim.

Silver Among the Gold

There were 100-200 miners looking for gold in the Virginia Range next to the Sierras. As they panned and dug, they kept finding a dark-colored, sandy substance. They kept the gold but threw away the other stuff. Little did they know they were throwing away silver.

The miners knew little about silver, but they could have done nothing with it anyway. Silver needs to be *refined*, and they had neither the knowledge nor the money for equipment.

One pair of miners, however, suspected that keeping the silver might be worthwhile. The two Grosh brothers worked in California in the winter and spent their summers in Carson Valley. They claimed to have found a "monster ledge" of silver and looked for investors to finance their digging.

Unfortunately for the Groshes, they never saw it happen. One died of an injury, and the other died from frostbite while crossing through the snowy Sierras a few weeks later.

Women Came Too

The pioneers who followed the Humboldt River to Carson Valley and beyond to California were not just men. Women and children also made the long journey by wagon. They often kept diaries or journals about their trip. Harriet Ward wrote about traveling through Nevada in 1853:

> We crossed the . . . Humboldt, which we found to be good. . . . Our camping ground is very beautiful, being almost surrounded by willows and roses. . . . Made about sixteen miles.

Another woman, Catherine Haun, didn't write such a glowing report:

> It was with . . . apprehension that we started to traverse the treeless region of the Great Basin or Sink of the Humboldt. Our wagons were badly worn, the animals much the worse for wear, food and stock feed was getting low with no chance of replenishing the supply. . . .
>
> The . . . dust of this territory was suffocating, irritating our throats and clouds of it often blinded us. . . . the water was unfit to drink or to use in any way.

Catherine Haun wrote about what she wore on the trail:

> When we started from Iowa I wore a dark woolen dress which served me almost constantly during the whole trip. Never without an apron and a three-cornered kerchief, . . . I presented a comfortable, neat appearance. The wool protected me from the sun's rays and [cold] prairie winds.

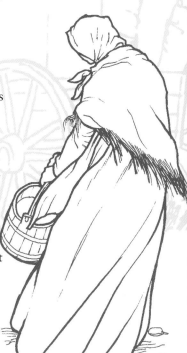

Brigham Young was governor of the Utah Territory, which included most of today's Nevada.

Squatter Government

At the time, Nevada was part of the Utah Territory. Brigham Young, president of the LDS Church, was also governor of the territory. Young and the other leaders lived far away in Salt Lake City.

To bring law and order to the settlements in Carson Valley, more than 100 men met at Mormon Station to create a "squatter" government. That meant that since they were far from any formal government, they would meet, elect officers, and vote on their own rules. They also sent word to the U.S. Congress across the country in Washington, D.C., to request "a *distinct* Territorial Government" for their area.

This was the start of a conflict that would *mar* the small settlement for the next decade. The population in Carson Valley was mostly miners and a few Mormons. Most of the miners wanted nothing to do with the LDS Church and its strict rules. However, the miners lived in a place run by Mormons. Clashes between the groups were bound to follow.

Mormons and Miners Respond

The Utah government did little in response to the requests of the Carson Valley settlers, so the settlers asked California to *annex* the area. Then they could be part of California instead of part of Utah. This never happened.

In Salt Lake City, officials finally responded by creating Carson County. But they appointed no officials to run the new county, so settlers were left exactly as they were before.

The people of Carson County hired a lawyer to draft a constitution setting up their own colony. Disturbed by news of the *proposed* colony, the territorial *legislature* appointed judges and gave Carson County a vote.

Salt Lake officials sent Orson Hyde, a high official in the LDS Church, to be a county judge. About 40 Mormons moved to Carson County with Hyde. The small settlements grew with the sound of children and teens who came to live in the foothills of the Sierras with their families. For about two years, the Mormons worked to build a religious community. They started new towns. Mormon Station was renamed Genoa. Sixty more families came to farm, bringing the total to about 500 people by 1857.

What do you think?

How might Nevada's history have been different if California had annexed Carson County?

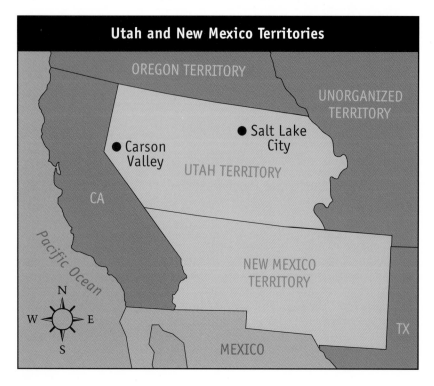

Utah and New Mexico Territories

OREGON TERRITORY

UNORGANIZED TERRITORY

● Salt Lake City

● Carson Valley

UTAH TERRITORY

CA

Pacific Ocean

NEW MEXICO TERRITORY

TX

MEXICO

N
W E
S

Nevada: A Journey of Discovery

Daniel Jacks drew this picture of pioneers camping along the Humboldt River in July 1859. What activities are going on in camp?

The Church Takes Charge

Orson Hyde asked California's governor to order a boundary survey to settle the issue of whether the eastern Sierra foothills belonged to California or to the Utah Territory. When the survey showed that Mormon Station was in Utah, Hyde held elections. The new arrivals won almost every office.

The miners and other non-Mormon settlers were no happier with the Mormon government than they were without any government at all. They again asked California to annex the area, but Congress, which would have to approve any boundary change, said that California was already large enough.

Filling the Mormon Corridor

The church officials who ran Utah Territory were doing more than responding to a need for government in Carson County. Brigham Young wanted his territory to be as independent as possible. He worked to make all the settlements productive, growing their own food and making the things they needed. As part of the plan, he mapped out a series of fort-missions from Salt Lake City to southern California. The Mormons in these settlements tried to introduce religion and farming to American Indians, sell supplies to overland travelers, and provide aid and comfort to other Mormons coming and going from Utah towns.

Settling the Muddy

Elizabeth Hunter was the fourth polygamous wife of Joseph Murdock. In 1856 they were called by Brigham Young to assist in colonizing Carson Valley. They moved from Salt Lake City with a group of Mormon pioneers. They carried seeds, planted crops, and with the first harvest bought a homestead from the Mexicans. Within a few years, however, they were called back to Utah, so they traded their land for horses and cash.

After three years, the Murdock family and others were again called to start a new settlement in Nevada, this time on the Muddy River. Families again made a long journey and planted cotton, grain, vegetables, and fruit in time to see grasshoppers devoure crops and swarms of mosquitoes bring malaria fever. Because of the extreme heat and mosquitoes, most of the farming was done at night in the dark.

In 1870 Brigham Young made the long trip from Salt Lake City to the Muddy by wagon. Tears came to his eyes when he saw the ragged, barefoot children and tired, worn-looking men and women. He released the settlers from any obligations to stay.

The Murdocks and others left in one group, leaving behind homes, fields, orchards, and vineyards. They received not a penny for their property, as no one wanted to settle on the Muddy. Alva Murdock, a boy of 13, drove one of the heavy wagons. As they crossed the last ridge beyond the Muddy, the family stopped to look back one last time, and all except one were shocked to see their cabin going up in smoke. Alva admitted he had set the fire and said, "I want to go someplace where there are schools and where my mother won't have to work so hard. We're never going back there!"

The Las Vegas Mission

Las Vegas Mission ●

Las Vegas was part of what was known as the Mormon Corridor, a string of new Mormon communities through Idaho, Utah, Nevada, Arizona, and into southern California. You can see a map of these settlements on page 73.

Brigham Young sent about 30 missionaries to establish the Las Vegas Mission and build a supply and rest station between southern Utah and San Bernardino, California. They arrived under the command of church official William Bringhurst.

Bringhurst and his group built an adobe fort and a mud-walled corral. They dug irrigation ditches from the creek to their farms. They also started an experimental farm where they hoped to teach the Paiutes how to grow their own food.

The following year more men arrived, some bringing their wives and children. The group grew to more than 100 people.

> Shortly after we arrived here, we assembled all the chiefs and made an agreement treaty with them for permission to make a settlement on their lands. We agreed to treat them well, and they were to observe the same conduct towards us, and with all white men. Peace was to be preserved with all emigrants traveling through this country, as well as with the settlers. If travelers through this country will use the Indians well, there will be no trouble with them.
>
> —William Bringhurst, July 10, 1855

"By the aid of irrigation [the land could] be highly productive. There is water enough in this rapid little stream to propel a **grist mill** *. . . and oh such water! It comes just at the end of a 50-mile stretch without a drop of water or a spear of grass."*

—Addison Pratt, passing through Las Vegas region, 1848

Lead Mining or Missionary Work?

After a while, the Mormon settlers at the mission became as divided as the settlers in Carson County, but for different reasons. Exploring the area one day, men found lead north of the mission at Mt. Potosi. Word of the find was sent back to Salt Lake City. Excited at the news, President Young sent Nathaniel Jones to get the lead out—literally.

The problem was that Bringhurst thought the Mormons were in Las Vegas to farm and to educate the Indians, not to mine. He and Jones wrestled for control of the mission. Finally, the need for lead prompted Young to remove Bringhurst from command. Unfortunately, the lead proved to be useless.

The missionaries were frustrated, not only over leadership issues, but over the Paiutes' lack of interest in farming and Mormonism. The scorching summers made life miserable. It was hard to grow enough food in the desert to feed all the people. About two years after starting the mission, Young released the missionaries, and almost all of them returned to Salt Lake City.

What do you think**?**

- What might be some of the reasons the Mormons wanted to settle in other places outside Salt Lake City?
- Why did Bringhurst make a treaty with the Indians?
- If the lead found in the region had been useful, would that have justified mining rather than teaching the Indians to farm?

Activity

Research

There are several ideas in this chapter that could be expanded by more research. Choose one of these subjects to learn more about. Use the Internet (see www.1st100.com) or library books.

1. Las Vegas Mission: What can you learn about the purpose of the mission and the lifestyle there? What was the result of the mission from the Indian point of view?
2. Lead: What was it used for in pioneer times and now?
3. Indian treaties in Nevada: Were they made often, and, if so, were they usually honored by both sides?

Early Mormon Settlements

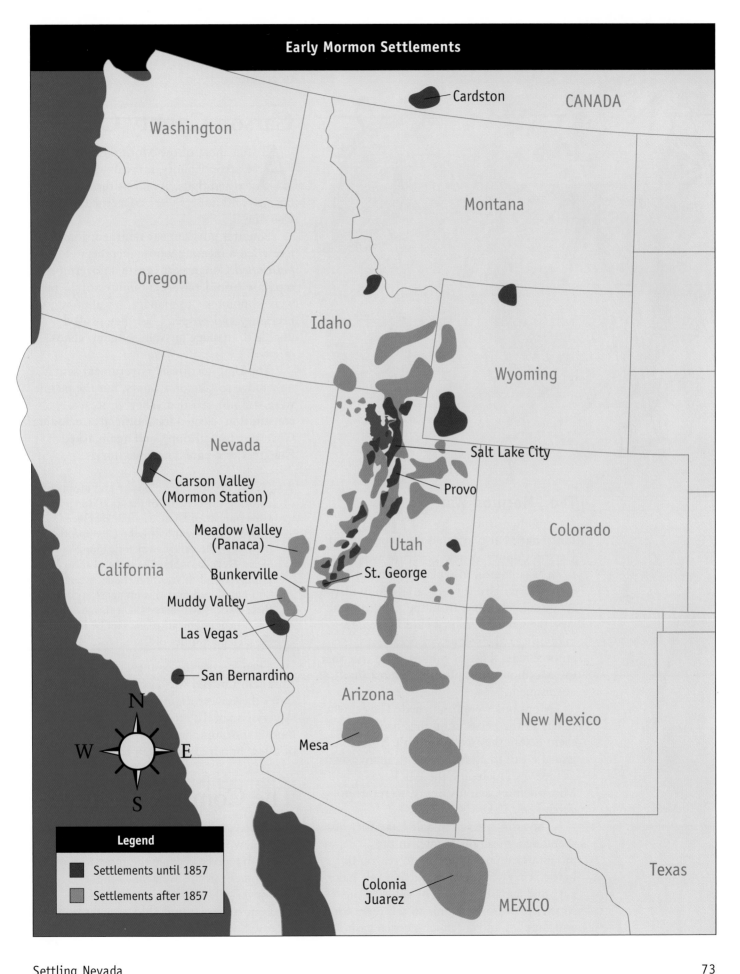

Cardston

CANADA

Washington

Montana

Oregon

Idaho

Wyoming

Nevada

Salt Lake City

Carson Valley
(Mormon Station)

Provo

Meadow Valley
(Panaca)

Utah

Colorado

Bunkerville

St. George

California

Muddy Valley

Las Vegas

San Bernardino

N

W   E

S

Arizona

Mesa

New Mexico

Legend

Settlements until 1857

Settlements after 1857

Colonia
Juarez

MEXICO

Texas

The "Mormon War"

Another problem for the Las Vegas missionaries also affected the Mormons of Carson County. A new governor was sent from Washington to replace Brigham Young as territorial governor. A large group of U.S. Army soldiers came from the East to make sure the new governor would be able to take office. The soldiers also came to enforce federal law if rumors were true that the Mormons were plotting against the U.S. government.

Mormons were frightened. They saw a replay of the persecution that had afflicted them before they came to Utah. Young issued a call to all Mormons in many towns in the West, including the Las Vegas Mission and Carson County, to return to defend Salt Lake City.

The army arrived in Salt Lake City after spending a miserable winter in the mountains, but they found no reason to battle. They set up camp outside Salt Lake City and actually proved of value to the Mormons, who were able to sell them food and supplies and get much-needed cash in exchange. The new governor took office with Brigham Young's promise of cooperation, and each vowed to do his best to get along.

Carson County Chaos

After most of the Mormons left Carson County, no real government existed there. As far as the remaining farmers and miners were concerned, that was fine.

Squatter government returned. John Reese led a meeting whose members *petitioned* Congress to create a government separate from Utah. A committee of 28 men were appointed "to manage . . . all matters necessary and proper," but they proved unable to manage anything. Again, chaos *reigned*.

The Utah territorial government sent a new judge to Carson County, but the people were still not satisfied. They wrote a constitution, elected local officials (including Governor Isaac Roop), and again asked Congress to create a new territory:

> We are destitute of all power and means of enjoying the benefits of the local Territorial Government of Utah, . . . The distance between the Great Salt Lake City and the [many] fertile valleys which lie along . . . the Sierra Nevada, where the most of the population of this section reside, is nearly 800 miles, and over this immense space there sweeps two deserts. On this account no . . . communication . . . can be held with the civil authorities of Utah.

Then, across the country in the East, Abraham Lincoln was elected president. The states there were arguing bitterly about slavery issues. The federal government had more important concerns than the problems of a few hundred settlers in the West.

The Comstock Lode

The Carson County settlers soon had new interests. The discovery of gold and silver became the most important development in the West since the California gold rush.

Four miners found gold at what became the town of Gold Hill. A few weeks later, thinking they had found all they could, the men sold their claim. James Finney received ten dollars and a horse. A few days later he fell off the horse and died.

The second discovery was in Six-Mile Canyon. Early in June miners Patrick McLaughlin and Peter O'Riley tried to improve the flow of a spring at the entry to the canyon. They found gold in the sand and soon dug their way to a ledge of gold and silver. The men went to town to celebrate, and when they returned, they found another miner, Henry Comstock, standing next to the spring. Comstock, long known for laziness, told them that he and another miner, Emanuel Penrod, had claimed the spring.

McLaughlin and O'Riley decided caution was the best policy. They made Comstock and Penrod their partners and claimed about 1,500 feet along the vein. They added two more partners who built a mill to crush the ore for processing.

Comstock spent the rest of his life wandering the West, talking about "my" claim. The Washoe Diggings, named after the nearby Indians, went down in history as the Comstock Lode.

The *Semi-Weekly Observer*, a California newspaper, featured the earliest known report of the discovery July 2, 1859:

We saw a **specimen** of the Carson Valley gold quartz yesterday. The rock is very different in appearance to the quartz in this vicinity. It has a bluish cast. . . . The sample we examined was full of gold, however, and . . . the owners have doubtless found a good thing.

What do you think?

Gold Hill discoverer James Finney actually may have been named James Fennimore. Many miners changed their names when they came west, hoping to escape the law or family members trying to find them. This began a Nevada tradition of people moving here to start over and be accepted for who they are, despite what they may have done in the past.

Have you ever based your feelings about someone on what you heard about him or her, instead of what you learned yourself by getting to know the person? Is there anything wrong with making judgments about people based on what others say?

Comstock's nickname was "old pancake" because he was too lazy to cook anything more difficult.

Mining towns like Gold Hill sprung up around Nevada.

From 1865 to 1880 the parish of St. Mary's had up to 5,000 members, most of whom were Irish miners. These were the boom days of Virginia City. More Irish emigrants came to work on the railroad. Father Patrick Manogue came in 1862.

The Word Spreads

Whenever a miner found a large vein of gold, the word got around fast. An *assay*, or evaluation, of the Comstock gold and silver lode found the value to be almost $4,000 per ton. At the time, $100 a ton would have been a great find. When this news spread, the "Rush to Washoe" had begun.

Small towns sprouted on the hillsides. Finney threw down a bottle and christened a new town in honor of his home state, "Ol' Virginny." The name stuck, and Virginia City grew. At first the business places and homes consisted only of tents or huts of mud, sagebrush, stone, or even barrels. Miners wanted to find gold and silver, not spend time building homes. In time, however, lumber was brought in from the mountain forests, and wood buildings dotted the hillsides.

Just as in California gold rush towns, cities grew up quickly, miners streamed in, and stores and other businesses opened to make money off the miners.

Nevada: A Journey of Discovery

An article in the *Mountain Democrat*, 1860, described the mining towns:

> I have noticed some eight or ten small buildings in the course of construction, but some of them have been stopped for the want of lumber. Nearly all of the "buildings" here are canvas; a few are of rough stone, and some of them are merely holes dug in the hillside, and covered over with brush and dried hides, presenting more the appearance of an Indian wigwam than that of a City. . . The principal business going on at present is eating, drinking, and gambling.

While some of the miners came from the East, more of them simply came back across the Sierra from California. The miners set up yet another form of local government. They set punishments for crimes and banned gambling—but obviously not forever, as Nevada's future history would prove.

Recording the Claims

One important job was recording claims. The Gold Hill Mining District

defined the duties of one official:

> The duty of the Recorder shall be to keep in a well-bound book a record of all claims, . . . with the names of the parties, . . . where situated, and the date of location or purchase; also to return a certificate for such claim or claims.

Sometimes records were "adjusted" according to greed. A Virginia City newspaper reporter and historian wrote:

> . . . the book of records was kept at a saloon, where it lay upon a shelf behind the bar. The "boys" were in the habit of taking it from behind the bar whenever they desired to consult it, and if they thought a location made by them was not [to their advantage] they altered the course of their lines, and fixed the whole thing up in good shape. . . . When the book was not wanted for this use, those lounging about the saloon were in the habit of snatching it up, and "batting" each other over the head with it.

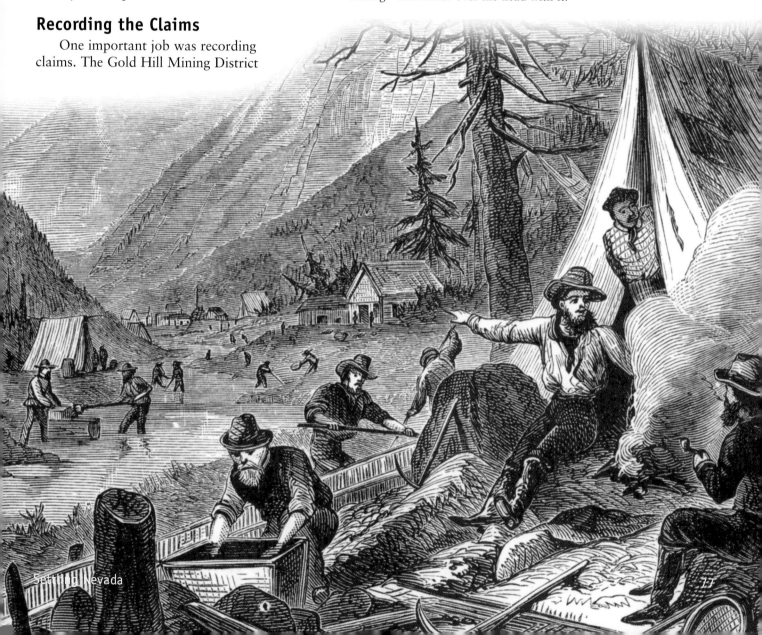

Native Americans and the Miners

The arrival of so many miners and other settlers created a new set of problems for Nevada's native people. Amid the squabbling in Carson County, both Mormons and miners largely ignored the Indians. But as the Washoe Diggings spread, Northern Paiutes and their allies—Bannocks from southern Oregon—met at Pyramid Lake. The Paiutes were concerned about the region in which they hunted, fished, and gathered food.

The Pyramid Lake War

After the meeting the Indians learned that two Indian women had been kidnapped at a trading post. The Bannocks then killed three whites and burned down the trading post. The usually peaceful Paiutes in the area readied for battle.

Miners and other settlers formed military companies, one led by Major William Ormsby, but there was no organized preparation. The Indians led them into an ambush, killing 76 of the 105 settlers who fought them. One of the dead was Major Ormsby.

Sarah Winnemucca had lived with the Ormsbys and was loyal to them. Sarah's brother tried to save Major Ormsby's life in the battle but was not successful. Sarah later wrote, "Brave deeds don't always get rewarded in this world."

Panic gripped the towns along the Comstock Lode. About 550 men volunteered to fight Indians, with more than 200 soldiers coming from California. They met along the Truckee River and finally defeated the Northern Paiutes and Bannock. The Indians never again gathered in such large numbers, but resorted to raiding emigrant wagon trains.

The army soldiers built a fort at Pyramid Lake, then another one on the Carson River. Nevada's native people were learning, to their sadness, and despite the peace that had existed between them and the settlers, that miners and other white settlers planned to control the area.

Activity

Two Points of View

Numaga

Numaga, a Northern Paiute leader, responded to his people after the battles at Pyramid Lake:

Could you defeat the whites in Nevada [when] from over the mountains in California would come to help them an army of white men that would cover your country like a blanket? What hope is there for the Pah-Ute? From where is to come your guns, your powder, your lead, your dried meats to live upon, and hay to feed your ponies with while you carry on this war. Your enemies have all of these things, more than they can use. They will come like the sand in a whirlwind and drive you from your homes.

Edward Bryant, a white man, described the events leading to the Pyramid Lake War in a different way:

They assembled at Pyramid Lake a few miles below Virginia City, held a council of war and determined to wipe out the whites. Then came daily news of massacres by the red villains. Ever since the discovery of these silver mines at Virginia City, they have complained and threatened. . . . The scene of the battleground . . . is horrible beyond description. The savages were not content with scalping their victims but after stripping them, mutilated their bodies in a horrible manner.

- When people disagree, it is difficult to see the other person's point of view. It's hard to understand why others act as they do. Take a side on the Pyramid Lake War, and debate the issue with your class.

- When you listen to world news, try to see both sides of an issue. How can trying to understand the other point of view help bring peace to a country, town, or family?

Nevada: A Journey of Discovery

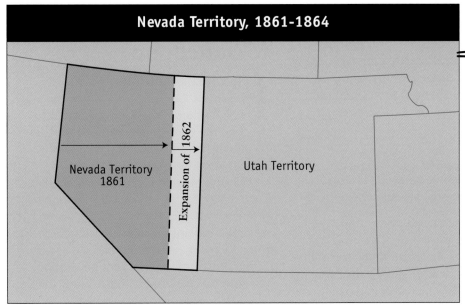

Nevada Territory, 1861-1864

Nevada Territory 1861

Expansion of 1862

Utah Territory

In 1861, the Nevada Territory did not have the same boundaries as Nevada State has today. Which of today's important cities and towns were part of the Nevada Territory? Which ones were not?

Birth of a Territory

A large number of people in the mining towns mined all day and played at night. They needed a government to keep their behavior under control. The census of 1860 showed a population of just under 7,000 in Carson County and the two counties next to it. The next year, the population had increased to about 10,000. Clearly, there was a need for a government separate from the Utah Territory.

National events also worked in the settlers' favor. Southern states began *seceding* from the Union rather than accepting the election of Abraham Lincoln, who worked to stop the spread of slavery.

When seven states left the Union, so did their votes in Congress. This meant the northern states gained more influence. In summary, one local event and one national event combined to make Nevada Territory possible:

- The Comstock Lode meant that enough people would be in Nevada to justify the creation of a territory.

- The secession of southern states meant that the question of whether or not slavery would be allowed in the territories was not as important as it had been, so Congress was not afraid to create more territories.

Congress passed a bill that created a new Nevada Territory. President James Buchanan signed it two days before he left office.

A Territorial Governor

When President Lincoln took office, he used the distant Nevada Territory to reward his supporters. He appointed James W. Nye, who had worked in New York state government, as the first territorial governor. Nye, traveling by wagon, reached the new territory just after the Fourth of July celebration. As he ordered a census and set up the election of officers, he visited Virginia City, Gold Hill, and Carson City, which was then a small town. Carson City would become the territorial capital.

NEVADA
P O R T R A I T

James Warren Nye
1814–1876

James Nye, born in upstate New York, became one of the most prominent residents of territorial Nevada and did a lot to shape the territory and the state.

As an adult, he left the Democratic Party, who were usually southern slave owners or sympathized with them, and joined the Republicans, who hoped to stop the spread of slavery.

President Lincoln appointed Nye to help organize Nevada's territorial government and serve as the first governor. He later worked for Nevada's statehood. When Nevada became a state, Nye realized his lifelong dream and was elected to be one of Nevada's members of the U.S. Senate.

In his eight years in Washington, Senator Nye strongly supported civil rights for African Americans newly freed from slavery.

Nye is remembered as the namesake of a Nevada county—and for standing up for the rights of the oppressed.

Nye and the legislature created services and passed laws that we now take for granted. They worked out a system of taxation to help fund needed services. They set up education and transportation systems.

> The public have an interest in the instruction of every child within our borders, and as a matter of economy, I [have] no doubt that it is much cheaper to furnish school houses and teachers than prisons and keepers.
> —Territorial Governor James W. Nye

Reflecting the racism of the time, the new government passed laws banning people of African American descent from marrying whites or testifying against them in court. Laws also banned horse racing and the theater on Sundays—laws common in many places at the time. Governor Nye also opposed gambling:

> I . . . recommend that you pass **stringent** laws to prevent gambling. . . . It captivates and ensnares the young, blunts all the moral sensibilities and ends in utter ruin. The thousand monuments that are reared along this pathway of ruin demand at your hands all the protection the law can give.

The Ghiradelli family posed for a picture in Genoa in 1880. How long after statehood was this picture taken?

The Winding Road to Statehood

Finally, a local bill was passed "to frame a Constitution . . . for the State of Washoe," the term then used to describe the Comstock mining region. The people of Nevada Territory voted in favor of statehood by a large majority.

Meanwhile, Nye visited Washington, D.C., to lobby for statehood. The only problem was that the U.S. Congress had yet to pass a bill authorizing Nevada Territory to make plans for statehood.

A constitutional convention—whose purpose was to write a constitution for the new state—was held anyway. Since 35 of the 39 **delegates** had come to the Nevada Territory from California, they used a lot of material from that state's constitution.

One important decision was to pick a name for the state. Despite much support for "Washoe," and less for "Humboldt" or "Esmeralda," the leaders stuck with "Nevada."

A Constitution and Corporations

The most **controversial** part of the proposed constitution had to do with mining. There were heated arguments between individual miners and large mining companies. The result was crucial to the development of mining.

Individual miners and small companies favored what was called the "multi-ledge

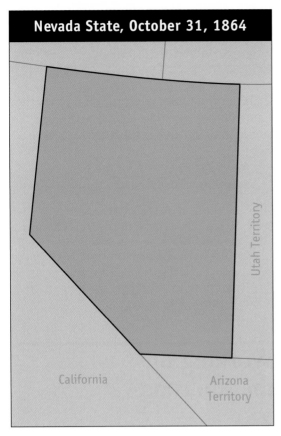

Nevada State, October 31, 1864

Utah Territory

California

Arizona Territory

theory." Veins of ore often break up and intersect under the ground. Under the multi-ledge theory, these veins were separate and anyone who found one could make a claim and make money.

But as larger corporations formed on the Comstock, they favored the "one-ledge theory." Their legal argument was that whoever found an ore body could follow it and all of its branches to its end and claim the profits from all the connecting veins of ore. That might be hundreds of feet under the earth.

Eventually, the large mining companies and the one-ledge idea won and it was written into the proposed constitution. When the people of Nevada voted, however, they voted down the first constitution by a large margin.

A New Constitution for a New State

The following year a new group of delegates met to write a new constitution. It proved to be much the same as the defeated one, with a key exception. Only mining profits—not all of a company's assets—would be taxed, which is what the large mining companies wanted.

The delegates also had new rules to follow. The bill that Lincoln signed, called an Enabling Act because it enabled Nevadans to move toward statehood, required Nevada to follow several rules:

- Slavery was banned.
- The government could not favor any one religion.
- Nevada had to give up rights to lands not already claimed by companies or individuals. The lands would be part of the state, but they would be owned by the federal government.

The voters accepted the new constitution. The vote was 10,375 for and 1,284 against. Then officials wired the document to Washington, D.C., so that Lincoln could proclaim statehood on October 31, 1864.

This letter was sent by James Nye, governor of the Nevada Territory, to Washington leaders to persuade them to approve statehood for Nevada.

Today, the federal government owns about 86 percent of Nevada. Only in Alaska does the federal government own more land.

An Opposing View

William Forbes, editor of *The Humboldt Register*, was famous in early Nevada for disagreeing with popular opinion. What do you think of his argument against the Nevada Constitution? Why would he feel this way?

DON'T WANT ANY CONSTITUTION—That's what's the matter. The Humboldt world is dead-set against engaging to help support any more lunk-heads till times get better. . . . If we have a State Government we'll have more fat-headed officers to support; and if we undertake to support them without taxing the mines, we'll run hopelessly into debt. If we do tax them, we'll stop the development of them.

The Civil War and Statehood

Legally, Nevada should have remained a territory. Under the Northwest Ordinance, a territory was supposed to have a population of 60,000 before it could become a state. Not until the first decade of the 20th century would Nevada's population reach that number.

The myth grew that Lincoln wanted statehood for Nevada because he needed the gold and silver it produced to finance the fighting of the Civil War. That is wrong for one simple reason: Nevada already belonged to the Union as a territory and still could have provided gold and silver.

Nevada became a state because Lincoln and his fellow Republicans were thinking of the future. First came the election of 1864. People were weary of the Civil War and wanted peace at any cost. Because of the raging war, Lincoln expected to be defeated for reelection. Some think that Lincoln wanted to make Nevada a state so Nevada would vote to reelect him. Most historians, however, doubt that Lincoln cared much about the three electoral votes that Nevada would provide.

More important to Lincoln and his party was the rebuilding of the Union when the war finally ended. Another state meant another vote for the Thirteenth Amendment, which would end slavery. Lincoln had other plans for the new nation. If Lincoln and the Republicans granted statehood to Nevada, they could expect support in return. Nevada's leaders did vote Republican, although Lincoln did not live to see it.

The War Affects Nevada

The North and the South fought no battles in Nevada, but the Civil War greatly affected the state just the same. First, hundreds of Nevadans left the mines to fight in the East.

Second, Lincoln and Congress passed laws that would affect Nevada universities for years to come. As part of rebuilding the country after the war, leaders in Washington encouraged education, especially in farming and *technology*. As part of the Morrill Act, the federal government would provide land for colleges. In return, the state would agree to create courses in agriculture, mechanics, and technology. Many states created schools in this way.

Third, the state constitution ensures the state will not leave the United States like the Southern States did at the beginning of the Civil War.

Article 1, Section 2, of the Nevada Constitution reads in part:

> . . . the paramount allegiance of every citizen is due to the Federal Government . . . . and [if] any portion of the States, . . . attempt to secede from the Federal Union, . . . the Federal Government may . . . employ armed force in compelling obedience to its authority.

Nevada cast two of its three electoral votes for Lincoln. Not that Lincoln really needed them—he was reelected by a vote of 212 to 21.

Linking the Past to the Present

Usually, if a college has A&M, A&T, or Tech in its name, it has some connection to the Morrill Act. In Nevada, the state university started out as a land-grant school, teaching mining technology. Today, the Mackay School of Mines is a key part of the University of Nevada, Reno.

Working on the Railroad

Before the Civil War, southerners wanted a *transcontinental* railroad built west from New Orleans and across Texas. Northerners wanted it built west from Chicago out to the gold rush in California. When the South left the Union, northerners approved a route across the northern part of the country.

The Union Pacific built west and the Central Pacific built east. They ended up meeting at Promontory Point, Utah, about four years after the end of the Civil War.

The railroads proved important to Nevada's growth and development. Trains made it possible to ship Nevada's ore throughout the country.

The federal government encouraged construction in several ways:

- It eased limits on emigrants from Asia so the Central Pacific could hire more Chinese workers to build the tracks.

- It gave loans to the builders and gave them *subsidies* to help pay for building the line.

- It gave the railroads land, which eventually meant that Nevada's second-biggest landowner, after the federal government, was the Central Pacific.

A Central Pacific train in the high Sierra was part of the transcontinental railroad. Chinese workers, who helped lay the track, watch the train go by.

Chapter 4 Review

What Do You Remember?

1. Who founded the first trading posts in Nevada, and why?
2. What kind of government did the original settlers around the trading posts set up?
3. What national events affected Nevada in this period?
4. How did Mormons and miners get along with one another? Why?
5. Was the Mormon mission in Las Vegas a success or a failure? Explain your answer.
6. How did the "Mormon War" affect the people in Nevada?
7. How was the Comstock Lode discovered? How did it get its name?
8. What events led to the Pyramid Lake War? What were its effects?
9. How did Nevada become a territory?
10. How did James Nye help Nevada?
11. What two groups argued about mining issues as part of the constitution?
12. How did it happen that Nevada became a state, even though its population was not large enough?
13. How did the Civil War affect Nevada?
14. How did the transcontinental railroad affect mining?

Geography Tie-In

1. On a map, find the approximate location of Mormon Station. How far was it from Salt Lake City? From San Francisco? From Las Vegas?

2. On a map, trace routes that would provide travelers with enough water as they went from Salt Lake City to northern California and to southern California. Were they different than the routes the settlers and miners really traveled?

Activity

Investigating the Past in Your Town

1. Visit an original building or marker from the founding of your Nevada town. Think about what went on in the building and what Nevada life was like during that time. Report on it to your classmates or talk about it with a friend.

2. Find out if your town or county has an organization to take care of old buildings. If so, find out what you can do to help.

3. Make a list of things in your home that you use a lot. On the list, circle the things that would have been available for use by the original Nevada settlers. Talk with your class about how the settlers got along without many of the things we think we have to have today.

What Did It Cost?

Here are prices for items at a trading post in Carson Valley in the winter of 1854-55:

Pants .... $5-$10
Woolen Shirts .... $3-$4
Panama Hats $5
Boots .... $5-$14
Bacon .... $ .50 per pound
Tea .... $1.25-$1.50 per pound
Coffee .... $.45 per pound
Sugar .... $.45 per pound

Examine the list of prices.

• Research the value of money to learn how it has changed from 1850 to today.

• Calculate what the items on the list would cost in today's money.

• Go to a store, and write down what the items actually cost today.

• Was the value of a shirt higher then or now? Boots? Sugar?

Nevada as Part of the United States

Can the history of a state be separated from national events? For example, the settlement of Nevada was due to a mining discovery that had nothing to do with the Battle of Gettysburg going on in Pennsylvania about the same time.

Choose one event in this chapter that happened in Nevada, then relate it to an event in another part of the United States. Then do one of the following:

1. Act out the events with a few classmates, and see if the rest of the class can guess what you are showing.

2. Draw pictures of Nevada and United States events and place them on a map of the U.S. where they happened.

3. Think of a national or international event that has affected you personally and tell the class about it, write about it, or develop a hypothesis about actions leading up to the event.

Settling Nevada

A Mining State

Timeline of Events

1861
Nevada Territory is created.
Samuel Clemens arrives.

1864
Nevada becomes a state.
Bank of California opens Virginia City branch.
Panaca and Callville are started.
Silver is discovered at Pioche and Eureka.

1860   1862   1864   1866

1860
Mining begins at Aurora.
Square-set timbering is invented.
The Pony Express begins riding across Nevada.

1865
Octavius Gass
starts a cattle
ranch at the Las
Vegas Mission.

1859
The Comstock Lode is discovered.

1865
Sutro Tunnel company is formed.

Chapter 5

WORDS TO UNDERSTAND
capital
circulation
economic downturn
influx
interchangeable
interlocking
investor
lavish
magnate
opportunist
sagacity
satire
seedy
shrewd
stock
strike

A hopeful prospector prepares to head for the gold fields.

WANTED
YOUNG, SKINNY,
wiry fellows not over 18. Must be expert riders, willing to risk death daily. Orphans preferred.

1870
Virginia and Truckee Railroad is completed to Carson City.
U.S. Mint is established in Carson City.
Crown Point strike

1874
William Sharon buys *Territorial Enterprise*.

1878
Sutro Tunnel is completed.

1877
Mormon farmers establish Bunkerville.

1868 | **1870** | **1872** | **1874** | **1876** | **1878**

1871
Mormons leave Muddy Valley.

1872
Virginia and Truckee Railroad extends to Reno.

1873
Silver Kings discover the Big Bonanza.

1875
Fire destroys Virginia City business district.

1869
Silver Kings get control of the Hale and Norcross mine.
Yellow Jacket Fire

SUTRO TUNNEL

The Gilded Age

The two decades of the Comstock and the two decades afterward are an era of American history known as the Gilded Age. Industrialization was at the heart of the Gilded Age. New metal plows, sewing machines, and *interchangeable* parts for machines were produced in factories. A huge *influx* of immigrants provided the labor to run the factories in eastern cities. Factory owners made huge profits because there were plenty of workers who accepted low wages rather than not work at all.

Owners became more powerful and made even more money by owning all parts of a business. For example, an oil company might buy the oil fields, the refinery, and the railroad that carried the oil.

The owners of large companies lived *lavishly*. In the East, steel *magnate* Andrew Carnegie bought a castle in his native Scotland. The Vanderbilts, who built railroads, also built a 138-room mansion in New York City. The combination of fabulously wealthy owners and poverty-stricken workers was bound to create unrest. And it did.

Strikes spread across the country several times, but workers on strike could easily be replaced by others who needed jobs. Skilled workers started forming unions to demand better wages and safer places to work. All of these traits of the Gilded Age would be true, in their own way, on the Comstock.

Early Comstock Days

From the discovery in 1859 until mining wound down years later, the lode brought profits to investors and workers. But only with new *capital* to finance the mines would great amounts of ore and large profits come from the region.

Most prospectors were hard-working but usually lacked the equipment and knowledge to pursue their dreams far beneath the surface. This led to the creation of large mining companies that sold shares of *stock* to *investors*. The money from the sale of stock was used to purchase equipment and hire workers. The Ophir Silver Mining Company sold more than $5 million in stock.

The large companies hired a knowledgeable boss called a superintendent. Then he hired miners and decided when and where to dig. The companies had the newest, best equipment to work with. Most of the profits, however, usually wound up back in San Francisco, where the investors lived, or in the pockets of the owners and supervisors. The miners got very little.

Labor Unions

Though working in the mines was always dangerous, the miners at least gained power and better wages by forming strong labor unions. The Virginia City and Gold Hill Miner's Unions won

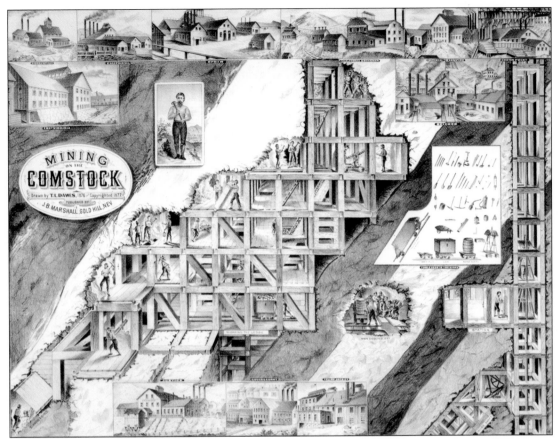

Philipp Deidesheimer never patented square-set timbering. He earned none of the huge profits that might have come from owning the plans to this life-saving invention that was instantly used in mines across the West and in other places in the world.

... over their heads towered a vast web of **interlocking** *timbers that held the walls of the gutted Comstock apart. These timbers were as large as a man's body, and the framework stretched upward so far that no eye could pierce to its top through the closing gloom. It was like peering up through the clean-picked ribs and bones of some colossal skeleton.*

—Mark Twain

their members a wage of four dollars a day. This was good pay at the time.

Miners certainly earned their pay. Dan DeQuille of the *Territorial Enterprise* wrote, "So many men have been killed in all of the principal mines that there is hardly a mine . . . that does not contain ghosts, if we are to believe what the miners say."

Creativity to Meet the Challenges

There were many problems to be solved. One problem of silver mining was that silver was harder to dig up and process than gold. Miners invented the Washoe pan process. It separated and crushed the ore, making it easier to transport. Stamp mills mixed ore and chemicals in large iron pans, then ground and heated it.

One problem was deadly. The deeper miners dug, the more dangerous it became. At depths of 180 feet, the earth was too soft for miners to work safely without the fear of constant cave-ins. The Ophir Company brought in a German engineer, Philipp Deidesheimer. He created square-set

timbering, framing wood in rectangular cubes to which more cubes could be added above and to the sides. Then miners could fill the cubes with rock and dirt and add flooring if necessary to keep the mines from caving in. This provided a network of support so great that Comstock miners were able to dig deeper than ever before.

Dangers of Mining

The following accidents killed miners in Comstock mines in 1878:

Falls in deep mining shafts.	6
Heat stroke	6
Premature explosions of powder	4
Cave-ins	4
Machinery that operated improperly	3
Hoisting machinery that failed	2
Crushed by a cage carrying supplies	1

V Is For V-Flume

Wood was needed for square-set timbering in the mines, for fuel, and for buildings. Only so much wood could be found around Virginia City and Gold Hill. The rest had to be brought down from the mountains—but how?

It was hard for horses to go up and down the mountains pulling or carrying heavy logs. The answer was the V-Flume, invented by a Virginia City man. Logs were put on the flume and sent flying down the mountainside. Some flumes were over 15 miles long.

In this illustration from Harper's Weekly, 1877, two daredevil lumberjacks "shoot the flume."

Living on the Lode

Like most Nevada towns, Virginia City had a split personality. There were miners and saloonkeepers, teachers and preachers. Most of the population, at least at first, was male. Women and children joined the men later.

Lavish homes stood near *seedy* hotels and rooming houses. Most mining towns developed this way. If the mines and the towns lasted, brick buildings would replace wood and families would arrive. One historian called it "a curious combination of industrial city and frontier town."

The author Samuel Clemens, later known as Mark Twain, came west and worked as a newspaper reporter in Virginia City during the early 1860s. He described the town in many of his reports. Here are some of them:

> [Virginia City] claimed a population of 15 thousand to 18 thousand, and all day long half of this little army swarmed the streets like bees and the other half swarmed among the drifts and tunnels of the Comstock, hundreds of feet down in the earth directly under those same streets. Often we felt our chairs jar, and heard the faint boom of a blast down in the bowels of the earth under the office.

> Virginia swarmed with men and vehicles to that degree that the place looked like a very hive—that is, when one's vision could pierce through the thick fog of alkali dust that was generally blowing in summer. . . . if you drove ten miles through it, you and your horses would . . . present an outward appearance that was a uniform pale-yellow.

> The cheapest and easiest way to become an influential man and be looked up to by the community . . . was to stand behind a bar, wear a cluster-diamond pin, and sell whisky. I am not sure but that the saloon-keeper had a shade higher rank than any other member of society.

A Cultural Center

Virginia City's wealth and population made it an important cultural center. Piper's Opera House welcomed performers and speakers. The nearby springs, streams, and mountains hosted family outings. Residents filled public and religious schools, and the whole community helped rebuild Catholic Bishop Patrick Manogue's 4th Ward Church when it burned.

Women on the Comstock

In Nevada, just like in other places, some women were happy to work at home cleaning, cooking, and caring for children. Some ran lodging houses and laundries. They created groups that provided social activities and service to others. Other women wanted to be more involved in politics, especially when it came to making laws about alcohol and gambling that affected family life.

Mary McNair Mathews was such a woman. She put aside housework to persuade people to sign petitions to prohibit the making, selling, and drinking of alcohol. She wrote:

> I used to take my paper and go to the post office, and there take names as the people came in for their mail. I got nearly a thousand names there. I also stood in front of my house twice a day for two weeks and took names.

Other women, like Anna Fitch, believed that women should stay out of politics and care for their homes and their husbands. She wrote:

> The true woman's sphere is . . . a charmed circle, radiating light and dispensing happiness, . . . there she unburdens man of his wearisome cares and girds him anew for the battle of life. . . . Oh! Who would thrust woman from her "sphere" of which she is the center and the sun.

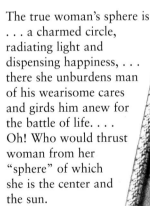

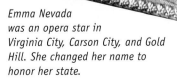

Emma Nevada was an opera star in Virginia City, Carson City, and Gold Hill. She changed her name to honor her state.

Comstock Children

Children on the Comstock differed little from today's children—they went to school. Virginia City had seven schools, Gold Hill had three, and other smaller towns had one each.

John Waldorf wrote a book about being a child growing up on the Comstock Lode. His first teacher wanted to kiss each child in her class at the end of the school week. The boys were unhappy:

> They sneaked through and trickled through and rushed through. . . . She never succeeded in kissing more than ten percent of the boys, despite the fact that our fathers advised us to submit; but still, she never would agree with anyone who called us savages.

A few miles south of Genoa, Mrs. Isaac Mott taught the first group of children in her home. In Franktown, Orson Hyde started the first school district and had the first schoolhouse built.

Children also played with toys, went to the homes of other kids, and played baseball in vacant lots and the streets.

Children and teens also worked for money to buy food for their families. A common job was gathering and selling wood for fireplaces and collecting glass, metal, and cloth to sell to junkyards.

Minorities

As in most cities, minorities often suffered. People of color were few and segregated.

The *Territorial Enterprise* reported the following about a would-be white voter in 1870:

Dr. Stephenson, a well-known colored citizen of this city . . . registered [to vote]. We understand that another person of lighter skin but darker heart refused to register because he would not place his name under the Doctor's.

The largest ethnic group was Chinese. Hundreds who helped build the Central Pacific wound up in a Virginia City slum. Local miners protested whenever their bosses tried to hire the Chinese, who would work for lower wages. Laws were passed so the Chinese could not own their own claims or even work in the mines. They could only take the lowest-paying jobs such as washing laundry, chopping wood, and cooking.

> They will do things for us I would not like to ask a white person to do; besides, they never tell any family affairs like white girls do.
>
> –Mary Mathews

Sometimes anti-Chinese feelings turned violent. Under cover of darkness, Chinese homes were burned and the owners taken out and beaten. Chinese men could be thrown in jail without much hope of a fair trial.

Both state and federal laws were passed to keep the Chinese out of the state. Later, federal laws banned Chinese immigration into the country.

Harper's Weekly *was an important magazine in the East. Study this page from the magazine to see how the artist drew the Chinese working in Virginia City. What work are the people doing? How did their hair and clothing differ from the white miners'?* ▶

BULL RUN ALLEY

CHOP AND SAUSAGE HOUSE

"WASHEE, WASHEE"

A STREET COBBLER

The railroad depot and main street of the little town of Elko were illustrated by Frank Leslie's Illustrated Newspaper in 1878. Elko had mineral springs that promised future tourist business. It was near several mining centers that always needed railroads to bring in supplies and carry away the gold or silver they produced.

Other Booms and Boomtowns

The Comstock was Nevada's most important mining boom—but not the only one. The Comstock prompted further mining in the region. About 30 percent of Nevada's mining production came from outside the Virginia City area.

Three miners staked claims in a place they called Aurora about 90 miles away from Virginia City. This boom lasted fewer than 10 years, but it helped populate a previously ignored region.

As the excitement began at Aurora, several Comstock miners heading east discovered gold at a place later called Unionville. That boom was as short-lived as Aurora. The Central Pacific Railroad built its own new town, Winnemucca, which became an important shipping center and a place to buy supplies.

Miners discovered ore at Reese River and sent it to Virginia City, where word of its value quickly spread. Since the Comstock was then in a slight *economic downturn*, the Reese River boom drew more attention than it otherwise might have. Several small towns grew near the river, but only Austin survived. It became a supply center for miners headed to the Comstock and other places to find more gold and silver.

Ho, then for Reese River! Have you a gold mine? Sell out and go to Reese! Are you the [owner] of lots in the city of Oakland, California? Give them to your worst enemy and go to Reese! Are you merchant, broker, doctor, lawyer, or mule driver? Buckle up your blankets and off with you to Reese, for there is the land of glittering bullion, there lies the pay streak.

—J. Ross Browne

Getting the Word Out —The Pony Express

With so many people moving to Nevada, friends and families wanted a way to send mail faster than by stagecoach. The most famous mailmen in early Nevada were Pony Express riders. They began riding on a regular schedule between Sacramento and Salt Lake City. With relay stations every 10 to 25 miles, riders took three days to cover the distance. Each rider went from 75 to 125 miles before a new rider took over. They averaged about 9 miles per hour.

The Pony Express hired young men between the ages of 14 and 18. They did not weigh very much, so their horses could run faster. Ads like this one appeared in newspapers across the country:

The Pony Express lasted only 18 months before it was put out of business by the telegraph. The telegraph could send messages across the country faster than riders on horseback.

Transporting People and Goods

Moving from place to place has always been important to people. They move to find better places to live and better jobs. They travel to visit relatives, to see new places, and to do business with people in faraway cities. They need fast and inexpensive ways to ship their farm, factory, and mining products to people who will buy them.

Toll Roads

From the 1850s to the 1880s, local businessmen built more than 100 toll roads in Nevada and through mountain passes to California. Why? Today, we take paved roads for granted. Back then, though, most of the roads were bumpy dirt trails. People were willing to pay for smoother roads that were cleared of brush, trees, and rocks.

Some of the toll roads made fantastic profits. The builders competed like businesses do today, with special rates, advertising, and efforts to outdo each other.

After a time, of course, people complained. They wanted the government to make roads and bridges for everyone to use for free. Politicians agreed and started hiring men to make public roads.

. . . It was believed that unless Congress gave the Territory another degree of longitude there would not be room enough to accommodate the toll roads. The ends of them were hanging over the boundary line everywhere like a fringe.

—Mark Twain

Companies cleared roads through the Sierras and charged a fee to use them. Later, the government hired workers to make roads in Nevada and into California. Most were dirt roads.

Camels in Nevada

The U.S. Congress paid to bring a small number of camels to America to test their usefulness for military and other travel purposes in the deserts of the West. Some carried ore from Nevada mines. Some helped build a road across Arizona. Brightly costumed camel drivers from Syria sang cheery Arabian songs to soothe the animals.

The experiment failed. Most camels were set free to live on their own in the deserts of Nevada and Arizona. Some were sold to a traveling circus.

One miner described camels as "ungainly looking animals bearing atlases upon their backs."

A camel train plods through Nevada's mining country.

End of the Civil War, Death of a President

While men in the West were under the ground digging ore at the Comstock, other men in the East were fighting the Civil War. When the telegraph wire brought news that the war had ended, residents of Virginia City and Gold Hill dropped their work and welcomed the news. One newspaperman wrote in his diary:

> At noon all the bells & whistles in the City were sounding—I helped ring St. Mary's . . . bell myself. . . . The military were all out . . . came up with 2 pieces of cannon & fired in streets—flags flying everywhere—anvils, guns, pistols, everything that could make a noise did so.
>
> —Alfred Doten

Five days after the end of the war, John Wilkes Booth crept into a theater in Washington, D.C., and shot President Abraham Lincoln. Lincoln died the next morning. When the news reached the Comstock, the *Gold Hill Daily News* reported:

> The flags of our town, which so lately waved and fluttered in the breeze in joyful honor of peace to our country, were raised in sorrow at half-mast; our church bells tolled the solemn hour; our local gun . . . fired its hourly shot in remembrance of the National calamity.

The Comstock held memorial services. Brass bands marched, as did a variety of groups, from the Jewish Order of B'nai B'rith and the Irish Fenian Brotherhood to the Odd Fellows and newspaper typesetters. Local African Americans joined in, carrying a banner: "He was our friend—faithful and just to us; though dead, he liveth. Hail! and Farewell."

William Sharon, part of the Bank Crowd, built a vast empire of wealth and power.

The Bank Crowd

A different quest for wealth soon affected the Comstock. After years of digging, miners seemed to have removed all of the ore in the mines. The real problem was the lack of funds needed to develop the technology and buy the equipment to dig deeper. More ore lay deep under the ground.

The money came—at a price. San Francisco investors founded the Bank of California and set up a Virginia City branch. William Sharon, a former miner, store owner, and real estate investor, managed the branch.

Sharon had the vision to take risks. Smaller banks loaned money to mining companies at five percent interest. Sharon undercut them by charging only two percent, but the mines had to repay the loan amount whenever Sharon said so. Because the mines were soon in debt to the bank, Sharon and the Bank of California soon controlled the Comstock's major mines.

Sharon was *shrewd* and found ways to make even more money. As Andrew Carnegie had done with the steel empire in the East, Sharon expanded the first business—in this case, mining—to include related businesses. The Bank Crowd, as it was known, bought mills to process ore from its mines, lumber and water companies to supply the mines, and a railroad to transport the ore. The bank and Sharon made money on all the industries.

To build the Virginia and Truckee Railroad, the Bank Crowd got money from local officials in Carson City and other towns who feared that the railroad line would bypass their towns. Sharon planned to build through Carson City all along, but he wanted others to pay for it.

A newspaper in Austin, a small mining town, expressed its opinion of men like Sharon when it criticized "the San Francisco leeches who incorporate mining companies but who do not develop the mines."

Challengers to the Throne

John Percival Jones was one of the many mine superintendents Sharon had hired. Superintendents were well paid, but they received nowhere near the compensation Sharon enjoyed. Jones wanted a taste of Sharon's riches and power. He found a vein in the Crown Point Mine, and he and a partner bought enough stock to take control of the mine. He also won five terms in the U.S. Senate. Sharon actually benefited from Jones's success, however. Sharon owned the mine next to the Crown Point, and the rich ore vein continued there, adding once again to Sharon's wealth.

The Silver Kings

Four men broke Sharon's grip on the Comstock. Two were mining superintendents in Virginia City. John Mackay, an Irish immigrant, was honest in business and treated miners with compassion and fairness. James Fair had a reputation of greed and trickery. Working with two stockbroker friends, they quietly bought stock in the Hale and Norcross Mine and slowly took control from Sharon and the Bank Crowd, making enough money to buy what were then unproductive claims. Then they struck the "Big Bonanza," a huge vein of gold and silver. In the next decade, the four shared about $75 million.

With success and money came power. The Bonanza Firm, owned by the Silver Kings, opened a bank and mills, obtained lumber and water companies, and threatened to build a railroad to compete with Sharon's whenever he threatened to raise their freight rates.

The California Big Four and the Railroad

Four railroad builders became wealthy from money they got from the federal government to aid construction of the Central Pacific Railroad. Once the railroad tracks were completed, they made money from carrying passengers and freight and developing land near the tracks. They gave free ride passes and other bribes to state and federal legislators so they would pass bills to help the railroad.

Trains brought a constant stream of people and supplies, which was good for business. Towns such as Reno, Lovelock, Winnemucca, Elko, and Carlin sprouted in response to the railroad.

Tale of a Tunnel

Adolph Sutro, a store owner, saw that square-set timbering cut the risks of mining, but that nothing could eliminate them—except, perhaps, a tunnel.

Sutro concentrated on digging a four-mile-long tunnel into Mount Davidson, the site of most of the mining. The tunnel would drain water, bring more air to the miners, and enable them to bring supplies in and take ore out more easily. At first, he received support from most Nevada leaders.

But Sutro had bigger plans than a tunnel. He wanted to build a new town at its entry. The town would be called Sutro and could replace Virginia City and Gold Hill as the Comstock's major city. Sharon, who owned many businesses in those cities, refused to allow his bank to loan money to build the tunnel or the new city.

Sutro built his tunnel anyway. European investors helped. So did tragedy. The Yellow Jacket Fire killed about three dozen miners. Sutro pointed out how his tunnel might have saved them, and the local miners' union donated $50,000 to his project. When it was completed, the tunnel was more than 20,000 feet long, went down 1,600 feet, and cost about $3.5 million.

Unfortunately, mining in the Comstock was in decline by then. It didn't help that

Adolph Sutro

most mines went deeper than the tunnel. Even though the tunnel wasn't a huge success, Sutro profited and took his money back to California. He later became mayor of San Francisco.

The Rancher Who Said No

Taxes on mining profits led to what might be called the first great political battle in the state of Nevada. Sharon and the Bank Crowd worked to pass laws that made sure large mines paid lower taxes.

Later, the legislature increased taxes on larger mining companies, but large mine owners said the tax law was against the constitution and refused to pay.

Mine owners failed to reckon with Governor Lewis Bradley, an Elko rancher. The livestock industry had grown around mining boomtowns in response to the need for food and other goods. Sheep and cattle ranching was a strong economic force in Elko. Understandably, ranchers often resented the power the Bank Crowd and the Silver Kings enjoyed.

Governor Bradley, the state's second governor, vetoed a bill that gave a tax cut to mines. As a result, he lost his reelection.

The Yellow Jacket Fire

The Yellow Jacket Fire resulted in Sutro getting funds for his tunnel. The raging fire spread into other mines. At one point, a mine superintendent put a lantern and the following note in a cage and sent it 1,000 feet below the ground:

We are fast [putting out] the fire. It is death to attempt to come up from where you are. We will get to you soon. The gas in the shaft is terrible and produces sure and speedy death. Write a word to us and send it up in the cage, and let us know how you are.

When workers pulled the cage back up, the note remained, and the light in the lantern had gone out.

NEVADA
PORTRAIT

Henry Goode Blasdel
1825–1900

The first governor of the state of Nevada is largely forgotten, but Henry Blasdel was well respected for his commitment to principles and morality.

An Indiana native, Blasdel came west during the California gold rush and worked at various jobs before coming to the Comstock. While working as a mine superintendent there, the devout Methodist won admiration for quitting a job because he objected to miners working on Sunday.

Loyal to the Republican Party, he was its first nominee for governor of Nevada. He easily won the election and was later reelected.

Blasdel worked for a state home for orphans. Wanting to see and represent more of Nevada than just Carson Valley, he visited farmers and ranchers who had started small towns in the southeast corner of today's Nevada. Blasdel nearly died of starvation on the trip, but he saved the lives of others when he left his group to find help.

Mining society could be wild, but Blasdel was not. He was called the "coffee and chocolate" governor because he served no alcohol at state receptions. He also vetoed several bills that would have made gambling legal.

After Blasdel left office, he invested in several mines before moving to northern California, where he did well in business. He is remembered for building a new state government and for standing up for what he believed in.

William Morris Stewart
1827?–1909

William Stewart was one of Nevada's most controversial figures. His biographer called him a "servant of power." He was smart, hard-working, and an *opportunist*. He was also committed to what he thought best for Nevada.

Born in New York, Stewart came to San Francisco during the gold rush. He became an attorney and worked in politics, becoming California's attorney general. Stewart moved to the Comstock, where his legal experience won him most of the mine owners as clients. Access to their money and power gave him money and power as well.

Later, when Stewart became Nevada's first U.S. senator, he arranged for a federal mint to be built in Carson City to coin money from Comstock silver and to provide jobs. The national mining laws he pushed through Congress aided mine owners and miners alike.

Stewart also played a controversial role in the Mint Act of 1873. The act stopped much of the *circulation* of silver as a form of money. Apparently misunderstanding the bill, Stewart voted for it. He spent the rest of his political career pleading against the bill that hurt his state's silver industry.

In Washington, Stewart wrote the final draft of the controversial Fifteenth Amendment to the U.S. Constitution. It said the right to vote could not be denied on account of race.

After his second term, Senator Stewart left office. Then he returned for three more terms. Besides the fight for silver, Stewart supported federal projects to irrigate Nevada farm and ranch lands.

Stewart left office for the last time when he was 80 years old. He started a new life in a southern Nevada boomtown, where he invested in mines, practiced law, and served on the school board. He is remembered as the elected leader with the most influence on Nevada's early history.

Mint Act of 1873, or the Crime of '73

While there was an oversupply of silver coming from Nevada, the U.S. Congress in Washington, D.C., passed an act that eliminated silver in many coins. Then the national mint produced gold dollars, but not silver. In fact, the act eliminated some coins altogether. The silver dollar, the half dime, a 2-cent piece, and a 3-cent piece were no longer produced, but the half-dollar, quarters, and dimes were still made of silver. There was so much pressure from silver miners, however, that years later, silver dollars were made again.

Freedom of the Press

One critic annoyed William Sharon daily—the *Territorial Enterprise*, Nevada's first newspaper. Editor Joseph Goodman accused Sharon of abusing power. In one election Sharon felt he lost his Senate bid because of attacks printed in the paper. When Sharon returned from out of town, this story greeted him:

> You are probably aware that you have returned to a community where you are feared, hated, and despised. . . . You cast honor, honesty, and [good manners] aside. You broke faith with men whenever you could [promote] your purpose by so doing.

To get rid of the printed attacks, Sharon bought the paper for a large sum of money. A new editor hailed Sharon's "*sagacity*, energy, and nerve." Sharon finally won the Senate seat—but he hardly ever showed up in Washington during his six-year term.

Two Famous Reporters

The Virginia City *Enterprise* boasted two now-famous reporters. One reporter, William Wright, adopted the pen name of Dan DeQuille. His work was said to be "dandy" even though he did not write with a quill. DeQuille wrote a book called *The Big Bonanza* about the Comstock Lode.

Another reporter, Samuel Clemens, became known as Mark Twain. Like his friend Dan DeQuille, Mark Twain wandered the streets and saloons and was in and out of the mines getting news stories. When he and DeQuille could find no news, they made it up—from new inventions to murders. When Clemens angered some people with his made-up stories and feared what they might do to him, he left town.

Mark Twain and Virginia City

Samuel Clemens was born in Missouri. As Mark Twain, he became one of the great names in American literature for books such as *The Adventures of Tom Sawyer* and *The Adventures of Huckleberry Finn*. He was also a well-known public speaker with strong opinions about everything.

Clemens came to Nevada because his older brother, Orion, received an appointment as territorial secretary. The younger Clemens hoped to get rich in the gold and silver mines. He worked as a clerk for his brother and for the territorial legislature for $8 a day.

He became Mark Twain at the *Territorial Enterprise*, where Goodman hired him after reading a couple of **satirical** news stories about the legislature where Twain had once worked as a clerk. His stories were full of inside information—and mockery. He once told readers, "Reports lie—I do not." But he soon left the paper, partly because he wrote such insulting stories about local people.

Mark Twain was far from finished with Nevada, however. He returned to Virginia City as a lecturer and brought Virginia City to the American public by publishing *Roughing It*. The book traced his trip across the continent to Nevada and his adventures in mining and journalism.

A noted historian and writer said:

> *In Washoe [Samuel Clemens] took the name that is known more widely than any other in our literature and will be known as long as any. It was in Washoe that Mark Twain was born. Not, one thinks, by chance.*

—Bernard DeVoto

More Mining Towns

Nevada was more than the Comstock, Winnemucca, and Elko. Discoveries of minerals led to new towns near the Utah-Arizona border. In Eureka, prospectors found silver and lead. Eureka's miners, however, lacked the money and knowledge to make the mine profitable. Later, when experts arrived from Wales, profits jumped from about $6 thousand to $2 million in three years. Lawmakers created a new county, with Eureka as the county seat.

The Treasure Hill boom peaked by 1870, although mineral production continued. About 30,000 people flocked to the White Pine mining region in the late 1860s, but by the 1870 census, the county's population was down to about 7,000 people, which shows how quickly mining booms came and went.

Eureka ●

Pioche ●
Panaca ●
Moapa ●
Overton

Mormon Farming Towns

Brigham Young sent Mormon settlers to start farming towns near the Utah/Nevada/Arizona borders and along the Colorado River. Mormons started farms and Indian missions along the Muddy River at Moapa, St. Thomas, and Overton. Francis Lee set up a colony at Panaca.

With plenty of river water nearby and mild winter weather, the Mormon farmers were able to grow many crops. Cotton was one of the main crops. Because of the cotton these towns were called the Cotton Mission. The farmers sent their crops up river by boat to communities in Utah. This was a much faster way of moving crops than by land with horses and wagons.

Anson Call started the farming and shipping center of Callville by the river.

Riverboats on the Colorado

In the mid-1800s, riverboats steamed up and down the Colorado River, bringing supplies to mines in Eldorado Canyon. Eldorado Canyon was a mining area in southern Nevada that was undergoing a boom at the time. The boats also brought supplies from California to towns in Arizona and southern Utah. The riverboat trade lasted for over 40 years.

Travel on a riverboat was very difficult. Cabins were hot and seating was very uncomfortable. There was little or no fresh food. The trip was also dangerous. Rapids made river navigation difficult. Large rocks, boulders, and sandbars seemed to be everywhere. But boat travel was faster than traveling overland. People sometimes rode boats for recreation.

However, few people wanted to live in the Mormon towns along the Colorado River. They were a long way away from their families and friends in Utah. In time, most of the people moved away, and the riverboats did less and less business.

The Las Vegas Mission, first started by Mormons as a mission to the Indians and a supply station for travelers, was taken over by Octavius Gass. It became a farm and cattle ranch. At the time, the region was still part of Arizona.

Today, Callville is beneath Lake Mead's waters. But in the 1860s, it was a port for steamboats that chugged up and down the Colorado River.

Octavius Gass tried to promote the port and even became its postmaster. He hoped to sell supplies to Mormon settlers up the river, but most of them were self-sufficient farmers and had little cash anyway. The steamboat business never made much money.

Silver Boom in Pioche

Mormon missionary William Hamblin found the silver ore that helped begin the town of Pioche. Mining in Pioche went through peaks and valleys. With the arrival of refining mills, Pioche boomed. Population topped 1,000, and the mines produced nearly $17 million in the next six years. But Pioche was isolated from the rest of Nevada, and it was hard to ship the ore when the Central Pacific was more than 250 miles away.

The Million Dollar Courthouse

The population of Pioche had grown enough to merit a new courthouse for the newly created Lincoln County. Building began in 1872, and the cost was bid at about $16,000. Extras were added over the years, bringing the cost to $75,000. Then bad budgeting and corruption by local officials and building companies drove the cost up even further. Pioche residents finally finished paying off the cost of the courthouse in 1938! The total cost was

about $800,000—not quite a million, but more than a small community could afford.

Gass's Station

While Mormons were settling mining and farming towns to the north of it, the Las Vegas Mission was largely ignored. Two church members at the mission, the Knapp brothers, ran a general store for miners in Eldorado Canyon and at Mt. Potosi.

One of the miners, Octavius Gass, often talked with the Knapp brothers and thought the lands around the Las Vegas Mission would make a good cattle ranch. He and two partners took it over and expanded the ranch to nearly 1,000 acres. Gass grew crops and owned 3,000 head of cattle. He also got married and became the father of several children.

Mrs. Mary Virginia Simpson Gass was known for shooting hawks that came after her chickens and for once refusing to move her mule team from the road to make way for a coach coming the other way. It turned out that she declined to get out of the way for Mormon Church leader Brigham Young, who raised his hat to her as she went by.

Gass enjoyed success while Las Vegas was part of Arizona. He was a member of the territorial legislature and helped create Pah-Ute County, Arizona. But Gass was in debt from lawsuits related to old investments. He mortgaged his ranch several times before finally losing ownership to Pioche businessman Archibald Stewart. The Gass family left for California.

Pioche●

End of the Line

Ironically, as Las Vegas changed hands from Gass to Stewart in 1881, the Comstock was closing down at the other side of the state. Many Nevadans blamed the Mint Act, often called the "Crime of '73" for reducing the value of silver.

The reality was different. First, fire had always been a grave danger to Virginia City—not just down in the mines, but because so many buildings were made of wood. One October day in 1875, a fire began in a small rooming house. Strong winds spread flames through the main business district. The fire kept going and extended 400 feet down into the Ophir mine. Three of the most important mines closed for a time.

An unknown author described the chaos:

On all sides was heard the roar of the fire, the crash of falling roofs and walls, and every few minutes tremendous explosions of black and giant powder, as buildings were blown up in various parts of the town. . . . In all directions and on all the streets the people were seen lugging along trunks, articles of furniture and bundles of bedding and clothing.

Another problem was the limits of mining—it was profitable and safe to dig only so deep. Whatever remained in the earth was too hard and costly to reach.

From a peak of nearly $37 million in 1876, Comstock ore production fell to just under $1.25 million five years later. Virginia City remained the Queen City of the Comstock, but she no longer had much of a throne. The boom was over, and the decline would be a steep one.

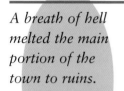

A breath of hell melted the main portion of the town to ruins.

—*The* Territorial Enterprise *on the great fire*

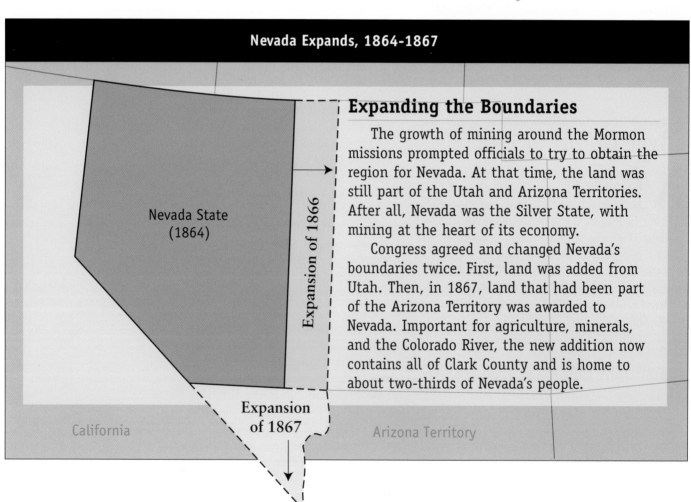

Nevada Expands, 1864-1867

Nevada State (1864)

Expansion of 1866

Expansion of 1867

California

Arizona Territory

Expanding the Boundaries

The growth of mining around the Mormon missions prompted officials to try to obtain the region for Nevada. At that time, the land was still part of the Utah and Arizona Territories. After all, Nevada was the Silver State, with mining at the heart of its economy.

Congress agreed and changed Nevada's boundaries twice. First, land was added from Utah. Then, in 1867, land that had been part of the Arizona Territory was awarded to Nevada. Important for agriculture, minerals, and the Colorado River, the new addition now contains all of Clark County and is home to about two-thirds of Nevada's people.

Chapter 5 Review

What Do You Remember?

1. Describe some features of the Gilded Age.
2. What kind of technology did mining companies develop to aid mining at the Comstock?
3. Describe the lifestyle of women, children, and minorities in the early years of Virginia City.
4. What were some ways mail and information were exchanged?
5. Describe some ways people traveled and the problems they faced.
6. How did early Nevadans react to the end of the Civil War and the death of Abraham Lincoln?
7. In what ways were the Bank Crowd and William Sharon important?
8. How did John P. Jones become a challenger to Sharon?
9. How did the Silver Kings take over the Comstock?
10. What was the purpose of the Sutro Tunnel?
11. What role did Lewis Bradley play in the fight over taxes?
12. What role did the *Territorial Enterprise* play in Virginia City?
13. Who was Henry Blasdel?
14. Name two things about the life of Senator William M. Stewart.
15. How was Virginia City important to Mark Twain's career?
16. What were two reasons Mormon towns started in southern Nevada?
17. Describe the factors that contributed to the end of prosperity in Virginia City.

Geography Tie-In

1. Plot the towns in this chapter on a map. Now plot the nearby mountain ranges, rivers, and lakes. Is there any connection between water and settlement? In what ways was water important for settlers?

2. On the Internet, in an atlas, or in library books, look up Nevada ghost towns and mining camps. Tell your class about them, write about a few of them, or draw and label them on a map.

Activity

Point of View

If you were alive at the time, would you have agreed more with Mary Mathews or with Anna Fitch? Why? (Review what they wrote on page 91.) What might be some ways that alcohol and gambling affected family life? Relate the issues of that day to today's issues of substance abuse, gambling, and women in politics. How are they the same? How are they different?

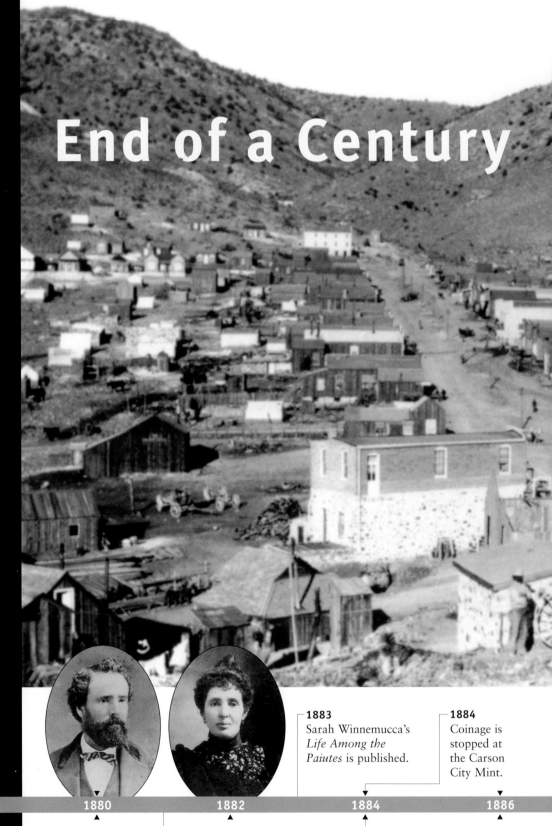

End of a Century

Timeline of Events

1880 **1882** **1884** **1886**

1883
Sarah Winnemucca's
*Life Among the
Paiutes* is published.

1884
Coinage is
stopped at
the Carson
City Mint.

1881
Archibald and Helen Stewart take
over the Las Vegas Ranch.

1884
Archibald Stewart dies;
Helen takes over the ranch.

WORDS TO UNDERSTAND
creditor
currency
industrialist
inquiry
luxury
monopoly
necessity
platform
prophecy
prosperous
reclamation
retaliation
supernatural
surplus

DeLamar looked like this in 1896. A year later DeLamar had over 3,000 residents.

1889
Silver Clubs
are created.

1890
Stewart Indian School opens in Carson City.
Sherman Silver Purchase Act is passed.

1893
National economic depression

1888   1890   1892

1891
DeLamar discovers gold near Pioche.
Sarah Winnemucca dies.

107

NEVADA
PORTRAIT

The First Lady of Las Vegas

Helen J. Stewart
1854–1926

Collector of Indian Culture

Stewart had a keen interest in the Indian culture and kept a large collection of Indian baskets. She signed over 10 acres of her land as a colony for the local Paiute Indians. Many still live on this property off Main Street in downtown Las Vegas.

Archibald and Helen Stewart were living in Pioche when they learned that Octavius Gass had financial problems and was losing his Las Vegas ranch. A successful businessman in Pioche, Archibald made a loan to Gass but ended up with the ranch instead of repayment of the loan. With promises to remain only a short while at the isolated ranch house beneath the cottonwood trees, and against the wishes of Helen, the Stewart family of three children packed their things and moved south.

At the ranch, Helen gave birth to another child and settled in to lead a quiet life as a housewife. Instead, she would end up running the large ranch.

Who was this amazing woman? Helen Jane Wiser grew up in Illinois and California and married 38-year-old Archibald Stewart when she was 18. A very social woman, Helen was happiest when visitors, especially other women with children, stopped at the ranch oasis in the desert.

Murder at the Ranch

The ranch was successful for the Stewarts, but problems developed with one of the neighbors. Conrad Kiel, one of Gass's friends from Ohio, came west to take over the old Indian farm. It was the same farm run earlier by Mormon missionaries for the Indians.

Kiel was sure that Stewart had swindled his friend Gass and was responsible for Gass's financial problems. Kiel had a reputation for creating a haven for outlaws at his ranch. The Stewart and Kiel families barely spoke to each other.

One hot July day, a Stewart ranch hand told Helen he was quitting and demanded his pay. Her husband was out of town, so Helen told the man he would have to wait for Mr. Stewart to return. The man left to work for Kiel and started spreading nasty rumors about the Stewarts.

When Archibald returned, Helen was very upset and told him what had happened. She claimed the man had a "black-hearted slanderer's tongue." Carrying a gun, Archibald mounted his horse and rode off.

A couple of hours later, a note arrived from Conrad Kiel that read,

Mrs. Sturd [Stewart] send a team and take Mr. Sturd away he is dead.

—C. Kiel

Helen rode over with some of their workers, picked up her husband's body, and buried him on the hill overlooking the ranch. Kiel and others claimed Stewart had approached looking for trouble and they had killed him in self-defense.

Despite a humble beginning, the ranch became an important rest station for travelers.

Helen Runs the Ranch

At the time of Archibald's death, Helen was expecting another child. But instead of leaving the ranch, she stayed for nearly two decades. She took care of nearly 1,000 acres at a time when few women managed such large operations.

From 1884 until she sold the ranch in 1902, Helen Stewart was the dominant figure at the Las Vegas ranch. She was in charge of all mail that came through town and she also ran a rest stop for weary travelers who traveled the dusty road between Los Angeles and Salt Lake.

Stewart hired several foremen to help her run the ranch. She even married one of them.

More Murders

One day, Helen's second husband and her son rode over to the Kiel Ranch. The sons of Conrad Kiel were now running the place, but they fought constantly. When the Stewarts got there, they found the Kiel sons dead from gunshot wounds.

An *inquiry* called it a murder-suicide, but later an investigation found it to be a double murder. Among the prime suspects was Helen's son Hiram. The question remains, could the Kiel boys have finally been the victims of *retaliation* even after 16 years? The answer remains a mystery.

Selling the Ranch

Helen and her children finally sold the Las Vegas ranch to William Clark, a wealthy Montana senator. Later, about 1,200 lots were auctioned off for a town. Helen Stewart is often called "the first lady of Las Vegas" because of her role in its early beginnings. You will read more about early Las Vegas and Helen Stewart in Chapter 7.

What do you think?

What might have been some reasons Helen Stewart stayed at the Las Vegas ranch after her husband died? What do people have to consider before moving to a new place? Does Helen Stewart fit the image of a typical 19th century woman?

A Boy, a Horse, and Another Stewart Death

Helen Stewart endured many tragedies, including the death of the son born after his father's death. Young Archie was sent to a California boarding school to get a good education. While home on a visit at age 14, he was chasing wild horses and died after a fall from his horse.

Daughter of the Paiute

Other women, in another part of Nevada, were also making history. You read about Sarah Winnemucca in Chapter 2. During the late 1800s, she devoted her time to helping her people.

Her knowledge of English, her ability as an interpreter and public speaker, and her intelligence prompted her fellow Paiutes to ask her to speak in their behalf. They even sent her to San Francisco to plead their case for more aid for their reservation.

> The proverb says the big fish eat the little fishes, and we Indians are the little fish and you eat us all up and drive us from home. Where can we poor Indians go if the government will not help us? If your people will help us, and you have good hearts, I will promise to educate my people and make them law-abiding citizens of the United States.
>
> —Sarah Winnemucca, in San Francisco pleading for the creation of a Northern Paiute reservation, 1879

The next year, Sarah met with federal leaders, including President Hayes, in Washington, D.C. She wanted them to understand the Indian people and their hard life dealing with the whites.

Sarah also gave talks in Boston and other eastern cities. Her efforts had an impact. She won attention for the plight of Northern Paiutes. Federal leaders, however, tried to stop her from speaking because they realized she could embarrass them. Sarah angered men at the Bureau of Indian Affairs, whom she accused of corruption.

Not only did she keep speaking, Sarah published a book, *Life Among the Paiutes: Their Wrongs and Claims*. White friends helped her write the book, but it was clearly her story and voice. It was the first book written by a Native American woman.

An Indian School

Just as she used her book to try to educate whites about the plight of native peoples, Sarah also tried to educate her people and started an Indian school in Lovelock. However, the government provided no support because officials preferred their own boarding schools.

Despite its educational success, her school closed, partly due to a lack of funds.

> Your children can learn much more than I know, and much easier, and it is your duty to see that they go to school. . . . A few years ago you owned this great country; today the white man owns it all, and you own nothing. Do you know what did it? Education. You see the miles and miles of railroad, the locomotive, the Mint in Carson where they make money. Education has done it all.
>
> —Sarah Winnemucca

A Place in History

Rivalries among the Northern Paiutes and the chance to be with family prompted Sarah Winnemucca to move to the Montana-Idaho border. Eventually, she died there, tired of fighting what proved to be a losing battle. Her efforts, however, won her a secure place in the history of the United States and Nevada.

Hannah Clapp Works for Women's Rights and Education

Hannah Clapp was a prominent fighter for women's rights. She lobbied the legislature for the female vote. When she arrived in Carson City in 1860, there were no schools. She started the Sierra Seminary, a private school, which was highly respected because of the education it offered.

When the University of Nevada moved from Elko to Reno, Clapp became one of the first faculty members, teaching history and English and advising young female students.

Sarah Winnemucca

Hannah Clapp

Wovoka
and the Ghost Dance

Wovoka, who sometimes used the white name Jack Wilson, grew up in the Mason Valley region. He was about 30 years old when he saw an eclipse of the sun on New Year's Day. His experience inspired a *prophecy* that became known as the "Ghost Dance."

> When the sun died I went to heaven and saw God and all the people who had died a long time ago. God told me to come back and tell my people they must be good and love one another, and not fight, or steal, or lie. He gave me this dance to give to my people.
>
> —Wovoka

The prophecy spoke of Native Americans and their ancestors dancing and enjoying happiness together. It spoke of restoring native lands and traditional native ways. Wovoka was a man of peace, opposed to fighting, but his message prompted many Indians to believe that if they wore a certain shirt, *supernatural* forces would protect them from bullets fired at them.

As Wovoka's vision spread among Native Americans across the United States, white people became nervous that new violence would soon erupt. It soon did at Wounded Knee in South Dakota, the site of one of the worst Indian massacres in all of American history.

Shortly after Sioux Indians gathered to dance, a nervous U.S. Army attacked, killing nearly 300 Native Americans. Wovoka was not there. Over the course of his lifetime, Wovoka rarely left the Mason Valley.

Grace Dangberg, a Nevada historian, wrote the following:

> I went to visit Jack early one sunny Sunday morning. Jack, in undershirt and trousers, was lying on a blanket in the shade on the north side of his cabin. When we approached he sat up in embarrassment, which I attributed to the fact that he was without his top shirt but which I . . . realized [was because] he was being seen WITHOUT his wide-brimmed black sombrero. His usual poise and dignity were restored as soon as he had reached for the hat and placed it on his head, still without a top shirt!

Wovoka

Activity

Two Points of View
   White people had different points of view on Indian issues. Read both of these statements below and discuss them with your class. Try to see both sides of the issue. What are the problems? Think about some possible solutions.

There should be assigned to each tribe, a country adapted to agriculture, . . . within which all . . . should be compelled to remain until such time as their general improvement and good conduct [proved they could leave].

In the meantime the government should supply them with animals, tools, and clothing; encourage and assist them in the erection of comfortable dwellings, and secure the means . . . of education—intellectual, moral, and religious.

— Luke Lea, Federal Commissioner of Indian Affairs, 1850

The only good Indians I ever saw were dead.

—General Phil Sheridan, head of the U.S. Army's troops dealing with Indians west of the Mississippi

The Stewart Indian School near Carson City housed students from many tribes—including Washo, Paiute, Hopi, Apache, Ute, and others from other states.

Treatment of Native People

"The next day the torture began. The first thing they did was cut our hair. While we were bathing, our breech clouts were taken and we were told to put on trousers. We'd lost our hair and our clothes; with those two, we'd lost our identity as Indians."

—Asa DeKlage, 1885

Federal treatment of Native Americans in the 1800s is an unhappy story. Reservations were created to teach Native Americans the ways of white people, to provide food for them, and to keep them off the lands wanted by white settlers.

Individuals as well as the U.S. Army attacked Native Americans. Some Indians also attacked whites. This clash resulted in the loss of native lands. Native Americans struggled to maintain their dignity and their way of life.

The federal government passed the Dawes Act to help native people get back some of the land they once lived on. The Dawes Act was supposed to provide land to individual Indians, not tribes. It was meant to provide a place for native people to farm and provide for their families. However, the plan was not successful because native people were not used to living in small family groups or taking care of their own private piece of land. They had always worked and lived together.

Stewart Indian School

One of the ways Nevadans tried to help native people was to create a school called the Stewart Indian School near Carson City. It was created to provide young Indians with a basic education, work skills, and language to help them fit into white culture.

Providing education for American Indians seemed like a good idea to many, but there were many problems with the plan. One problem was that it was a boarding school that forced even young children to leave their families for most of the year. Boys and girls were separated by age, so brothers and sisters were rarely together. One student said, "I still remember my folks just standing there crying and I was missing them. I got on the train and my mind was so full of unhappiness." Students lost most of their native culture because they were punished when they spoke their native language or lived according to native ways.

These two students attended the school in the early 1900s:

Thurman Murphy Jr. was forcefully taken by the BIA (Bureau of Indian Affairs) from his home at age six and placed in the

Stewart Indian School, where he lived until he joined the Marine Corps in World War II. He fought the Japanese at Iwo Jima and got a Purple Heart.

Florence Frances Pacheco Hooper was a Paiute. She said:

> I was born in Tonopah, Nevada. Before I was five years old, my mother . . . was unable to take care of us children, so we were placed in foster homes. I attended 1st through 3rd grades at the school in Fallon and the 4th through 12th grades at Stewart Indian School.
>
> My husband, Ernest Hooper, a Shoshone Indian, . . . also attended the school. Today, Ernie is a minister to help American Indians. He practices his ministry and is employed as a heavy equipment operator. I help Ernie whenever I can by playing hymns on the piano for church.

Economic Struggles

The end of the Comstock era marked the end of Nevada's *prosperous* beginning. By 1881, the state was headed for two decades of economic decline. Nevadans worried about their economic survival after the gold and silver ran out. People moved away to earn a living in other places. The state's population dropped from 62,000 in 1880 to 42,000 in 1900.

Nevada's depression was so bad that all Comstock mine managers had their salaries cut in half, and the Virginia and Truckee Railroad considered ending its local passenger service.

The Mines Decline

With the Comstock Lode in decline, Nevadans looked to other mines. Austin, Eureka, and Pioche continued to produce ore but not enough to pick up the slack. The mining town of Candelaria produced $5 million but was virtually a ghost town 10 years later. Tuscarora had the same problem.

The DeLamar Boom

The end of the 1800s brought Nevada only one mining boom—and it was at the opposite end of the state. Two men found gold 40 miles away from Pioche. Captain Joseph DeLamar began developing the area a few years later. This boom created a new town, named after the captain, and produced about $9 million. That was not much in relation to other mines, but by then, Nevadans welcomed any good news.

The DeLamar boom, however, came at a price. The dust from the mine created serious health problems for miners by lodging in their lungs. The mine was called the "Widow-Maker."

Mining booms always attracted other businesses, and agriculture was one of the most successful. After all, miners had to eat. When mining declined, however, so did farming and ranching in mining regions. Most settlers moved to other places.

Old mining towns were often very rough places. The Candelaria newspaper once boasted, "No one killed or half-murdered during the past week."

DeLamar ghost town

Empire was a typical small town in the 1890s. The whole town turned out for a rare photograph.

The Farm Problem

The farming industries had many problems. The good news was that factory growth and a rise in immigration created new and larger markets for food. The bad news was that many farmers tried to take advantage of this growth and ran into trouble of their own.

For many years, farmers grew what they needed to survive and then sold or traded their *surpluses* for additional *necessities* and sometimes even *luxuries*. Things changed, however, when the Civil War began in 1861. The war affected Nevada farming in at least two ways. First, it took many farm workers away to fight in the war. But improvements to farming equipment meant farmers could produce more food with fewer workers.

Second, supplying the needs of soldiers showed farmers that if they produced crops and goods for market, and not just for themselves, they could make large profits.

Irrigation provided water for farming in 1910.

The Blame Game

Farmers got caught in a blame game as they tried to figure out how to increase crop production. Growing one large crop or product for sale meant they would need more seed and equipment. With little cash on hand, how could they pay for these things? Farmers had to borrow money. This started them on a spiral of debt. Many lost their land or owed *creditors* more money than they could ever repay.

Farmers had additional troubles. Not only did they owe money to people and banks, they were mad at railroad owners who carried their crops to market.

In the west, farmers attacked the Central Pacific Railroad for what became known as long-haul/short-haul discrimination. If a farmer shipped his goods one-way from Reno to Elko, the railroad might charge for the round-trip. Farmers saw this as corrupt, but, of course, railroad officials disagreed. They argued that they provided a service. They said they had no need to send their trains to some stops where farmers wanted to send their goods, so farmers should pay the round-trip cost.

What do you think?

Do you think bankers and the railroad deserved the blame for the problems of farmers?

Irrigation and Reclamation

Nevada's leaders began seeking federal aid to support irrigation and *reclamation* projects. Reclamation projects help to "reclaim" lands by making them more usable. In the arid West, reclamation means dams, irrigation, and controlled use of river water.

Other western states saw they could also benefit from irrigation projects, so they joined Nevadans who were seeking government money and support. Several western cities hosted National Irrigation Congress meetings, which helped keep the issue alive.

As mining died down and Nevada's economy became more depressed, Nevada leaders focused their attention on water. You will read more how the government answered the call for dams and irrigation in later chapters.

Factory and Railroad Problems

Just like farmers and miners, factory and railroad workers had money problems. They resented low wages and dangerous working conditions, especially while eastern *industrialists* like Andrew Carnegie and John D. Rockefeller and the Central Pacific Big Four grew wealthier. Labor violence broke out in several waves. Workers in Nevada and other places all over the nation began to strike.

The federal government's reaction to strikes was to send in the army to take over the jobs of striking railroad workers. They made sure the mail was delivered and tried to control the strikers.

Trade and Monopolies

The government also created the Interstate Commerce Act to regulate trade and the Sherman Anti-Trust Act to prevent *monopolies*. Monopolies are large businesses that have no competition and too much control over what is bought and sold, and for what prices.

Sadly, none of the acts really worked. Businessmen who were supposed to be regulated took control of the Interstate Commerce Commission, and government did little to stop big business monopolies. Farmers, miners, and factory and railroad workers simply got angrier.

The Populist Movement

Farmers in the Midwest and the South began forming clubs, called the Grange, where they met and talked about their problems. Eventually, the Grange evolved into the People's or Populist Party. This national political party worked for workers against big business.

The Populists nominated a presidential candidate whose *platform* included several ideas designed to appeal to Nevada's working class people. These included:

1. **Government aid to farmers**

   The federal government would have to buy the farmers' crops if they didn't sell at market.

2. **Government ownership of railroads**

   The federal government would take over management of the railroads. Farmers believed this would eliminate the long-haul/short-haul problem.

3. **Government printing of paper money**

   Populists hoped that with more dollars in circulation, farmers would have more money to pay their debts.

These ideas were of little interest to urban factory workers in the East and the Midwest. All they seemed designed to do was increase the price of food and other farm products.

The Populists needed to find a way to broaden their base of support. Why should the additional currency be paper? Why not silver? So, the Populists came out in favor of restoring silver as coined currency, and Nevadans happily supported their platform.

Silver or Gold Coins?

National leaders believed strongly in the use of gold as *currency*. They showed little interest in using silver for coins. Matters took a turn for the worse when Grover Cleveland was elected president and favored gold coins. Cleveland stopped silver coin production at Nevada's Carson City Mint.

When Benjamin Harrison came into office, Nevada finally began to get help. Harrison and Congress approved statehood for several western territories that depended upon mining. They passed the Sherman Silver Purchase Act to buy 4.5 million ounces of silver a month. Still, the people in the West, who wanted the government to use more silver coins, were not happy.

Silver Clubs, Silver Party

Bringing back silver coins was still Nevada's goal. A young editor and businessman thought he knew how Nevadans could do this. George Nixon's life became a true Nevada success story. At age 26, Nixon put together a group of investors who opened the First National Bank of Winnemucca. He also published the local newspaper, *The Silver State*. In its pages, Nixon called for Nevadans to organize in behalf of their silver cause. Residents of Winnemucca and Eureka listened and started Silver Clubs.

The Silver Clubs met in Reno to create their own Silver Party. They vowed to support only those candidates who agreed with their fight to bring back silver coins.

> We, the undersigned, solemnly pledge, each to the other, our sacred word of honor, not to vote for or in any way assist any candidate for office who will not pledge himself to use every honorable means to obtain . . . [silver's] free and unlimited coinage.
>
> —The Silver League pledge

Activity

Analyze a Historic Poem

1. To understand this poem below, you need to understand the Mint Act of 1873. Think about the poem and how people who made a living from silver felt about Sherman's bill.

2. What words in the poem show support for the silver leagues? What words show the Silver League was against the silver coinage bill?

> The silver leagues are moving,
> You have heard their cheery tone;
> The bugle calls for freedom—
> For our fathers' silver coin.
> They are on the track of Sherman
> And his tricky coinage bill
> It robbed millions of our people,
> The bankers vaults to fill.
>
> —A member of Winnemucca's Silver League

Chapter **6** Review

What Do You Remember?

1. Tell some events from the life of Helen J. Stewart, including some of her contributions to the Las Vegas region.
2. Tell some events from the life of Sarah Winnemucca. How did she try to help Native Americans?
3. Who was Wovoka?
4. How did the federal government try to help Native Americans during this time?
5. What was the state of Nevada's mining industry during the last two decades of the 1800s?
6. Why was the nationwide farm industry depressed at the same time as Nevada's mining industry?
7. Why were reclamation projects needed?
8. What were the main causes of unrest among workers in the South and Midwest?
9. Describe the beliefs of the People's Party.
10. What were the origins of Nevada's Silver Clubs? How did they evolve into the Silver Party?

Geography Tie-In

Research and discuss with your class at least three uses of Nevada's gold and silver during the 1800s. Then learn what they are used for today. Make a poster showing gold and silver use during both time periods. Learn where gold and silver are mined in Nevada today.

Activity

Research and Perform

Divide your class into small groups, and choose an important person from this chapter to research. Each group must prepare and perform a skit about the person. Here are some ideas to help you:

- **Helen Stewart**. Portray some events from her active life. Look on this website: www.1st100.com and in encyclopedias and library books.
- **Sarah Winnemucca** Locate and read her book, *Life Among the Paiutes*. Include a speech about the plight of her people. Dress and speak like you think she did.
- **Wovoka**. Learn more about this man and show the class some events from his life. Don't forget the hat!

Timeline of Events

1898 — 1900 — 1902 — 1904 — 1906

1899
Nevada approves direct vote of U.S. senators.

1900
Copper is discovered in Ely area.
Gold is discovered at Tonopah.

1902
Helen Stewart sells most of the Las Vegas Ranch.

1902
Newlands Reclamation Act

1902
Goldfield booms.

1904
Referendum amendment is added to Nevada's constitution.

1905
Auction creates the railroad town of Las Vegas.

Chapter 7

WORDS TO UNDERSTAND
Allies
conservationist
draft
gender
high grading
initiative
mass production
moral
pacifist
posthumous
preferential vote
Progressive Era
radical
ration
recall
referendum
regulate
scrip
socialism
workmen's compensation

Progressive Nevada

A parade through Tonopah is captured on film in 1907. Cover the photo with a piece of paper and then slide the paper gradually to the right to help you learn more about this time period in a mining town.

1911
Legislature approves workmen's compensation and outlaws gambling.

1914
Nevada approves women's suffrage in state elections.

1916
Nevada City, a socialist colony, is created.

1920
U.S. Congress passes the Nineteenth Amendment, granting the vote to women.

I WANT YOU FOR U.S. ARMY
NEAREST RECRUITING STATION

1908	1910	1912	1914	1916	1918	1920

1918
Pittman Silver Act

1909
Clark County is created, with Las Vegas as its seat.

1911
Nevada Equal Franchise Society is created.

1912
Initiative amendment is added to Nevada's constitution.

1914–1918
World War I
The U.S. enters the war in 1917.

A Progressive Nation

People in the West, like others across the nation, enjoyed new inventions by people from the Midwest and the East. Thomas Edison had invented the light bulb and the motion picture; Alexander Graham Bell's telephone, invented in 1876, was showing up in more houses; Orville and Wilbur Wright's flight at Kitty Hawk, North Carolina, in 1903 showed new ways for people to go from one place to the other. Add in the *mass production* of automobiles pioneered by Henry Ford, and people could more easily reach and communicate with one another.

Progressive Reform

It was clear, however, that major reform was needed. Progressive reforms began near the end of the 1800s, but historians call the first two decades of the 20th century the *Progressive Era* because it was a time of great reform and change.

Progressives believed in improving society. They fought for *moral* reform by trying to prohibit the making and drinking of alcoholic drinks. They supported changes in America's criminal code and believed the severity of punishment should be equal to the severity of the crime. They demanded better treatment for the mentally ill, who were often locked away in dark and dirty hospitals. They sought laws to limit the workday from 10 or 12 hours to 8 hours.

Nevada's Progressive Era

Nevada's governors supported progressive reforms. Governor Denver Dickerson wanted changes in the state prison system and mental hospital. He fought for a more honest voting system. Lawmakers approved *workmen's compensation*—money workers can get when they are injured and unable to work.

Then Tasker Oddie became governor. He helped change divorce laws to hold more marriages together. Those filing for divorce would have to live in Nevada for one year instead of just six months. In a day when few people got divorced, most people

Governor Tasker Oddie worked to reform the state's divorce and gambling laws.

felt a couple should work out their problems and stay together.

Governor Oddie worked to ban all forms of gambling. Progressives thought gambling was harmful to individuals and to families.

A cartoonist at the *Reno Evening Gazette* included this poem in an anti-gambling cartoon:

> O' Nevada, wicked state,
> Cut the gambling, ere too late;
> Lift yourself out of the mire,
> Throw the crap game in the fire.

However, both quick divorces and gambling attracted visitors who spent money in the state, and within a few years both restrictions were dropped.

The Dark Side of Progressivism

Across the country, progressives and others believed that foreigners were inferior to Americans already living in the country. Immigrants were expected to give up their cultural traditions, and segregation was everywhere.

A state law was passed that allowed only English to be spoken in Nevada mines. Supporters claimed this would promote safety; if a miner could not understand what was being said, how could he hope to avoid danger? Critics believed the law was really intended to keep foreigners from taking jobs.

> "Our country . . . should prevent the immigration into this country of all peoples other than those of the white race. . . . We should confer citizenship upon no one but people of the white race, and . . . we should write the word white into our constitution."
>
> —Francis Newlands

What do you think?

Why did the progressives believe in moral reforms, such as laws against divorce and gambling, but ignore civil rights of ethnic groups?

What is your responsibility to question current thinking about moral issues?

Agencies of Government

Progressive reform eventually led to the creation of federal agencies to *regulate* business. Today, the Federal Reserve Board sets interest rates and monitors our supply of money. The Food and Drug Administration evaluates the safety and use of prescription and over-the-counter drugs. The Federal Deposit Insurance Corporation (FDIC) protects savings deposits. Both the federal government and the state bank examiner protect our money.

Progressive legislators approved a commission to regulate railroads, telephones, and telegraphs. It became known as the Public Utilities Commission. Electricity, natural gas, and the companies that supply them were also regulated.

Nevada's Tax Commission started regulating how property values were decided. Years later it began regulating casinos and other agencies.

Boards were created all across the United States to make sure no one business in an industry had too much power. In Nevada, however, mining and ranching were both powerful industries. Boards feared too much regulation would anger leaders of these vital industries, causing the economy to suffer, so regulation was minimal.

Electing U.S. Senators

Progressives believed that political corruption such as bribery and other unlawful acts needed to be stopped. They believed the best way to do this was to give the people a bigger voice in government.

At the time, all U.S. senators were chosen by state representatives, and not by the people in an election as they are today.

Governor Jewett Adams and state representatives approved a *preferential vote*, which meant the citizens could vote for the man they preferred for the U.S. Senate, and then state lawmakers would follow their wishes.

Voice of the People

Voting in elections is an important American responsibility. But, what if an elected official fails to listen to the people he or she represents? What if the office holder is corrupt or turns out to be simply the wrong person for the job? Across the United States, progressives passed state constitutional amendments to give voters a greater voice in civic affairs. Nevadans were among those backing the *initiative*, *referendum*, and *recall* amendments.

Nevada voters approved a **referendum**. The referendum allows voters to request that legislators put a law (already passed) on the ballot at the next election. Then voters can either keep or reject the law.

An **initiative** allows voters to propose their own laws. If 10 percent of the voters in three-fourths of Nevada's counties sign a petition, the ballot must include that initiative. If the voters approve it twice, it becomes a state law legislators cannot change.

Then Nevadans approved the **recall**. It requires 25 percent of the voters in a district to sign a petition, calling for an officeholder's name to appear on the ballot. The people then vote to keep or remove the official from office.

The initiative, referendum, and recall have made our state stronger by giving voters more direct voice in government.

Linking the Past to the Present

Nevada has passed several constitutional amendments through the initiative process. For example, due to a vote by the people, legislators may now serve only limited terms in office.

Another example of a modern initiative is that all tax increases must now receive a two-thirds majority vote in the legislature to become law.

Senator Newlands speaks at the opening of the Carson River Canal. Newlands brought federal dollars to build dams, reservoirs, and canal systems to dry Nevada.

Conservation and the West

Far away from Nevada, in Washington, D.C., President Theodore Roosevelt, a progressive, got political support from *conservationists*. This group believed in using the environment wisely and in protecting natural resources. Conservation became a large part of Roosevelt's policy. He supported many projects in the western United States and helped bring water to arid western lands.

The *Reno Evening Gazette* said in 1901:

> If President Roosevelt takes the stand for irrigation that it is believed he will, it will double the population of Nevada before his term of office expires. Double—did we say—it will triple, and quadruple it, and those who have been hanging on in Nevada . . . will be glad they didn't have money to get away.

Newlands Reclamation Act

Francis Newlands, Nevada's representative in Congress, worked with others to find funding for reclamation projects that would enable farmers to make the desert bloom. Their solution was the Newlands Reclamation Act. The federal government would sell federal lands in 16 states and use the profits to pay for building dams, canals, and irrigation ditches. The act fit perfectly with President Roosevelt's vision for the wise use of land. Dams and canals were built in Nevada. The state's farms and ranches greatly benefited, and Nevada became one of the nation's leading growers of alfalfa. You will read about building Hoover Dam in Chapter 8.

Newlands said about reclamation:

> I ask, who should undertake this work? Who can undertake the work? The view of the people of the arid region is that this is a public work . . . that ought to be undertaken by the government of the United States.

Nevada: A Journey of Discovery

Francis G. Newlands
1848–1917

Francis Newlands inherited wealth from the Comstock boom and was a key player in events that shaped Nevada's future.

Newlands attended Yale and Columbia Universities and then moved to California to practice law. There he married the daughter of William Sharon. Several years later, Newlands' young wife died, leaving him with young children to raise and a large estate to manage.

Francis Newlands moved to Nevada and entered politics. He was intelligent, wealthy, and full of political ambition. He also had a desire to serve the people. He worked with the National Irrigation Congress to promote federal assistance in building dams and canals. He won the office of Nevada's lone member to the U.S. House of Representatives, where he introduced several reclamation bills.

Finally, Newlands' efforts for irrigation succeeded. The Bureau of Reclamation was organized to take charge of building dams. Newlands did more than water the West. He helped design such agencies as the Federal Trade Commission to protect consumers' rights.

Unfortunately, Newlands also sought the repeal of the Fifteenth Amendment, which stated that the right to vote could not be denied on account of race. He did not think African Americans should have the right to vote. Newlands, born in the slave state of Mississippi, was deeply affected by its attitudes toward people of color. His attitudes were common at the time.

After five terms in the U.S. House, Newlands won the office of U.S. senator. He died in office after serving his state in Congress for a quarter of a century.

Newlands' irrigation project brought water to farms. Notice the horses hauling away the dirt from the canal.

The Tale of Butler's Burro

Jim Butler, a farmer and would-be businessman in the small mining town of Belmont, had been prospecting. One day in May, he found some gold sticking out of the earth—an outcropping, as it is called. Some said he found it the morning after a windstorm while searching for his burro, which had become lost during the night.

Whatever story you prefer, Butler thought he might have struck it rich. The problem was that he had no money to have the ore evaluated. He turned to another prospector, Tasker Oddie, a young lawyer who also had no money. Oddie knew a science teacher who had the tools to evaluate the ore. He found it to be valuable.

> One of the most interesting things about the Tonopah discovery was the fact that Jim Butler walked over the only spot on that mountain where the vein appeared on the surface, and the mountain was the only spot anywhere in the district where ore-bearing rocks could be found.
>
> —Mrs. Hugh Brown,
> a longtime Tonopah resident

A New Lease on Life

Butler was both a lawyer and a rancher, so he had other duties to perform, including harvesting hay. But once they were done, he and the other men went to work. They managed to dig out two tons of ore and sent it to Salt Lake City. In return, they received a check for $500 and a lot of attention.

> I was the cook for the outfit and I never learned the expanding power of beans. I'd make the fire and throw some beans into the pot and fill the pot to the brim with water. Then I'd climb down the hole that was getting to be a shaft, and every day I'd come back and find those dang beans swelled all over the place, and all over the pot, and down into the fire. I never did learn to keep those things harnessed.
>
> —Tasker Oddie, describing mining
> with Butler and friends

A new boom was on. People and miners came from all directions, many hoping to get rich and others hoping to make a profit by supplying the miners.

The town that grew up around this discovery became known as Tonopah. Roughly translated, Tonopah means "place of little water" or "brush springs."

> Tasker [Oddie] went on to tell me that he hired a young man who had just come into camp from Arizona. His name was Wyatt Earp. Had I ever heard about him? He was a fancy crackshot. Earp hired twenty men to help him keep the jumpers off the Mizpah claim, and Tasker paid them twenty dollars a day for six days. "That was . . . expensive . . . ," Tasker said, "but I never spent money [better]. . . . It established all the Tonopah Mining Company's claims, and we never had another lawsuit."
>
> —Mrs. Hugh Brown

It wasn't long before the men needed more money to run the mine. The $500 would hardly be enough to buy everything that Butler, Oddie, and the science teacher needed to dig out the gold and silver in the area.

Jim Butler found gold while looking for his burro.

They solved their problem with the lease system. Butler staked as many mining claims as he could, then leased portions of land along the vein. Whoever leased the claim dug for ore and had to pay the mine owners one-fourth of what was produced. This meant that working miners could make a lot of money if their luck was good.

Tonopah's success inspired outside investors from California and the East Coast to form the Tonopah Mining Company and buy out Butler and his partners in July 1901, a little more than a year after the discovery. Butler requested that they allow the lessees to continue to dig until January 1, 1902.

In that year, Butler and other Tonopah leaders helped promote other discoveries, beginning a mining boom that saved Nevada from economic depression.

What do you think

Legends surround the discovery of the Comstock (for example, how Henry Comstock may have tricked Patrick McLaughlin and Peter O'Riley into giving him a percentage of their claim). Another legend is about Butler's burro and Tonopah.

Why might people tell these stories? Do they help you understand how history is often from one person's viewpoint and can be changed over time as stories are told over and over again? In what ways can history be proven as fact?

Goldfield mining camps grew into a town with wide streets and modern buildings.

Miners prepare to enter a shaft in Goldfield.

The Last Gold Rush

Little did Nevada know it was beginning one of its last big mining booms. Jim Butler, the discoverer of Tonopah, gave prospectors money and equipment to look for gold in return for a percentage of the profits. Two men found gold about 30 miles south of Tonopah. They were the first to stake claims in what later became known as the Goldfield District.

One carload of ore from a mine in the Goldfield District brought the owners an eye-popping check of almost $575,000. Once the word of the rich discovery got out, its population shot up in just a few weeks. At its peak, mining production reached nearly $121 million. Gold, silver, copper, and lead were all mined in the area.

More than 100 mining companies worked in the Goldfield District at one time or another, and Goldfield's population grew to over 20,000, making it Nevada's largest city.

Taking Over Goldfield

It didn't take long for money and power in Goldfield to be held in just a few hands, just as it had in the Comstock region years before. George Nixon, already a millionaire businessman and banker before the Goldfield boom, saw an additional opportunity. He sent a smart young man, George Wingfield, to check out investments in Goldfield. Wingfield, a cowboy, bartender, and

Nevada: A Journey of Discovery

professional gambler, had already been working in Tonopah. He and Nixon formed a partnership that quickly produced great profits. Wingfield later said their relationship "depended merely upon the personal honor and integrity of the two men," and did not rely on legal documents.

At only 30 years of age, Wingfield dominated Goldfield. He bought several mines and owned a large mill that processed ore. Wingfield and Nixon owned entire city blocks. They owned banks in Goldfield and in several other Nevada towns.

One Humboldt County man wrote about Nixon's varied enterprises in a letter:

> Mr. Nixon is a cashier in a bank, a stock man, runs a saloon and hotel, has gone into the merchandise business, is an insurance agent, and sells stock, cattle, wool, etc. . . . and monkeys with mines. . . . Nixon is strong and powerful with his friends and [with] a large element who support him because they fear him.

Eventually the partnership dissolved, with Nixon keeping the banks and Wingfield keeping the mines.

Autos in the Boomtowns

Tonopah and Goldfield were the first Nevada boomtowns to use automobiles. They also became among the first Nevada towns to have speed limits for cars—4 miles per hour in Tonopah and 6 miles per hour in Goldfield. The new laws also stated that "vehicles drawn by horse, at all times, have the right of way."

Life in the Camps

> *Goldfield is a sadly hideous group of tents, huts, shacks, adobes, frame houses, and three good stone buildings. The climate is, perhaps, the worst in the world. For three months it scorches the life out of you; freezes and chills you for another three, and blows what's left of you into dust for the remaining six.*
>
> —Parmeter Kent, editor of a local paper

Tonopah●
●Goldfield

The mining camps in southern Nevada, like those in the rest of the state, started out mostly male and mostly wild. Then, if the boom continued—as it did in Tonopah and Goldfield—more people arrived and opened churches and schools.

Groups such as the Masons and Eagles formed in several towns. Tonopah and Goldfield opened public libraries and built theaters to welcome the latest traveling road shows. Circuses were frequent visitors to town. Both towns formed baseball teams and hosted boxing matches. Sports became crucial to local pride and recreation.

Towns hired sheriffs and policemen. Wyatt Earp, the legendary gunman involved in the shootout at the OK Corral in Tombstone, Arizona, lived in Tonopah for a few years, worked at the Northern Saloon, and sometimes helped defend the law.

Both Tonopah and Goldfield had terrible fires. Despite hiring more firemen, blazes continued to destroy parts of the mining towns, thanks to wooden buildings, summer heat, and winds.

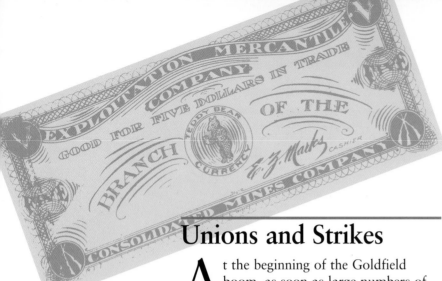

Scrip was paper certificates paid to miners. It could only be used in company stores. This scrip makes fun of the real scrip that was one of the issues of the miners' strike of 1907.

Unions and Strikes

At the beginning of the Goldfield boom, as soon as large numbers of miners started arriving, union organizers were close behind. The most important were from the Western Federation of Miners (WFM), whose members had grown increasingly *radical* until it joined with other unions to form the Industrial Workers of the World (IWW). Members of the IWW were often called "Wobblies."

Labor and management enjoyed a temporary peace, but members of the union struggled to get along. Tensions were high between union members and between the union and mine owners. State government leaders did not encourage working people to seek better pay or safer working conditions. According to the leaders, improvements were to be given, not demanded.

Eventually miners voted to strike. The reasons for the strike were many. Mine owners were wealthy, but the workers who went down in the mines every day, in dangerous conditions, got little of the wealth. Another issue was that mine owners sometimes paid workers in *scrip*. Scrip was like coupons, used instead of money.

Mine owners also tried to ban a practice called *high grading*. High grading was when miners hid gold in their clothing, so they could carry it out of the mine and sell it.

When the miners went on strike that November, Wingfield and other mine owners asked Governor Sparks to call for federal troops to control violence. President Roosevelt sent U.S. soldiers, who stayed for several weeks.

Then Sparks created a state police force and sent it to Goldfield to keep the peace. Wingfield hired non-union workers to take the place of those on strike.

There was always fear of violence in mining towns during the strike. One man visited his friend during the labor battles of 1907 and said of Wingfield, who owned the mine:

> He was carrying five revolvers and had four . . . detectives. . . . He was afraid of nothing.

Political cartoons are written to showcase the artist's point of view on things going on in the town. What does this cartoon say about the miners' strike of 1907? Who does the large man with the badge represent?

Historical Research

Research can serve many purposes. One of them can be to right wrongs. The labor violence in Goldfield serves as a good example. Two union organizers were accused of shooting the owner of a local restaurant. Lawyers and witnesses against the two were hired and paid for by Wingfield.

The two men proclaimed their innocence, and even some of the jury agreed, but the men were convicted and sent to jail.

Over 50 years later, the University of Nevada Press published a book on the case. Authors found new evidence in favor of the convicted men. The Nevada Board of Pardons voted to give them the first *posthumous* (after death) pardons in Nevada's history. One man's family member said, "I can tell my children that justice does prevail."

Miners in the town of McGill, 1912, strike for safer mines and higher wages. What does the photo tell you about the dangers faced by the striking miners?

129

Booms and Busts

When a railroad reached Beatty, the town celebrated. One man wrote, "The entire population was on hand with dynamite bombs, sky rockets, and hurrahs. . . . The corks popped, men threw their arms round each other and shouted their joy at the final coming of the railway that linked the great little camp to the outside world.

Just as the Tonopah boom led to Goldfield, the Goldfield boom led to other discoveries. Just east of Death Valley, two men found gold. It was only one strike, but it marked the beginning of the Bullfrog mining district. The name Bullfrog described the ore's unusual greenish color. The boom quickly turned to bust.

Other towns began. Beatty grew and remains important today. Pahrump is an important gateway to Death Valley. The town of Rawhide was born, but a fire destroyed it within two years. Rhyolite grew to more than 5,000 people but was down to 14 people within 20 years.

The Tonopah-Goldfield boom created not only other mining towns, but also other companies. New water companies provided a supply to the mines. Small companies provided electricity until they were bought out by larger power companies that installed miles of power lines and supplied electricity to Nevada and to mining districts in California. Railroad lines shipped ore, supplies, and workers from camp to camp.

Ely—Nevada's Copper Town

Just as southern Nevadans needed the railroad in order to build a city, eastern Nevadans needed copper. Copper discoveries in White Pine County led to a brief spurt of development, but the low-grade ore wasn't in great demand. It was also too far from water and population areas to merit much attention. Ely started as a stagecoach station and post office, then became the county seat of White Pine County.

In 1900, two prospectors found rich copper deposits in a nearby mountain, and a mining rush began. Mark Requa bought their claims and started looking for investors. Fortunately for Ely, Requa turned to the Guggenheim family in New York.

The Guggenheim family was gaining control of most of the world's copper production, including mines in Utah. They helped fund the Nevada Consolidated Copper Company and the Nevada Northern Railroad that linked Ely with the transcontinental railroad near Elko.

Life of Luxury in Ely

Mark Requa's daughter remembered the two cabins her father built in 1903:

There was no running water in either house, although I vaguely remember a pump in the kitchen sink. Wash bowls and pitchers did service in the bedrooms. . . . We were pretty proud that we had the only real bathtub in White Pine County. . . . Papa, who thought of everything, had it freighted in and installed in a small room next to the hoisting works at the mine. . . . We had candles for light and drum stoves for heat in the bedrooms, kerosene lamps elsewhere, and cord upon cord of pinewood stacked back of the kitchen to feed the cook stove.

Ely could be as rip-roaring a mining town as any other. A deputy sheriff explains why the jail was built near the main local saloon:

It is very hard work to carry a drunken man up hill three or four hundred yards in order to lock him up. . . . it would be very much easier to roll him downhill an equal distance for the same purpose.

Some say Ely was named for John Ely (left), a tall, adventurous miner who used his watch as part payment for a mine that made over $5 million. Others say the town was named for a man by the name of Smith Ely, or a town in the East.

Miners in Ruth, six miles from Ely, started mining copper underground, but five great open pits were dug a level at a time and yielded the rich copper ore. Tons of ore were hauled by train to the smelter at McGill.

Unfortunately for Requa, the Guggenheims then removed him from control of their copper investments. They spent more than $4 million to develop the Ely area before they made any money. But by 1909, copper production there had topped $6 million. Another mining boom was underway.

Copper Company Towns

The Guggenheims created their own towns for miners. Ruth, McGill, and Kimberly were built and owned by Nevada Consolidated Copper Company.

These towns were different from most mining camps. The small wooden houses looked alike. Unlike the 100 saloons Goldfield boasted, copper company towns had few or no saloons and no hotels. Because the company literally owned the town, workers who wanted to gamble or buy liquor had to do so at company stores, dance halls, and bars.

No town government existed, which meant the local population had no voice in local affairs. Workers were often paid in scrip they could spend only at company-owned stores.

The copper boom brought a new set of immigrants to Nevada. Greeks and Serbs came from Europe to work in the mining towns. They, like other immigrants, were often victims of discrimination. The copper company decided where people would live, and they segregated foreign-born workers.

Not everything about living in a company town was bad, of course. Company towns provided medical and recreational facilities, free utilities, and towns that were relatively crime-free.

Another Strike

Low wages, segregation, payment only in scrip, and tight control over the miners' lives, however, prompted workers to try again to organize labor unions. The unions went on strike against all Guggenheim properties. To keep the peace and keep the mines operating, the company hired 30 armed guards, which led to three shootings. Two of them were fatal. Governor Oddie declared martial law and the strike ended with a small wage hike for the miners.

What do you think?

The *Ely Mining Record* was concerned about the arrival of immigrants:

A systematic effort has been undertaken . . . to supplant American labor by the employment of Greeks. Several hundred of them have arrived during the past few weeks, and as they are not in the habit of traveling for their health, it can be set down as a fact that they are here under the promise of employment.

Why did immigrants inspire such reactions among local miners and townspeople?

• Ely
Tonopah •
Bullfrog • Beatty
• Pahrump

Las Vegas, a Railroad Town

As you read in Chapter 6, after nearly two decades of running her ranch, Helen J. Stewart found a buyer. William Clark, a senator from Montana, owned many profitable copper mines and hoped to take advantage of a boom in California by building a railroad from southern California to Salt Lake City. The route would go through the desert oasis of Stewart's Las Vegas ranch.

Clark planned to build a railroad town where travelers could stop, stay overnight, and get a good meal. Stewart kept part of her land for herself, built a new home, and remained active in the Las Vegas community.

Clark immediately began making plans to build what would become the San Pedro, Los Angeles, and Salt Lake Railroad, but others had similar plans. The Union Pacific Railroad started another line within yards of Clark's road. Separate construction crews started laying track in the hot summer sun. Tempers were short, and fighting between workers of the companies began, including shooting at one another. These conflicts helped convince railroad owners that they needed to reach an agreement.

The Union Pacific and Clark decided to evenly share ownership of one railroad, and Clark would operate it. It took nearly two years, but passenger service finally began.

Two weeks after the trains started carrying passengers through Las Vegas, Clark's assistants held an auction and in two days sold off half the lots of the original Las Vegas townsite. They received $265,000—nearly five times what Clark paid for the land.

A 24-Hour Town

At its beginning, the railroad made Las Vegas a 24-hour town long before gambling or other activities were permanent parts of the city. Since the trains came through at any hour, lodges and restaurants were almost always open.

The Las Vegas Land and Water Company, owned by the railroad, controlled many of the town's services. Since the railroad was concer-ned mainly with its tracks and depot, it paid little attention to other public needs. Streets were left unpaved, and the land and water company refused to build water lines beyond the business district. Residents outside the townsite had to dig their own wells.

Walter Bracken, who worked for the Las Vegas Land and Water Company, developed a reputation as the true ruler of Las Vegas. So did Edward W. Clark, who owned a mailing company, part of a store, part of the main local bank, and part of the

Las Vegas ●

The Las Vegas and Tonopah Railroad, 1914, helped build the southern part of the state.

part of the main local bank, and part of the local electric and telephone company. Clark later worked toward the building of Hoover Dam.

Charles P. Squires built the first hotel in Las Vegas—in a tent. Later he bought a weekly newspaper, the *Las Vegas Age*, which he edited for nearly 40 years.

The women of Las Vegas were also committed to building the community. At the time, most women worked caring for their families at home, though some worked as teachers or nurses. Las Vegas women did more. They formed a club to help charities and to beautify their city. They asked Helen Stewart, one of their founding members, to pick a name for their group. She chose the Mesquite Club, named after a desert plant that lives a long time. The Mesquite Club is still the oldest women's group in Las Vegas.

Despite all the positive things in the town, certain aspects of life in early Las Vegas were not pleasant. Railroad

executives wanted to limit liquor sales to one area of town, which became famous for its lawlessness. Sadly, discrimination in Las Vegas got worse before it got better. The city was racially segregated. City leaders gave ethnic minorities, especially African Americans, Mexicans, and Chinese, no choice but to live in certain parts of town.

Clark County

Las Vegas leaders worked together to separate Las Vegas and its surrounding area from Lincoln County, whose county seat was more than 150 miles away. In 1909 they succeeded, and the area became known as Clark County, named after the railroad and copper giant William Clark. Las Vegas was the county seat.

Lincoln County

Clark County

Las Vegas ★
(County Seat)

Back in Time

Reading the direct words from people of the past often gives an interesting picture of a place. What do these quotes tell you about Las Vegas in the early 1900s? Would you read any of these accounts in newspapers today?

Longtime sheriff Sam Gay recalled Las Vegas before he became the law:

From 1905 to 1910, Las Vegas was a rough and tumble western town. Five men dead for breakfast one Sunday morning and 10 men wounded.

Charles P. Squires was asked to buy the city newspaper, the *Las Vegas Age*, and replied:

What on earth would I do with a newspaper? I have troubles enough already. . . . But something had started a train of thought which I was unable to sidetrack. Now, just suppose I had a newspaper in Las Vegas; perhaps I could help revive the poor, sick little town.

Peter Buol, the first mayor of Las Vegas, explained how he became mayor:

Somebody got an idea the town needed a mayor, so Bill Hawkins and I decided to run against each other. Nobody else wanted to run. Some little accident happened and I beat him by about 10 votes.

A Socialist Town

In Nevada and across the country, workers, especially miners, felt progressive reforms fell short of meeting their needs for improved living and working conditions. They began to give increasing support to the *socialist* movement. In socialism, the government, not powerful companies or individuals, owns and runs businesses and controls the distribution of goods. Another aspect of socialism is equal ownership of property and goods by the common people. How much the workers of Nevada actually believed in the idea that government should own business is not known. In Nevada, the main purpose for worker support of socialist unions was focused on the need for better wages and working conditions.

Socialists created their own colony, organized as the Nevada Colony Corporation, and called it Nevada City. The members of the colony grew and shared their own food and worked to become self-sufficient. They hoped that the number of socialists in Nevada might be enough to support the kind of community they had created.

> The object of the Nevada Colony Corporation is to organize and establish co-operative colonies to engage in agriculture, stock raising, and manufacturing industries.
>
> —From the colony's Declaration of Purposes and Plans

The colony's newspaper, the *Cooperative Colonist*, featured this song meant to show that starvation and sadness would come to those who continued to pursue their old ways outside the colony:

> My stomach, 'tis of thee
> So full of misery
> Of thee I sing.
> I used to fill my craw
> With beefsteak hard to chaw,
> But now a bone I gnaw
> Or any old thing.

Nevada City, a socialist experiment, existed until World War I, when it was abandoned.

• Nevada City

Activity

Exploring a Photograph

What do you see in this photograph of Nevada City that gives you clues to the lifestyle there? What was the land and climate like? What were the buildings made of?

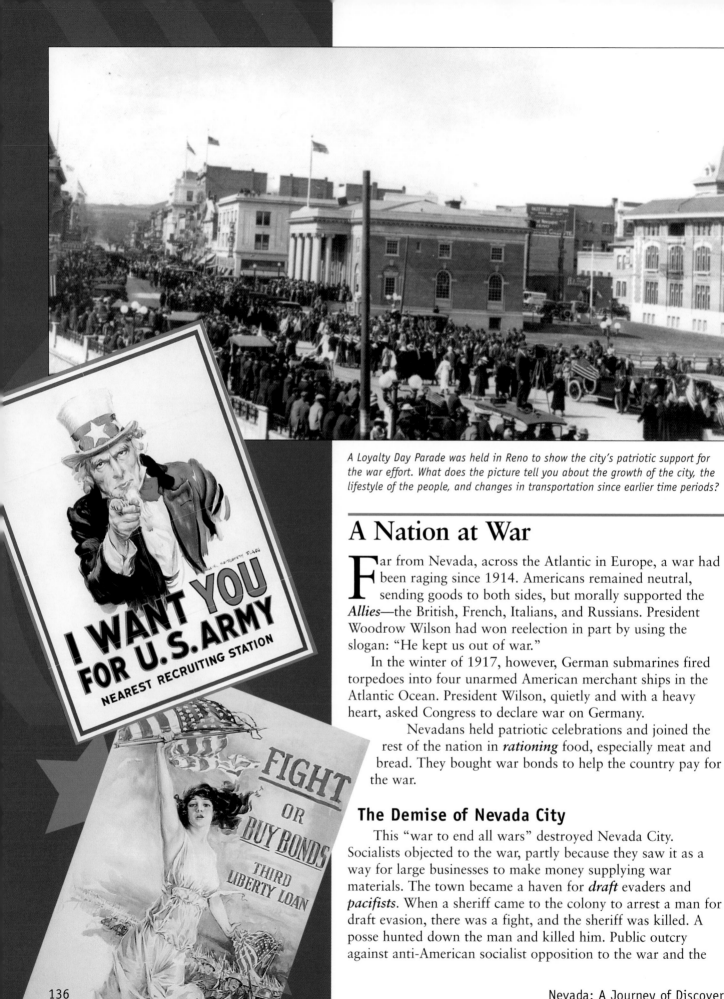

A Loyalty Day Parade was held in Reno to show the city's patriotic support for the war effort. What does the picture tell you about the growth of the city, the lifestyle of the people, and changes in transportation since earlier time periods?

A Nation at War

Far from Nevada, across the Atlantic in Europe, a war had been raging since 1914. Americans remained neutral, sending goods to both sides, but morally supported the *Allies*—the British, French, Italians, and Russians. President Woodrow Wilson had won reelection in part by using the slogan: "He kept us out of war."

In the winter of 1917, however, German submarines fired torpedoes into four unarmed American merchant ships in the Atlantic Ocean. President Wilson, quietly and with a heavy heart, asked Congress to declare war on Germany.

Nevadans held patriotic celebrations and joined the rest of the nation in *rationing* food, especially meat and bread. They bought war bonds to help the country pay for the war.

The Demise of Nevada City

This "war to end all wars" destroyed Nevada City. Socialists objected to the war, partly because they saw it as a way for large businesses to make money supplying war materials. The town became a haven for *draft* evaders and *pacifists*. When a sheriff came to the colony to arrest a man for draft evasion, there was a fight, and the sheriff was killed. A posse hunted down the man and killed him. Public outcry against anti-American socialist opposition to the war and the

Nevada: A Journey of Discovery

death of the sheriff led to the breakup of the colony.

Prejudice and Patriotism

Once again, prejudice entered everyday life as Nevadans worried about the loyalty of German and Serbian immigrants. At the request of the students, many of whom were of German descent, the Douglas County School Board stopped teaching German at the local high school. Socialists worked to pass a law banning the teaching of German in the state's elementary schools. Most foreign workers, however, supported their new state and their new country.

The *White Pine News* reported on a patriotic rally in Ruth:

> One of the notable features was the patriotic spirit expressed by the large number of foreign-born men who are employed here. There is no doubt that these men are not only willing, but anxious for the opportunity to defend the flag of the country of their adoption.

Russell Elliott, a Nevada historian, grew up in McGill and recalled,

> My Irish mother was extremely anti-British and deplored our entrance [to the war] on the side of the British government. She sent away for a piece of sheet music, titled "I Didn't Raise My Boy to Be a Soldier."

The U.S. propaganda machine must have been in high gear at the time, for when she received a package from the music company, it was for the piece ordered, but one with exactly the opposite sentiment: "I Raised My Boy to Be a Soldier." Mom was disgusted and angry and threw the music in the garbage.

A Soaring Economy

The war helped Nevada's economy. Copper production tripled within two years and the production of minerals rose higher than during the peak of the Comstock Lode. The war also prompted Congress to pass the Pittman Silver Act, guaranteeing silver producers a high price for their ore. This continued until 1923, when production dropped sharply.

Finally, the war was over. Most of Nevada's fathers, sons, and brothers came home.

Activity

Political Cartoon

This cartoon refers to the British practice of flying a neutral flag (especially American) over their ships in the war zone. The German sailor asks, with a German accent, "Who iss it?" Vat boat?"

The British admiral points to an American flag and shouts back in a British accent, "Cawn't you see 'Im a blooming Yankee!!"

Ironically, the British *Lusitania*, shown in this cartoon, would end up being torpedoed two months after this cartoon was published.

1. Why did the British fly an American flag?
2. How does the cartoonist show the British admiral is not American?
3. How does the cartoonist show the identity of the German sailor?
4. In what way does this cartoon make fun of the Germans?

Jeanne Elizabeth Wier did a lot more than fight for women's suffrage. She was a professor of history at the University of Nevada. She helped organize and run the Nevada Historical Society for more than 40 years. She published several historical papers and collected original documents, all of which help today's historians. Many of these documents are in the Nevada Historical Society in Reno. Others are in museums in Carson City and Las Vegas.

Surrounded by suffragists who had worked so long to see it passed, Governor Emmet Boyle signs a resolution for ratification of the Nineteenth Amendment to the U.S. Constitution on Feb 7, 1920.

Should Women Vote?

While progressives had no problem denying people the right to vote on the basis of skin color, *gender* proved to be an even bigger issue.

Four efforts to allow women to vote in Nevada during the 1880s failed. Another effort fell short in the 1890s. By 1911, the women's suffrage movement had become an international effort, not just a cause in the United States.

Nevada joined in the cause when Jeanne Elizabeth Wier organized the Nevada Equal Franchise Society. The next year the group's new president, Anne Martin, stepped in and started lobbying legislators. She went from town to town around the state, giving fiery speeches on women's rights.

Women Win the Right to Vote

Finally, in 1914, Nevada's male voters approved an amendment to the state constitution that allowed women to vote.

> We are heartened rather than disheartened by the signs of protest against this long delayed measure of justice. . . . We are convinced there are enough broadminded and courageous women, enough just men who want fair play, to carry an amendment through in Nevada.
>
> —Anne Martin, 1914

The fight continued at the national level. Anne Martin traveled across the country, working for women's rights. Finally, in 1920, the Nineteenth Amendment was added to the U.S. Constitution, just in time for women to vote in the upcoming presidential election.

> The right of citizens of the United States to vote shall not be denied or abridged by the United States or by any state on account of sex.
>
> —Nineteenth Amendment, U.S. Constitution

Anne Martin
1875–1951

Anne Martin was one of the most important leaders of her time in the fight for women's rights. She took risks and dared to speak out.

Anne was born in Empire, a small town just east of Carson City. She went to a school for girls in Reno and earned a degree from the University of Nevada. Later, she traveled to California and attended Stanford University, where she earned degrees in history. Then she became head of the history department at the University of Nevada. Soon after, she left to travel across Europe, where she learned more about the fight for women's rights. In England, she was arrested during a demonstration.

Following her return from Europe, Martin was president of the Nevada Equal Franchise Society. She drove all over the state, meeting with women and men who supported the fight for women's rights. Most of the small mining camps supported her cause, but larger towns, such as Reno and Carson City, did not. To make matters worse, serious conflicts in personalities and other issues drove the women apart.

Meanwhile, Martin joined the national fight for a U.S. amendment for women's suffrage and organized a demonstration outside the White House.

After leading Nevada's fight to win the vote for women, Martin ran for a seat in the U.S. Senate. She received 18 percent of the vote—a respectable number, but not enough to win. She ran again two years later and received a smaller percentage of votes.

She said about running for office:

> I want to knock the fear out of the hearts of women. Even if I should not win, it will never seem so strange again when a woman tries it.

No other woman in Nevada had yet run for federal office or been so deeply involved in national women's suffrage issues. Anne spent the rest of her life discussing women's rights and reform in speeches and articles.

NEVADA PORTRAIT

On the side of the car is a sign that reads, "Vote for Anne Martin." The tour was part of Martin's bid for the U.S. Senate, which she lost.

Two Opinions

Senator Francis Newlands told Anne Martin:

> *The social and moral conditions of Nevada would be vastly improved by the aid of women's votes.*

George Wingfield, who owned much of the wealth in mining districts in eastern Nevada, opposed women's suffrage and threatened to leave the state and take his wealth with him. A woman responded:

> We'll be sorry, George, to lose you,
> But where are you going to go
> Now that the women are voting
> From Florida to Idaho.
>
> Nevada's not the greatest state,
> And if it ever hopes
> To be among the best ones, let
> The women have their votes.

Chapter 7 Review

What Do You Remember?

1. What are some examples of progressive laws?
2. Explain the dark side of progressivism.
3. What were the state boards and agencies created during the Progressive Era intended to do?
4. How did President Theodore Roosevelt's ideas benefit Nevada and other western states?
5. List three things you learned about Francis Newlands and his contributions to Nevada.
6. Why did Goldfield miners go on strike in 1907? What was the result?
7. Describe how Jim Butler found gold and got rich in Tonopah.
8. Describe everyday life in Ely.
9. What was it like to live in the copper company towns?
10. Describe everyday life in Goldfield.
11. How did the railroad influence the development of Las Vegas?
12. What were the roles of Ed W. Clark and Charles P. Squires in early Las Vegas?
13. List some of the good and bad things about life in early Las Vegas.
14. Describe the purposes of Nevada City. Did it succeed or fail?
15. List two examples of the impact of World War I on Nevada's people.
16. How was Nevada ahead of other states in giving women the vote?
17. How did Anne Martin work to change things for women in Nevada and in other places?
18. What amendment gave U.S. women the right to vote in all elections? What year was it?

Activity

You Choose!

1. On an Internet search engine, look up the Lahontan Dam and then choose one of the following activities to report what you learned about the dam and the reservoir.

   • Write a one-page report
   • Make a poster showing a map and life in the district, including farming, cattle, tourism, etc.
   • Write a short skit about the dam or life in the region.
   • Write a poem or song about the above.

2. Set up a mock election in your class and try to pass an initiative petition. Choose a subject that is of current interest to your community.

3. Make a list of the kinds of homes and businesses you see in a day. Could one of the businesses build and run a company town? What might the advantages be? What might the disadvantages be? Discuss the issues with your class or a small group.

1. On the Internet, locate websites for the Truckee-Carson Irrigation District.

   - Discuss with your class the contribution of the irrigation district to everyday life in Carson Valley today.
   - Find the dams and canals that are part of the irrigation district and draw them on a map.

2. On a Nevada map, pinpoint the mining towns created from the founding of Goldfield to the end of World War I. Do you see any patterns?

Activity

What Can You Learn About Nevada From the U.S. Census?

Every 10 years in this country, the federal government collects information about its citizens. The information includes the number of people in each state and each county, their gender and race, the size of their household, how much money the household earns, and a lot more. You can see the results of the last census at www.census.gov.

Study this chart of census figures from 1860 to 1920. Remember that Nevada was first the home of Native Americans, then the home of a few white settlers. When gold and silver were discovered, the white population grew. Chinese workers came to build the railroad and work for mining companies. Other ethnic groups came in smaller numbers to find work.

Look for population trends on the chart. Then review Nevada's history to get clues as to why the population figures changed.

1. What was the reason the total number of people increased so much from 1860 to 1870?
2. Look at the number of males compared to females on the chart. Why do you think the female population was so low in the earlier time periods, but grew later? Why do you think there were always more men than women in the state?
3. Look at the Chinese population. Can you find historical evidence to explain why their numbers grew, and then declined?
4. Read the note at the bottom of the chart to explain why the Indian population was so low, even though there were many more Indian people than white settlers in the early years of the state. What might have prevented an accurate counting of Indians?

Now it's your turn. Make either a line or pie graph, using all or part of the information from the chart. What trends do you see more clearly when the information is shown on a graph?

Year	1860	1870	1880	1890	1900	1910	1920
Total Population	6,812	42,491	62,266	45,761	42,335	81,875	77,407
Men	NA	33,279	42,019	30,031	25,603	52,551	46,240
Women	NA	9,212	20,247	15,730	16,732	29,324	31,167
White (includes Mexican)	6,812	38,959	53,556	39,084	35,405	74,276	70,699
Indian*	0	23	2,803	3,599	5,216	5,240	4,907
Chinese	0	3,152	5,419	2,836	1,352	927	689
Black	45	357	488	242	134	513	346
Japanese	0	0	0	0	228	864	754
Other	0	0	0	0	0	55	12

* Until 1880 only tax-paying Indians were counted.

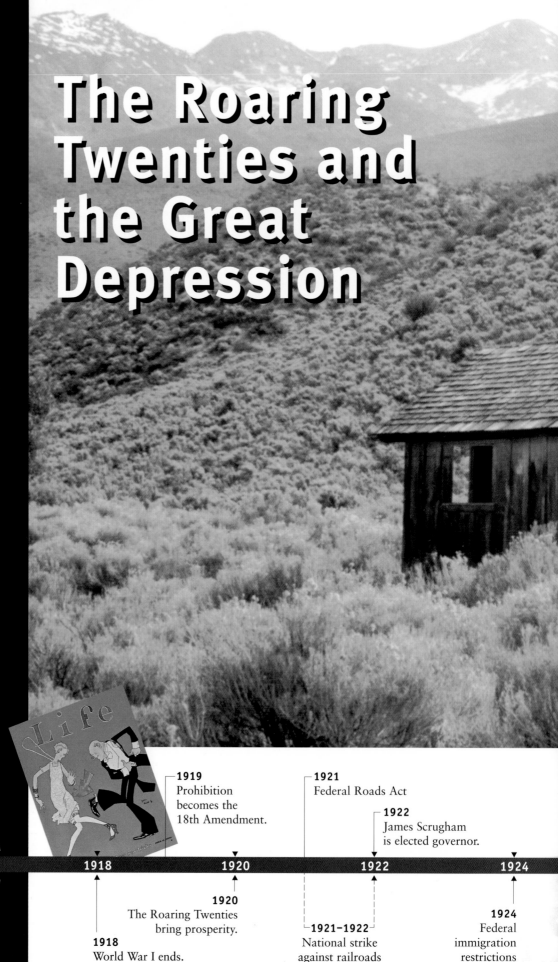

The Roaring Twenties and the Great Depression

Timeline of Events

1919
Prohibition becomes the 18th Amendment.

1921
Federal Roads Act

1922
James Scrugham is elected governor.

1918   1920   1922   1924

1920
The Roaring Twenties bring prosperity.

1918
World War I ends.

1921–1922
National strike against railroads

1924
Federal immigration restrictions

WORDS TO UNDERSTAND
bankrupt
communist
conclude
deport
depression
destination
fluctuation
glut
inflate
intimidate
plummet
residency
suspicious
temperance
vaudeville

The Baranagus School in Lee did not always look so forlorn. During the 1920s through the 1950s many isolated rural students boarded at the home of the Baranagus family so they could go to school. The first Elko Basque Festival was held in an apple orchard across the creek from the school.

Photo by Travis Miller

1926
Daily passenger air service begins in Las Vegas.

1928
Boulder Canyon Project Act is approved by Congress.

1928
Hawthorne Naval Ammunition Depot is started.

1931
Residency requirement for divorce is reduced, and gambling is legalized again.

1932
Wingfield's banks close due to the Great Depression.

1935
President Roosevelt dedicates Boulder (Hoover) Dam.

| 1926 | 1928 | 1930 | 1932 | 1934 | 1936 |

1931
Construction on Boulder Dam begins.

1933
The 21st Amendment repeals Prohibition.

1929
The Great Depression begins.

143

Roaring Nevada

The 1920s became known as the "Roaring Twenties," and Americans certainly made their share of noise. After the reforms of the Progressive Era and the lack of luxuries during World War I, Americans were in the mood to celebrate.

Vaudeville was at its peak, with entertainers traveling the country. Movies were becoming increasingly popular. New movies with sound, called "talkies," were all the rage. Women, who had just won the right to vote, wore shorter skirts and cut their hair short. Men and women learned to dance the Charleston and had all-night dancing parties.

The Great Red Scare

World War I marked an end and a beginning for many countries. After several years of turmoil, Russia overthrew the czar, first with a democratic government, then with a *communist* one. Karl Marx and Friedrich Engels, who wrote *The Communist Manifesto*, argued that communism would spread throughout the world.

As communists and socialists gained support in some European countries, Americans worried about what might happen in their country. Americans were also *suspicious* of those who had criticized progressives for doing too little to promote social justice. They thought some of these people would go too far and turn to violence to get change. In fact, several acts of violence, including bombings, appeared to be related to radical socialist groups in the country.

These concerns led to the *deportation* of 4,000 U.S. citizens suspected of disloyalty to the United States.

Nevada Targets Radicals

Nevada leaders passed a law that resembled one adopted in other states. It provided for up to 10 years in prison and/or a $5,000 fine for anyone who promoted "doctrine which advocates or teaches crime, sabotage, violence or unlawful methods of terrorism as a means of . . . industrial or political reform."

Later, another law required all of the state's college graduates to have completed classes on the national and state constitutions. It was agreed that citizens needed a better understanding of government.

Women who wore the new styles and cut their hair short were called "flappers."

Nevadans were far more concerned, though, about what was happening in the mining industry. Mine owners were worried about their profits. The end of the war meant the end of *inflated* prices for ore.

> The Department of Justice has undertaken to tear out the radical seeds that have entangled American ideas in their poisonous theories.
>
> —A. Mitchell Palmer

More Mining Strikes

Mining unions were also becoming more and more radical. After World War I, the cost of things workers needed to live rose, while wages did not. Many unions had pledged not to strike during the war, but with the war over, miners at the company towns of Ruth and McGill went on strike. Mine owners and politicians blamed the IWW for the unrest.

In Tonopah, mine owners rejected the miners' request for a raise, and the IWW organized a strike. Governor Emmet Boyle helped negotiate a settlement that most of the miners endorsed. But the IWW found it unacceptable and union supporters refused to come back to work. Only after mine owners and miners organized a new union was an agreement reached, and all the miners went back to work.

> The IWW . . . with its faults and brutal philosophy, has not been and will not be successfully combatted by mob rule or by methods which do not lie wholly within the law.
>
> — Governor Emmet Boyle's message to the legislature in 1919

What do you think?

Governor Emmet Boyle and other Nevada officials persuaded a judge to issue an order banning "all persons from publishing a statement that a strike exists, . . . or circulating any . . . libelous or false statements concerning Tonopah."

Why do you think the judge would issue such an order? According to the U.S. Bill of Rights, was the judge within his legal rights to issue that kind of order?

The Red Scare

The color red was a symbol of the Communist Party, so anyone suspected of being a communist was called a "Red." People who sympathized with communists were called "Pink."

Women of the Silent Screen

For many, the symbol of the 1920s woman was silent screen actress Clara Bow. She played women who were hard-working but liked to have fun. She married western film actor Rex Bell, and they lived on a ranch in Searchlight. Clara's husband and their son later held political offices in Nevada.

146

Prohibition—Roaring or Boring?

One reform movement of the postwar period might be called progressivism taken to the extreme. Prohibition was an effort to stop the drinking of alcohol. That in itself was nothing new—*temperance* movements had been popular since the 1800s. The idea of passing laws against alcohol received a boost from the progressive belief in moral reform and also sentiment against Germany. Not only was Germany the enemy in World War I, but Germans owned many major breweries.

The Eighteenth Amendment to the Constitution, forbidding the making, selling, transporting, importing, or exporting of alcoholic drinks took effect in 1919.

> The sale or manufacture of intoxicating liquors is forbidden. After one year . . . the manufacture, sale, or transportation of intoxicating liquors within, the importation thereof into, or the exportation thereof from the United States . . . for beverage purposes, is hereby prohibited.
>
> —Eighteenth Amendment, U.S. Constitution

Prohibition proved unpopular, especially in urban areas. Neither Reno nor Las Vegas showed much interest in enforcing it and people continued to buy, sell, and drink alcohol.

An unplanned result of Prohibition was it provided an income for many immigrants. How did this happen? From 1880 until 1924, millions of oppressed people left southern and eastern Europe and immigrated to the United States. As in other periods of American history, many of these recent arrivals lacked money, did not speak English, and suffered discrimination over their appearance, customs, or religion.

The new immigrants could accept low-paying respectable jobs or make more money providing illegal whiskey. The immigrants were mostly Italian Catholics or Slavic Jews who were less opposed to drinking alcohol than were the American Protestants.

> I don't believe in prohibition or any kind of reform that takes from any man or woman their right to find happiness in their own way. . . . I would make Reno the playground of the world.
>
> —Mayor E.E. Roberts, Reno

The Tunnels of North Las Vegas

One Nevadan who opposed Prohibition was Tom Williams. He arrived in the area from Utah and bought a large piece of land a mile down the hill north of Las Vegas. He built a house, dug wells, built roads and irrigation ditches, and started selling lots. People bought the lots, built homes, and moved in.

Williams dug tunnels under his town to help those who were making liquor hide their business. Local officials had little objection. One policeman drove up and down the street, warning that federal investigators were in the area. "The feds are coming! The feds are coming!" he yelled.

Another Las Vegas policeman said Williams's land was "a maze of tunnels. But I'm not saying where they are or who built them. It was sure one wet town, though."

The area became known as Old Town. Williams built a second house and opened the Oasis Auto Court, complete with a grocery store, post office, community center, campground, and telephone—the only one in town. Eventually, the town evolved into North Las Vegas.

Finally, in 1933, the Twenty-First Amendment repealed Prohibition, and alcohol came out in the open once again.

White Sheets

Sadly, prejudice toward people of different races and backgrounds led to a national revival of the Ku Klux Klan. The organization was born in the South just after the Civil War. It was a combination of a social club for Confederate veterans and a force to *intimidate* African Americans whenever they tried to use their new freedoms. However, the KKK also targeted immigrant groups, especially those belonging to the Catholic Church.

During the 1920s, the KKK's membership spread well beyond the South, and the hooded men attacked different ethnic groups. In many states, prominent men in the community donned their white sheets to disguise who they were and marched on main streets. In Las Vegas, they went down Fremont Street.

Harley Harmon, a Las Vegas businessman, remembered from his childhood seeing a burned-out KKK cross on Fremont Street. Harmon's father helped eliminate the local Klan by threatening to tell the public the names of the Klan members.

Highway Building

The popularity of automobiles pushed the need for better roads. What good was a car if you couldn't drive it quickly from one town to the next or out of state?

The U.S. Congress passed several acts to help states build highways. In 1921 the Federal Roads Act stated that the federal government would match money put up by the state. For every dollar Nevada put up to build a highway, the federal government would contribute about $6. This helped build several highways that are still widely traveled today.

Progressive Governors

The 1920s began with Emmet Boyle in the governor's mansion. His attempts to handle postwar labor strife in a balanced way and his support for road building made him very popular.

James Scrugham, the next governor, also supported highway building, pushing for taxes he wanted spent on roads. Then he began setting aside land for what became the Nevada State Park system. He took an interest in historic preservation, exploring ancient Native American sites.

> It is a wise move to preserve for future generations every evidence that can be found of a pre-historic race which once inhabited this country, and also to preserve the scenic beauties of Nevada's wonderful mountains. These may someday become an actual asset to the state.
>
> — J.L. Earl in a letter to Governor Scrugham

What do you think?

Some, like Governor Scrugham, say historic preservation is important for its own sake. Others say we should preserve the past only if it pays off financially. What arguments can you make for either side?

Linking the Past to the Present

Today, as in the past, highways go through towns. How else would you get to stop for gas and food? Highways 6, 50, and 95 go through many towns. The first Highway 91 through Las Vegas was Fifth Street, now called Las Vegas Boulevard. Freeways, however, make it possible for drivers to travel faster by going around towns instead of through them. In Las Vegas you can drive through the city on I-15 or I-93/95.

James G. Scrugham
1880–1945

James Scrugham is unique in Nevada history. No one else has been elected governor and a member of both the U.S. House of Representatives and the U.S. Senate. His life shows the importance of education, work, and appreciating the environment.

Scrugham was born in Lexington, Kentucky. As a young man, he trained to be an engineer and was hired in several states, including the University of Nevada in Reno.

Scrugham became the state engineer. That gave him the power to decide who received water from various rivers and lakes. He also joined the military during World War I and helped start the American Legion—a national patriotic organization.

After the war Scrugham ran for office for the first time and was elected governor of Nevada. He supported the building of highways because cars were becoming more popular and common. He also liked to drive around the state and visit voters, so he was nicknamed "Gasoline Jim" and "The Governor on Wheels."

Scrugham thought that southern Nevada had the potential to grow if it had cheap water and power. This inspired him to strongly support the building of a dam on the Colorado River.

The governor also wanted the state to set aside land for the public to use for recreation. He worked to create game refuges—areas where animals would be protected. This was the beginning of what later became the Nevada Division of State Parks. Long after Scrugham left the governor's mansion, Valley of Fire, near Las Vegas, became the first state park. Twenty-three other areas have been preserved.

While Nevadans liked the parks, they voted Scrugham out of office after one term. His political career, however, was far from over. He bought the *Nevada State Journal*, a daily newspaper in Reno. This gave him the chance to keep Nevadans aware of his opinions. He ran for the House of Representatives and was elected. He won four more terms before his election to the U.S. Senate.

During his years in Congress Scrugham made sure Nevada received federal money to help preserve park areas. He also helped start national recreation areas. One of them was Lake Mead.

When Scrugham died, a newspaper editor wrote, "He didn't know what it meant to relax. He regarded an hour lost if he wasn't doing something for Nevada."

Governor Scrugham (right) and John Chaloner (left) explore Pueblo Grande in 1925.

The first airmail flight left Las Vegas in April, 1926.

Las Vegas of the Future

As the 1920s began, the population of Las Vegas had barely passed 2,300. But that was more than double the number from the previous census. Despite a small population, Las Vegas began to take the shape of a tourist-oriented city.

Part of the motivation for becoming a tourist town was a long national strike against railroad operators. Workers in the Las Vegas railroad repair shops were dedicated union members who worked to shut down railroads until wages increased, but the effort ended in defeat for the strikers.

Las Vegas suffered an even worse defeat. The Union Pacific Railroad announced it would move its repair shops up the line to Caliente, taking many jobs with it.

Las Vegas leaders came up with a solution. Rather than just stopping off in Las Vegas en route to somewhere else, they hoped to encourage people to make Las Vegas their **destination**. They took small steps, but important ones. A businessman bought the old Kiel Ranch and turned it into a dude ranch for those who wanted to come west and live like cowboys. New highways brought in more tourists, and so did small airplanes, a new invention at the time. Airplanes began daily passenger flights at Rockwell Field, behind what is now the Sahara Hotel.

It would provide "a dustless and smooth highway all the way from the California to the Arizona state lines and will bring much more traffic into Las Vegas."

— James Cashman,
a Clark County auto dealer
who promoted new highways

The first Las Vegas golf course was opened, always an attraction for visitors. It had no grass—it was a dirt course. It was located next to the airfield, meaning that planes might land while golfers were driving or putting. If you have ever seen a golf competition, you know golfers often want everything around them to be quiet. Las Vegas had yet to perfect how it should attract and treat tourists.

Making new roads contributed to tourism in Las Vegas. This photo was taken in 1935.

Nevada: A Journey of Discovery

Maude Frazier
1881–1963

Few educators have been more important to Nevada's history than Maude Frazier. She was born in Wisconsin and grew up on a farm. At the time, women rarely had careers unless they were nurses or teachers. Frazier eagerly moved west to take a job as a teacher and principal in Genoa, the first settlement in Nevada. Then she taught at schools all around the state—Lovelock, Beatty, Goldfield, and Sparks.

Miss Frazier worked her way up to the job of state superintendent in the Nevada Department of Education. Based in Las Vegas, the department was in charge of all public schools in four counties. Frazier traveled from county to county in a used Dodge. She may have been the first person ever to drive the 180 miles from Las Vegas to Goldfield in one day.

Then, having had enough of the travel, Maude Frazier became superintendent of the Las Vegas Union School District, running two elementary schools and the local high school.

She persuaded voters to approve construction of what became Las Vegas High School, now the Las Vegas Academy. It had room for 500 students, and some Las Vegas leaders objected that the city would never have that many high school students.

Frazier proved them wrong several times over the next 20 years of running the local schools. She worked hard, hired good teachers, and maintained discipline. She carried a key chain with the keys to every local schoolroom, and whenever class got too rowdy, she would shake her keys as she walked past the door. The room would immediately become quiet.

After retiring, Miss Frazier was elected to the state legislature, where she served for 12 years. Her major project was getting a college for southern Nevada. The University of Nevada, Las Vegas, was born.

Then the teacher turned politician was appointed the first female lieutenant governor in the state. She died the next year.

> I was well aware that when a woman takes over work done by a man, she has to do it better, has more of it to do, and usually for less pay.
>
> — Maude Frazier

Maude Frazier wrote these thoughts about her work:

"There was never a complaint about too much homework. There was no playing hooky. [The school had] the two essentials important to any good school—pupils who wanted to learn and a teacher who wanted to teach." (Written about the schoolhouse at Seven Troughs, where the school lacked even a heater.)

"A good school is a thing of the mind and spirit, and not a thing of gadgets."

"Instead of trying to make people to fit into a certain mold, we should encourage them to furnish their own mold."

The Great Depression

The 1920s were a time of prosperity and change. Americans elected Herbert Hoover as president. "I have no fears for the future of our country," Hoover announced at his inauguration. "It is bright with hope." Like people in most states, Nevadans looked forward to a new decade of peace and prosperity.

All of this prosperity would suddenly change when a wave of panic spread over Wall Street—the nation's financial center—in New York City. On October 29, 1929, later called "Black Tuesday," the largest selling day in the history of the New York Stock Exchange began. Since so many people were selling their stock, and few were buying, prices *plummeted*. In just two months, the stock market lost 40 percent of its value.

Some people lost everything they had overnight. Many millionaires went *bankrupt*. Although few believed it at the time, the country was about to fall into the worst economic *depression* in its history. By 1930, the optimism of the 1920s was replaced by gloom and fear.

What was the cause of the Great Depression?

- Manufacturers and farmers had produced more goods than consumers could use, *glutting* the market and lowering prices.
- Banks recklessly invested depositors' money without having any way to protect the depositors' savings.
- The stock market was unregulated, allowing for wild *fluctuations* and many scams.

When the market crashed in October 1929, prosperity quickly ended for much of the population. Around the country, people lost their jobs, life savings, and homes. Makeshift little towns of tents and campsites, filled with the unemployed, became known as "Hoovervilles." They were named for President Herbert Hoover, whom many blamed for the depression. By 1932, national unemployment had climbed well over 20 percent.

At first, the depression affected Nevada only slightly. Mining and federal projects such as the Hawthorne Federal Naval Ammunition Depot continued to support the state. The depot brought many jobs in construction and public services, expanded the town of Hawthorne, and created the town of Babbitt.

Then mining production dropped by one-half. Within two years, both the price for silver and the income from Nevada's farming and ranching had fallen by more than two-thirds. Nevada's two leading industries were suffering.

Singing to Chase the Blues Away

"Happy Days Are Here Again" was written by Milton Ager and Jack Yellen. They introduced it to Americans on the eve of the stock market crash in October 1929. While happy days were really far away, people needed cheering up.

The song became famous as the theme song of Franklin D. Roosevelt's presidential campaign and has been sung at Democratic Party national conventions ever since.

So long, sad times;
Go along, bad times!
We are rid of you at last.
Howdy, gay times!
Cloudy gray times,
You are now a thing of the past.

Happy days are here again!
The skies above are clear again.
Let us sing a song of cheer again
Happy days are here again!

Taming a River

In 1905, the Colorado River flooded the Imperial Valley, creating the Salton Sea. This led to serious discussions in Las Vegas about whether it would be possible to tame what was known as America's wildest river. A dam across the Colorado River would regulate how much water would flow downstream, preventing floods. The rest of the water would be held in a reservoir behind the dam until it was needed. The dam would hold generators that would produce electricity.

Talks finally began on the Colorado River Compact. The seven states through which the river flowed had to agree on how much water each state could use. Since the states could not agree, it took seven years to settle the issues.

Las Vegas resident Leon Rockwell remembered:

> When the bill was passed, that's when the excitement was. . . . We got the fire truck out, and . . . everybody that could hooked on to it! In carts and baby buggies and everything else—just like they were nuts.

Then men from the Bureau of Reclamation started looking for a site for a dam. The men examined more than 70 locations before settling on one in Black Canyon. Since the original plan had talked about Boulder Canyon, Boulder remained the name of the dam. (Later, the official name was Hoover Dam, but many people still called it Boulder.)

A Mighty Dam

In 1930, Congress approved the plans for the dam and sent out a call for bids. The prospect of building the dam excited many throughout the Southwest. Californians welcomed the possibilities for inexpensive electricity and abundant water. In Nevada, officials saw that the dam would mean not only water, less flooding, and electric power, but also jobs for workers.

More than 13,000 men worked on the construction of Boulder Dam. Their jobs varied from menial to dangerous—from carrying water to climbing the cliffs above the Colorado River.

The employer was Six Companies, Inc., a group of six corporations that came together to build the dam. They hired a longtime dam builder, Frank Crowe, to supervise construction.

Crowe was determined to build the dam on time, despite all obstacles, and there were plenty. In the summer, the heat was almost unbearable, but the work went on. Railroad tracks had to be built to bring in

Out of work during the Great Depression, this man camped outside of Las Vegas, hoping to get a job on the Boulder Dam project.

supplies from Las Vegas. Workers came from all over the country and had to be trained. Some men brought their families, so an entire town was built to provide homes.

A worker wrote of Frank Crowe:

> [Crowe would] get you a job, like he got me a job here, but if I'd have got fired . . . it would have been too bad. And that's the type he was. He'd give you a boost, but you'd better look out for yourself.
> — Marion Allen

Despite Crowe's no-nonsense work ethic, he was admired for being dedicated to the work.

> If he wasn't in his office, he was down at the dam. It'd never surprise me to see him down there at 2 o'clock in the morning looking around. . . . If something went wrong he was there.
> — Saul "Red" Wixon

Crowe pushed his men hard—too hard, in the opinion of union representatives, including some from the IWW. The union tried to organize the workers in the quest for better pay and working conditions, but their efforts were unsuccessful. During the depression, workers were not willing to walk off the job. They knew they would have a hard time getting another one.

Tommy Nelson, during an interview years later, said this about getting a job at the dam:

> I'm a musician, a trumpet player. Things were pretty rough back in that era—people couldn't afford to dance . . . and things was getting a little rough. My father was down in this area, so he told me, "If you come on down, I can get you a job." So I did.

Joe Kine lost his job in Oklahoma and headed west to work on the dam.

> I picked strawberries to make a little money. . . . But I heard about this going on out here, so I bought a Model T Ford for $10 and drove it out. . . . I sold my Model T Ford after I got here, for $2.50. I wish I had it back now. I could drive it in parades.

Danger on the Job

Workers took great risks to do their jobs, and great pride in what they accomplished. They poured more than 3 million cubic yards of concrete to produce a structure weighing 6.6 million tons, more than 700 feet high, and 660 feet wide at its

Buried in Concrete?

One of the great myths about the dam is that men are buried in its concrete. That is not true. Dam worker William McCullough saw a man fall into the concrete, dead. He said:

> Frank Crowe supervised the job of taking that guy out. When they got down to his body, the concrete had set, of course, and they had pavement busters and jackhammers. When they got down to where they saw one of his hands or one of his legs, Mr. Crowe made them take small picks to get that body out.

Staying on the job was not easy, as Curley Francis remembered:

> We were making $5 a day . . . driving a truck. We had four days off a year. We worked seven days a week, and we had two days off at Christmas and two days off at Fourth of July. Anytime that you got sick and missed more than two days, you were out of a job.

base. They had to build more than 200 miles of power lines from San Bernardino, California, to bring the electricity they needed. They also had to build diversion tunnels to move the water of the Colorado River during construction.

The following statements give a glimpse into the dangerous work of building concrete tunnels to divert river water away from the building site.

Carl Merrill recalled:

Concrete is normally hot. And it was extremely warm. . . . They say the temperature got up to 150, 160 degrees back in there, and men were working. They'd go back in and work for 15 minutes, come out and rest for 15 minutes, back and forth like that.

Steve Chubbs described the day when the Colorado was shifted from its bed to the diversion tunnels.

I remember they were really excited about taking the river out of its channel because it's quite a task. . . . They worked all night. I forgot when they started, but I know by dawn the riverbed was dry.

Building the high cement structure between two steep canyon walls was a real engineering feat and a credit to the men who worked 700 feet above the canyon floor, blasting off the face of the cliff.

I've been told that a lot of these guys were pretty hungry that came to work. Some of them would come down to the job on the bus, and when they looked up where they had to work, why, they said, "It's too high for me." They weren't that hungry.

—Tommy Nelson

Tommy Nelson also saw a man die.

This fellow fell. . . . I went over to him real fast. . . . Along came a hard-boiled superintendent. I won't use the language he used. But he said, "Get those blankety-blank trucks moving." I said, "Carl, there's a man killed over here." "Well, he won't hurt anybody; get 'em going."

Prejudice at the Site

Though the Six Companies hired Native Americans, they refused to hire black workers. African Americans fought back and formed a Colored Citizens Labor and Protective Association two months after construction began. One member wrote:

The leaders of this association are law abiding citizens; standing for justice. Is it patriotic on the part of the white community to stand by and see the eagle torn down from its lofty perch and the flag used as a dishrag? Union and liberty are inseparable.

Finally, the Six Companies did hire a few black workers.

Boulder City was built to provide workers and their families a place to live.

While their fathers worked on the dam, these eighth-graders from all over the country went to school together in Boulder City.

Boulder City— a Company Town

Dam workers lived in what can best be described as a government company town. The town included barracks for single men and small wooden houses for families. Workers bought goods at a company store and ate at a company mess hall.

On weekends, workers often drove north to Las Vegas. But if they stayed out too late, the entrance to the city was closed, and they ended up sleeping on the highway. Sims Ely, who ran Boulder City, imposed a curfew on the workers to make sure they were ready to work the next morning.

Bob Parker recalled River Camp, a barracks set up for employees:

> They called us cliff dwellers down there, because the dormitories were built on stilts at the side of the canyon. . . . It was very hot down there that summer. The temperature got to 112. . . . In the kitchen, with all those big ranges and cook stoves, it was a fright in there. In those days we didn't have any air conditioning.

Rose Lawson talked about the first houses built in Boulder City:

> We didn't have any plumbing; we didn't have any water. We did have electricity—one outlet in each room and a light hanging from the ceiling. We had a stove, a gas range. . . . The house was built exactly like a shoebox: two rooms with a little porch. They were sitting on sand. Two steps, you were out into the sand. . . . Every house was exactly alike. You couldn't tell your own house. . . . Men coming home from work— if they weren't thinking, they'd come into the wrong house.

Lillian Whalen frequented the Boulder Theatre, which survives today as a theatre for musical and dance performances.

Mr. Brothers, who was the manager of the theater, started his shows at eleven in the morning so that the men who went to work at three in the afternoon could come in and rest and watch a movie or sleep. . . . A great many men who lived in those little houses where they had absolutely no way of cooling and couldn't sleep because it was so hot during the day would spend hours down in the theater. Mr. Brothers was very happy to have them do it. He had matinees and children's parties.

Boulder City also offered its depression-era workers free meals, as Wilfred Voss remembers:

When people came here, they hadn't had a square meal for a long time. . . . I remember one morning a man I had never seen before was sitting next to me at the breakfast table. There was a platter of 15 eggs. I asked him to please pass the eggs. He took them up, and he scooped the whole platterful off on his plate and gave me the empty platter. I never saw anything like it.

Most women, like Lillian Whalen, stayed home and took care of their children while their husbands worked on the dam.

Of course, with the building of the dam being the center of our lives, it was the center of the children's lives, and they built dams all over the backyard. They snitched their mothers' tablespoons and teaspoons to dig in the soft sand, so some of us had silver-plated backyards, I think. But they had fun.

Elbert Edwards explained what else the children did:

When people became aware of the fact that there were no schools, the people still wanted their children to get an education. There were people in the city with teaching experience. They began holding private classes. Parents would provide the books. Parents paid tuition—around $5 a month per student.

Later, a public school was built.

Boulder or Hoover Dam?

Many people today are unsure exactly whether the name of the dam is Boulder Dam or Hoover Dam. The correct answer is that when plans for the dam began, a site called Boulder Canyon was chosen, and the dam was named after it, even though the dam ended up being built in a different canyon. When construction started, the dam was named for President Herbert Hoover, who had helped negotiate the Colorado River Compact.

Then, when Franklin Roosevelt became president, the name was changed back to Boulder Dam, which was what everyone was calling it anyway. In 1947, the name was officially changed back to Hoover Dam, and so it remains. Today it is not uncommon, however, for the dam to be called Boulder Dam.

The waters of the Colorado River back up behind Hoover Dam to form Lake Mead.

▲ Photo by Larry Prossor

Finished at Last

Finally the gigantic project was almost completed. The last day of September, 1935, President Franklin D. Roosevelt came to dedicate the dam. In his speech, the president said, "Ten years ago, the place where we are gathered was an unpeopled, forbidding desert. . . . The site of Boulder City was a cactus-covered waste. The transformation wrought here is a twentieth century marvel."

Workers helped fix a road so President Franklin Roosevelt could visit the dam when he came to dedicate it.

> Everybody was excited. . . . That was quite impressive, hearing him dedicate that dam. After that we went right back to work, moving that pipe again.
>
> —Dean Pulsipher

By the following March, 1936, Six Companies had finished construction and turned control of Hoover Dam over to the U.S. Bureau of Reclamation. Some of those who had helped build the dam went to work for the government, while others left town.

Building a Tourist Economy

The dam proved beneficial to tourism in southern Nevada. When it was completed, 250,000 people a year came to look at the dam and marvel at the Colorado River backed up behind it, forming the serene Lake Mead in the desert. Once they had done that, tourists wanted something else to do. Boulder City was in no position to provide entertainment.

New Divorce Laws

The Nevada legislature passed two crucial laws designed to attract visitors. One law reduced the *residency* requirement (the time a couple had to live in the state before they could get a divorce here) from 12 weeks to 6 weeks. The goal was to persuade people who wanted to end their marriages to come and spend money in Nevada. Before long, every year, thousands of men and women visited what was then the state's largest city, Reno. They were, as people at the time said, "Reno-vated."

New Gambling Laws

Nevada also made gambling legal once again. Under the new law, cities and counties could license, regulate, and tax casinos, with some money going to the state. Small casinos, some of which had already been open, dotted the main streets of several Nevada towns, including Virginia Street in Reno and Fremont Street in Las Vegas.

This statement appeared in the *Las Vegas Review-Journal*, March 19, 1931, in response to legal gambling:

> People should not get overly excited over the effects of the new gambling bill—conditions will be little different than they are at the present time, except that some things will be done openly that have previously been done in secret.

The *Carson City Daily Appeal* reported:

> The passing of the six weeks divorce law and the gambling law is nothing to be proud of. Both measures could have been forgotten and the state would have been better off from a moral standpoint.

Gambling once again made money for Las Vegas as the Boulder Club in downtown Las Vegas attracted tourists.

Historical Interpretation

A lot of people believe history never changes. It may be true that the facts themselves remain the same—but we often learn more facts as time goes on. This leads to changes in how we interpret history. And, our thinking today about what is right and wrong influences how we think about the past.

Nevada's decision to legalize gambling is an example of changing historical views. Was it legalized because taxing it could make money for the state, or because people wanted to gamble?

As Russell Elliott, a leading Nevada historian, pointed out, most people believed state leaders took the action of legalizing gambling to help the depressed economy. While that was true, he said, the belief was based on the industry's later success. At the time, gambling was not as profitable. Elliott added that a greater reason for legalizing gambling

was that since it was going on anyway, and people enjoyed the games, why not just make it legal and make money from it?

But it was not so simple. Eric Moody, a curator with the Nevada Historical Society in Reno, published an article based on careful study of newspapers and private letters. He **concluded** that legalizing gambling was actually part of an economic plan. Nevada saw that tourism offered great opportunities for profit, and gambling was another way to attract tourists.

What do you think?

What should be the most important—the quest for the state to make money off gambling, or people's desire to have fun and maybe get rich by gambling? What could be the bad effects of gambling? Should they be considered?

Building a New Leadership

While the Great Depression was still raging, Franklin Roosevelt became president of the United States. Roosevelt made few promises during his campaign, except to call for "a new deal for the American people." That deal proved to be numerous federal agencies to provide jobs and laws to combat the depression. Roosevelt was highly popular with voters.

Because of his position in the Senate, Nevada's Senator Key Pittman was just behind the president and vice president in rank. This meant he had a lot of influence in Washington, D.C., and that would help Nevada.

George Wingfield

Meanwhile, back in Nevada, George Wingfield's banks had made many loans to ranchers and businessmen, but the depression made it impossible for them to repay their loans. The banks' resources were dropping steadily as other banks began closing due to similar problems.

When Wingfield's banks no longer could meet their obligations, Governor Fred Balzar requested a two-week bank holiday, which meant the banks would close. That would prevent depositors from massing at Nevada's banks and demanding their money, which would only make matters worse. At the end of the two weeks, those banks that were sound enough financially would reopen.

The Wingfield banking empire collapsed under the financial strain. When Wingfield's banks closed and his depositors lost their money, Reno citizens dumped garbage on the steps of his house. Bodyguards took him and his family to safety.

Wingfield eventually regained his wealth, but he never again would be called the most powerful man in Nevada. In the next two decades, that role would belong to Pat McCarran.

"Our condition out there is most serious. . . . We have practically all our State funds deposited with the Wingfield banks."

— Governor Fred Balzar

Patrick McCarran
1876–1954

Born near Reno, Patrick McCarran was the son of a sheep rancher and took over the ranch work when his father became ill. McCarran didn't graduate from high school until he was 21; he had missed too much school while helping to support his family. He later attended the University of Nevada and was an outstanding debater.

Entering politics, McCarran was elected to the state Assembly. Then he ran for state senator but lost, so he headed for the Tonopah-Goldfield boomtowns. He studied law and was quickly elected district attorney of Nye County.

Eventually, McCarran realized his chances of any great political success were diminishing, as were profits from the mining boom. He returned to Reno, still hoping to someday become a U.S. senator.

Later, McCarran served a term on the Nevada Supreme Court and wrote opinions supporting progressive ideals. He ran for reelection, was defeated, went back to practicing law, and waited for yet another chance. His chance came when he went on the road to gain support.

I made five laps of this state. I visited every water hole, town, hamlet, valley and place within the State. There was scarcely a man, woman, or child in that State that I did not see personally.

McCarran finally won a seat on the U.S. Senate in 1932 and served until his death.

How did Pat McCarran prove that persistence pays off?

Chapter 8 Review

What Do You Remember?

1. What were the characteristics of America in the 1920s?

2. What was the Great Red Scare? What was the reaction in Nevada?

3. What caused labor disputes after World War I? How did events compare with the earlier disputes at Goldfield and in the copper towns?

4. What was Prohibition? How did Nevadans feel about it?

5. What was the Ku Klux Klan? How did one Las Vegas man help end their activities in that city?

6. How did highway-building in Nevada and the West during the 1920s help the people of the state?

7. In what ways was Nevada progressive in the 1920s? In what ways was it not?

8. How did the 1920s change Las Vegas? In what ways did the city plan for the future?

9. What were some of the personal characteristics of Maude Frazier?

10. What were the causes of the Great Depression? What were its effects nationally, and in Nevada?

11. Why was Hoover Dam built? Why did it take so long to make the plans for it?

12. Why was Boulder City built? What was it like to live there?

13. Why did Nevada legislators pass bills to reduce the residency requirement for divorce and to make gambling legal?

Geography Tie-In

1. Find out where the Bureau of Reclamation has built dams in the West and pinpoint them on a map. What patterns do you see?

2. Find the following 1920s federal projects on a Nevada map: Hoover Dam, Hawthorne Naval Ammunition Depot, and Highway 50. Are any of them near a town where you have lived?

Activity

You Choose

Choose one of these activities to gain a better understanding of the events of this chapter.

1. Build a scale model of Hoover Dam.

2. Watch an old movie featuring Clara Bow. Compare hers with other movies you have seen.

3. Prepare a skit or reader's theater presentation on the life of either George Wingfield, Patrick McCarran, or Maude Frazier.

4. Interview a family member, relative, or friend who remembers the Great Depression or working on Hoover Dam.

Remaking Nevada

Timeline of Events

1933
Franklin Roosevelt becomes president.

1933
Adolf Hitler takes power in Germany.

1933	1934	1935	1936	1937	1938

1934
Pittman Silver Purchase Act

1936
Harold's Club opens in Reno.

1938
California anti-gambling reforms help Nevada.

Chapter 9

WORDS TO UNDERSTAND
amenities
arbitrator
civilian
concentration camp
dictatorship
envision
Holocaust
illegal
illicit
interference
internment camp
isolationist
per capita
resemblance
roulette
stabilize
surrender
suspected

Gambling laws in both Reno and Las Vegas resulted in growth of those cities, along with increased corruption when colorful outsiders came to town.

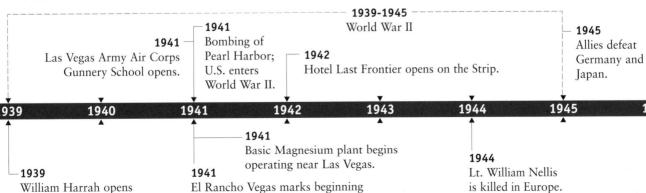

1939-1945
World War II

1941
Bombing of Pearl Harbor; U.S. enters World War II.

1941
Las Vegas Army Air Corps Gunnery School opens.

1942
Hotel Last Frontier opens on the Strip.

1945
Allies defeat Germany and Japan.

| 1939 | 1940 | 1941 | 1942 | 1943 | 1944 | 1945 | 1946 |

1941
Basic Magnesium plant begins operating near Las Vegas.

1939
William Harrah opens his first casino in Reno.

1941
El Rancho Vegas marks beginning of the Las Vegas Strip.

1944
Lt. William Nellis is killed in Europe.

163

President Franklin D. Roosevelt delivered his inaugural address at the U.S. Capitol, 1937.

What Was the New Deal?

As he accepted the nomination for president, Franklin Roosevelt had pledged "a new deal for the American people." Exactly what he meant was unclear until he took office. It became clear that Roosevelt and Congress were changing the role of the federal government. He created dozens of new agencies based on three principles:

- **Relief**—providing jobs to the unemployed
- **Recovery**—restoring the nation's prosperity
- **Reform**—making sure a large depression never happens again

In changing the nation, Roosevelt changed Nevada. New jobs were created. The economy started to improve.

> Franklin Roosevelt was God in our house. He was, . . . in my mother's view, everything Progressives had stood for. . . . For the first time, government seemed to feel a responsibility to see that people were fairly treated. . . .
>
> — Ralph Denton of Caliente

The government grew with all the new agencies, but many Nevada leaders disagreed with Roosevelt. They wanted to keep government small. They thought a large government had too much power.

"Take a method and try it," Roosevelt said. *"If it fails, try another."*

What do you think?

Why would Nevadans disagree with any of Roosevelt's policies when they had supported him in elections? Talk about this now, and think about it as you read on.

New Deal Legislation

The following are many New Deal acts and agencies. Do you know which agencies are still around today?

- **Emergency Banking Act (1933).** The government closed all banks across the country while deciding which ones were doing well enough to be reopened.
- **The Federal Deposit Insurance Corporation (1933).** The FDIC was created to insure money you put in the bank. It also set up regulation of banks.
- **Federal Emergency Relief Administration (1933).** State and local governments received $500 million to pay people to work.
- **Civilian Conservation Corps (1933).** Men between the ages of 18 and 25 joined the CCC and moved to rural camps, including several throughout

Nevada, to build roads, plant trees, and fight soil erosion. They got a place to sleep, three meals a day, and $30 a month to spend in the nearest town or send home to their families.

- **Public Works Administration (1933).** Over $3 billion was spent to help build roads, dams, bridges, sewers, schools, and airports. PWA workers built many of these in Nevada communities.

- **Agricultural Adjustment Act (1933).** Companies who produced food were taxed and the money was used to pay farmers. The farmers agreed to produce less so prices would go higher.

- **The National Recovery Administration (1933).** The agency abolished child labor, set a 30- to 40-hour work week, set a minimum wage, and gave workers the right to form unions.

- **Silver Purchase Act (1934).** The government bought more of the precious metal, helping to raise the price on the world market and encourage mining in western states, including Nevada.

- **Taylor Grazing Act (1934).** This act reduced livestock grazing on public lands to help protect natural resources.

- **Federal Housing Administration (1934).** The FHA even today loans money to people to buy or improve their homes.

- **National Labor Relations Board (1935).** This group protected the rights of labor unions.

- **Works Progress Administration (1935).** The WPA was over public works jobs,

much like the CCC and PWA. It also hired artists to paint murals, photographers to capture everyday life on film, and historians to write state histories and guides.

- **Social Security Act (1935).** This act provided income and insurance to seniors, the handicapped, and the unemployed.

Nevada and the New Deal

No state received more federal money *per capita* during the New Deal than Nevada. (Per capita means per person.)

Why did Nevada receive so much money? For one thing, Nevada asked for the money. For example, many towns needed paved roads and sewer lines, so they applied for funding and got it. That was especially true in Las Vegas. Another reason was that Nevada had a lot of open land on which the government could set up CCC camps. This brought money into the state.

It also helped that the elected legislators from Nevada were Democrats, and Roosevelt rewarded those who helped him.

> I am heart and soul in sympathy with Franklin Roosevelt's "New Deal" and I have given it active and loyal support with all of the mental and physical powers that I possess. No doubt exists in my mind with regard to the "New Deal."
>
> — Key Pittman, 1934

During the 1930s, men came from all over the country to work at the CCC camp in Humboldt.

New Deal Accomplishments

New Deal money did a lot to help Nevada. It provided jobs, and workers spent their paychecks in the state, which helped businesses. The Silver Purchase Act of 1934 helped miners when the government bought silver, and the National Recovery Administration helped *stabilize* the copper market. Mining came out of its slump in Pioche, Eureka, Tonopah, and the White Pine copper towns.

The WPA workers produced artwork and a book on Nevada history that was used in schools for many years. The CCC employed about 4,000 men in 24 camps from Reno to Westgate to the mountains outside Las Vegas. The PWA hired thousands who labeled street signs, painted buildings, dug wells, set up historic markers, and repaired roads.

The New Deal also redefined the two main political parties. Many Americans thought of Republicans as the party of business and wealth in large cities, and Democrats as the party of the poor in smaller towns and rural areas. Nevada became a strongly Democratic state, and remained so for the next 50 years.

> It has given work to millions of destitute people through the most dreadful period in our history. It has brought to our people a new courage, which will bring lasting victory over depression.
>
> —Key Pittman on the New Deal

One Sound State

Nevadans may have resented outside *interference*, but they had no problem accepting outsiders' money. During the 1930s, state leaders adopted "One Sound State" as a slogan to attract the wealthy from other places. The leaders wanted others to know they could move to Nevada and pay no income tax. In turn, they would buy property, which the

Eva Adams
1910–1991

Eva Adams was born in Wonder, a mining camp not far from Fallon. She attended one-room schoolhouses in mining camps, moving many times. As a teen, Eva was worried about being overweight and too short—she was only 5-foot-1. Although she couldn't run very fast, she was persistent and did well at sports as well as in class. She attended the University of Nevada and by age 19 taught at Las Vegas High School. Then she attended Columbia University in New York. Returning to the West, she was teaching in the University of Nevada English Department when Senator McCarran hired her to run his office in Washington, D.C.

Eva Adams's reputation for good management spread throughout the Senate. She wound up holding classes for other senators and their staff members on how to run a Senate office. At the same time, she also went to law school and graduated.

When McCarran died, Adams stayed on to run the office. The new senator suggested that Adams would be an excellent choice for the director of the United States Mint. For almost 10 years in that position, she was in charge of making coins.

The mint was a mess. Nobody had ordered new presses to produce coins and many weren't working well. Adams took presses from the old Carson City Mint and put them back into service. The mint began making "sandwich money" with common metals sandwiched in between the silver. Most all-silver coins disappeared as people started collecting them, which meant the country needed even more coins. Adams turned things around, and the mint ran smoothly.

Eva Adams worked in other jobs in Washington, then retired to Reno.

"Dress like a queen. Act like a lady. Think like a man. Work like a dog."

— Eva Adams

state had plenty of. Many took advantage of the opportunity, including Max Fleischmann of the yeast and margarine company and car manufacturer Erret Cord, who bought a large ranch in Fish Lake Valley.

> No income tax, no inheritance tax, no sales tax . . . but a balanced budget and a surplus.
>
> — "One Sound State" promotional announcement

Nevadans had other ways of getting other people's money. With the shorter time it took to get a divorce in the state, thousands came to end their marriages. Spending six weeks in Nevada, usually in the Reno-Lake Tahoe area, men and women spent money at local businesses, dude ranches, hotels, and casinos. Nevada's economy was also boosted when the same tourists stayed to remarry. Soon marriages were bringing in about as much money as divorces.

Sagebrush Casinos

When gambling became legal, many Nevada towns benefited. Reno, the state's largest city at the time, had the most tourists and quickly became famous for its casinos.

Harold Smith opened Harolds Club on Virginia Street. Smith and his family became known for using live mice in *roulette*.

Harolds Club hired an advertising agency to write historical articles called "Pioneer Nevada" for newspapers. Then a covered wagon posting large signs that read "Harolds Club or Bust" traveled around the country. It was the first time a casino had advertised itself much like any other business.

A few years after Harolds Club opened, William Harrah arrived from California and opened bingo parlors. He kept expanding, pouring money back into the parlors while building a world-class car collection. Harrah had two key rules he applied to his business:

- Treat people like you would like to be treated yourself.
- Do the impossible; please everyone.

No sales tax helped bring outsiders into Nevada.

Virginia Street in downtown Reno was a busy place in the 1930s.

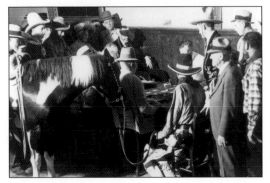

Gamblers in western garb attend the Helldorado celebration in Las Vegas.

Recreating Las Vegas

Like Reno, born a railroad town with *illegal* casinos, Las Vegas had always been open 24 hours. Legalized gambling merely made life easier for the owners of clubs. The first gaming license in Las Vegas was given to J.H. Morgan and Mayme Stocker for the Northern Club. Las Vegas's early casino row was Fremont Street, later to be known to the world as "Glitter Gulch." Fremont street was downtown—nowhere near today's famous Las Vegas strip.

While Reno had a built-in customer base of divorce-seekers, Las Vegas relied on Boulder Dam workers who came to town to enjoy some of the fun and visitors who wanted to look at the dam.

Many of the early casinos had a western theme. Their names included the Boulder, Eldorado, and Apache. Many of them had sawdust on the floor. Las Vegas advertised these casinos as "the Old West in modern splendor." Realizing that the end of dam construction could reduce the number of tourists who came to look at it being built, Las Vegas leaders started an annual Helldorado celebration with a rodeo, parade, and beard-growing contest.

Another way to attract tourists was used by a unique Las Vegas casino, the Meadows. It was built outside the casino district on the road to Hoover Dam. It was considered luxurious, with carpeted floors and entertainment, long before other Las Vegas casinos had these things. Its main operators were said to have connections to organized crime in California and other states.

One of the big-name acts that performed at the Meadows was the Gumm Sisters. One of the sisters, Frances, adopted the stage name of Judy Garland and was Dorothy in *The Wizard of Oz*.

The California Connection

California's attorney general, Earl Warren, wanted to reform California by cracking down on illegal gambling on cruise ships. The ships would sail from southern California ports and offer gambling once they reached international waters three miles from shore. It was known that the gambling began long before the boats reached international waters. The ships were closed, along with their gambling. Stopped from working on the cruise ships, dealer Sam Boyd headed to Las Vegas and built a gaming empire, and Tony Cornero returned to Las Vegas to run a downtown casino.

When the mayor of Los Angeles sought to eliminate illegal gambling there, the boss of the local casinos there left for Las Vegas, opened a casino, and built the Golden Nugget with several partners. The result of the California reforms was an influx of casino professionals, including Harrah and Cornero, who became part of an already successful gambling industry in Nevada.

Nevada: A Journey of Discovery

The Apache Casino was one of many downtown Las Vegas casinos that used an Old West theme to attract tourists.

Remaking Nevada

Birth of the Strip

The El Rancho Vegas, a low-rise, hotel-casino, opened on the corner of Highway 91 and San Francisco Street across from where the Sahara stands today. At that time, the region was outside the city limits and several miles from downtown Las Vegas, so taxes were low. At a time when women were prohibited from working as dealers in a casino, the El Rancho Vegas hired Maxine Lewis to find performers for the showroom.

> The dining room was built sort of in the form of a corral, with the dance floor the center of the corral.
>
> — John Cahlan, editor of the *Las Vegas Review Journal*

Then the second resort on the block opened. The Hotel Last Frontier was not a high-rise either. It boasted a wedding chapel called the Hitching Post. It also had Frontier Village and a stagecoach that was used as a shuttle bus to the airport. Both new hotels were marketed as part of the Old West, just as downtown Las Vegas had been doing.

While a few nightclubs already dotted the two-lane highway, these two small hotels were the beginning of the Las Vegas Strip. At the time, the street bore no *resemblance* to the Strip today. But great changes were on the horizon.

A New Breed Downtown

At about the same time the Strip was growing, the first high-rise hotel opened downtown. It was the modern six-story El Cortez. The El Cortez quickly became the elite casino in the area. Its success brought it to the attention of two men with an *illicit* past—Meyer Lansky and his friend "Bugsy" Siegel. Siegel, an out-of-town gangster, had come to Las Vegas to run a horse racing business; he also became involved with the El Cortez.

The venture proved successful enough for Lansky to include other friends. When Minneapolis officials started shutting down their illegal casinos, the operators headed for Las Vegas. The new arrivals bought a casino while the El Cortez was sold for a handsome profit. Then he tried to buy a hotel on the fast-growing Strip, but was rejected.

> I don't want Bugsy Siegel and people of his stripe in here.
>
> — Las Vegas City Commissioner Al Coradetti, 1944

Meyer Lansky and Benjamin "Bugsy" Siegel

Las Vegas has an image as "Sin City," where anything goes, whether it is legal or illegal. The reputation is usually associated with the arrival of Meyer Lansky and Bugsy Siegel.

Lansky and Siegel knew each other as young boys on the Lower East Side of New York. They belonged to eastern European Jewish immigrant families and faced a lot of discrimination over their religion and accents. Lansky was small but learned how to talk other boys out of beating him up. Siegel was larger and fought back—and was known to start many fights on his own.

During Prohibition, Lansky and Siegel teamed up with other Jewish and Italian immigrants to provide illegal whiskey. Later, they turned to other illegal activities, and branched out from New York City to other cities.

One of those cities was Hollywood. Siegel moved west during the 1930s. One of his reasons was to become involved in illegal gambling and what was called protection—forcing people to pay to be left alone. Another reason was that Siegel, considered handsome, wanted to be a movie star and even took a screen test.

Siegel's acting career went nowhere, but his performances in real life earned him a nickname that he hated. Bugsy was a word associated with crazy behavior; Bugs Bunny is a good example.

Siegel became a violent killer who certainly deserves no admiration. Yet those who knew him often described him as a gentleman, except when he lost his temper.

Lansky was less associated with violence and better known as an *arbitrator* in disputes between organized crime groups. He had a mathematical mind and helped divide up the ill-gotten gains of his partners, who often fought with one another. He *envisioned* beautiful resorts for Las Vegas because, he said, the town was too hot and isolated for anything else!

> No one wanted to go to Vegas to gamble. Air connections were bad. And the trip by car was bothersome. It was so hot that the wires in the car would melt.
>
> — Meyer Lansky on Las Vegas in the 1940s

While Siegel was a handsome man with many important friends, including many with links to organized crime, he didn't know much about business. Several builders overcharged him or stole from him. He financed the building of the Flamingo, but when it finally opened, rain kept away many of the Hollywood stars whom Siegel had expected to attend. Within two days, the casino was nearly empty. Siegel closed the casino and reopened during the spring.

The Flamingo began making money, but not fast enough to please some of the men to whom Siegel owed money. In 1947, as he was reading the newspaper one night in a friend's California apartment, Siegel was killed by flying bullets.

Within minutes after Siegel's death, a new management team entered the Flamingo. Within months, they made the Flamingo hugely profitable. Other groups with criminal connections noticed the success and came to Las Vegas.

With his murder, Siegel became a legend. He had a vision of the kinds of luxury resorts, complete with *amenities*, that would dot the Las Vegas Strip in years to come.

Bugsy Siegel

The Coming of War

*D*ictatorships were gaining power in Europe and Asia. In Germany, Adolf Hitler had gained power. He was rebuilding a strong army and starting a campaign of terror against Jews and others. In Italy, Benito Mussolini took over Ethiopia and joined Hitler. In Asia, Japan sought to build an empire by conquering Manchuria and attacking China.

Then German armies invaded Poland. England and France declared war. World War II had begun, but the United States did not enter the fighting. The country did, however, ship supplies to its allies.

The American Response

Before the war, many Americans, including those in Nevada, were *isolationists*, meaning they saw no reason for the country to be involved with the world beyond its borders. They wanted to leave Europe's problems in Europe. With the Great Depression, Americans had enough to worry about at home. And they had already been through the horrors of World War I.

President Roosevelt wanted the U.S. to be more active in world affairs, but isolationist ideas were strong. As Foreign Relations Committee chairman, Nevada's Senator Key Pittman was in the middle of the issue. He started out as an isolationist, but later said he had been wrong. Pittman also said the United States should be concerned about the growth of Japan's military.

Once German armies started defeating small countries of Western Europe, Roosevelt convinced Congress that the country needed to help in the fight against Hitler. With Pittman's support, Roosevelt was able to provide weapons and other war supplies to Great Britain and other European countries.

Then, on December 7, 1941, the Japanese bombed the U.S. naval base at Pearl Harbor, Hawaii. Congress declared war the next day. The United States and the Allies—Great Britain, France, and the Soviet Union—were at war with the three Axis powers—Germany, Italy, and Japan.

Nevadans did their patriotic duty. They marched in parades, enrolled for the draft, and made sacrifices to provide more rubber, aluminum, and food for soldiers and victims of the war.

After the Japanese attacked Pearl Harbor, the United States entered World War II.

Kristallnacht and the Holocaust

When the Nazis ruled much of Europe, including Germany and Austria, Jewish people living there were severely persecuted. Some of the worst violence occurred during two November nights in 1938, called *Kristallnacht*, meaning "Night of Broken Glass." Angry mobs organized by the Nazis looted and burned thousands of Jewish synagogues and businesses, and cemeteries and schools were vandalized. Thirty thousand innocent Jews were taken from their homes and sent to ***concentration camps***.

Many historians consider Kristallnacht to be the beginning of the ***Holocaust***, in which millions of Jewish people were murdered. Millions of others also died in the camps.

Nevada: A Journey of Discovery

Changing Nevada's Economy

Both preparing for war and the war itself helped Nevada's economy. Mineral production nearly doubled, especially in the White Pine copper towns. With the increased demand came better pay for miners and workers in related jobs.

For the first time, the federal government built large-scale military bases and training schools in Nevada. The same thing happened throughout the West. Why? The federal government already owned more land there than in other parts of the United States, meaning that more land was available for its use.

Military bases brought thousands of jobs. The Las Vegas Army Air Corps Gunnery School opened north of town. The Stead air base north of Reno began training pilots and navigators, and the U.S. Army opened another air base at Tonopah. While the army air base at Wendover was across the Utah border, men stationed there often went to the other side of town in Nevada. The Naval Air Corps built a station at Fallon, and the ammunition depot near Hawthorne got busier. Members of the armed forces spent some of their pay in nearby communities, contributing to the local economy.

> World War II, as much as any other event, shaped the present economy of Nevada.
>
> — Russell Elliott, Nevada historian

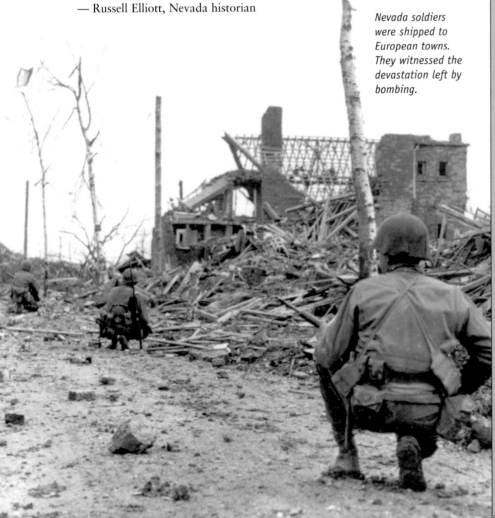

Nevada soldiers were shipped to European towns. They witnessed the devastation left by bombing.

NEVADA
PORTRAIT

Lt. William Nellis
1916–1944

William Nellis was probably Nevada's most famous World War II hero.

Nellis came from a long line of families in the small town of Searchlight. He lived with his grandmother, who ran the local hotel. Bill moved to Las Vegas and worked at a gas station. His family had abandoned him, and he lived in a rented room he paid for with money from his job.

Bill played football at Las Vegas High School. From there, he returned to Searchlight to work in the mines. He married and found a job as a brakeman with the Union Pacific Railroad. Because keeping the trains running was so important to the country, he could have avoided the draft. But he chose to serve his country, joining the Army Air Corps and training to be a pilot.

Bill Nellis was sent to Europe, where he flew many missions. One time, when the dials in his plane failed and the plane was going to crash, he rammed the glass cover with his head until it broke loose, badly cutting his head. Soldiers found him hanging from a tree, unconscious. Medics patched him up and he returned to flying.

Nellis flew 69 missions over enemy territory. He could have missed his 70th, but he volunteered to go. His plane was shot down two days after Christmas during the Battle of the Bulge over Belgium, and Nellis died.

Bill Nellis received just about every medal it was possible to get, including the Purple Heart. His widow and children were there when he received another honor. On a spring day in 1950, the Las Vegas air force base was renamed for him.

Enormous asbestos mittens are worn by the worker handling the hot magnesium ingots produced at the Basic Magnesium Incorporated plant in the southern Nevada desert.

Basic Magnesium

While all of the military bases were important, no federal project had a greater impact than Basic Magnesium, Incorporated (BMI). Howard Eells, a Cleveland industrialist, owned a magnesium deposit in Gabbs Valley. He wanted to build a factory to convert the ore into magnesium that could be used in building airplanes and bombs—both of which, of course, the U.S. could use in the war.

Two sources of power made southern Nevada the logical place for the plant. Electricity from Boulder Dam made southern Nevada a good place for the plant. Also important was Pat McCarran's influence in the U.S. Senate. He persuaded the federal government to promise $150 million to build the plant, and construction began even before the attack on Pearl Harbor. By the time the plant closed near the end of the war, it had produced about one-fourth of the magnesium used by the Allies.

A government town was built for Basic workers. At one time it was larger than every town in Nevada except Reno.

Nearby, Las Vegas benefited from the magnesium plant and the new town. Workers and their families spent a great deal of time and money in Las Vegas, and many chose to remain in the area after the plant closed and the war ended.

Even more important, Nevada leaders saw that an industrial plant could help their economy. They agreed to buy the site. The result was an industrial complex that contributed greatly to the economy and the creation of a town. They named the town for the former senator from Nevada who worked for the agency that made the plant and the town possible—Charles Henderson.

As with other factories around the country, women at Basic took on the jobs of men because so many men were off at war. At the time, many people believed that women could not do men's work. Working with molten metal at Basic was very dangerous. But one woman said, "It's nothing more than working over a hot cook stove."

Race and War

During World War II, Americans fought for freedom against Hitler, a dictator who believed in a master white race. Sadly, though, for two groups of Americans, World War II showed that Americans had a lot to change in their own country. The first of these groups, African Americans, faced racism in a segregated military and in looking for work in Nevada.

In two years, the number of African Americans living in Nevada had jumped from fewer than 700 to about 3,000. They came from two depressed southern towns in Louisiana and Arkansas, looking for work at Basic Magnesium. They hoped to find work, and they did. They also hoped to

Nevada: A Journey of Discovery

escape the racism they had known in the South, and they did not.

Upon arriving, the workers were shuttled to an area in Henderson where there was no electricity, running water, or paved roads. Carver Park, named for the black scientist George Washington Carver, was segregated. Just as bad, while BMI hired many African Americans, it not only gave them lower-paying jobs, it paid them less than whites who did the same job.

The first African American family to live in Carver came to work at BMI.

Japanese Americans

Japanese families in California, Oregon, and Washington faced an even more difficult problem. Many of them had already been victims of discrimination, but with the Japanese attack on Pearl Harbor, they were *suspected* of disloyalty to the U.S. The government moved thousands of Japanese-Americans into *internment camps*, depriving them not only of their freedom, but also of their property.

When the government began planning internment camps in Nevada, Nevadans were upset, and Governor Carville wisely urged fair treatment of Japanese citizens, as did Nevada newspapers. The camps were never built in Nevada.

The Tomiyasu farm provided vegetables to nearby communities for many years.

NEVADA
PORTRAIT

Bill Tomiyasu

One Japanese immigrant became one of the more respected members of the Las Vegas community.

Born near Nagasaki, Japan, Yonema "Bill" Tomiyasu settled first in California, where he worked at picking fruit, taking care of property, and cooking. But California had passed a law that said the Japanese could not own land. Nevada had no such law, so Tomiyasu bought 40 acres of Las Vegas property. He grew alfalfa while he studied the best way to grow other crops in the hot dusty valley. Soon he was supplying area restaurants and residents with melons, peppers, brussels sprouts, lettuce, cabbage, onions, carrots, radishes, and beets.

Tomiyasu expanded his business and his land. He grew crops in the Searchlight area. He sold produce not only in Las Vegas and the surrounding area, but in Beatty, Jean, Goodsprings, and Sloan. He won a contract from the Six Companies to supply food for the mess halls for Hoover Dam workers.

During the war, Bill's children kept working on their father's ranch. Bill Tomiyasu had permission from the FBI to drive across the dam, which the government had restricted out of fear that it would be a target of Japanese bombers.

Eventually, Tomiyasu lost ownership of his ranch in a bad business deal, but he ran a plant nursery until he died at age 87. One of his sons kept the family business going until 2002. A street on their old property is named for Tomiyasu, as is an elementary school.

War = Tourism?

One of the effects of the war was related to Nevada's growing tourist industry. Servicemen (and servicewomen, who were far fewer in number) from bases in California, Arizona, and Utah, spent some of their free time—and their money—in Nevada. *Civilians* in nearby states, who could not travel too far because of gas rationing, came to Nevada tourist cities on vacation.

Tourist businesses did whatever they could think of to attract these visitors. The Reno-Tahoe area started promoting great skiing. In Elko, the Commercial Hotel owner offered big-name entertainment at hotel-casinos. Reno and Las Vegas casinos followed suit.

End of the Beginning

The Allies had defeated Italy in 1943. Then, in 1945, two events came within a month of each other that caused both sorrow and rejoicing among the people of the world. Franklin Roosevelt died after 12 years in office. Then Germany surrendered on what came to be known as V-E Day for "Victory over Europe" and set off wild celebrations across the country.

But the United States and Japan remained at war. The Soviet Union agreed to join the invasion of the Japanese mainland, which was expected to take more than a year and cause at least a million deaths.

Then President Harry Truman warned the Japanese that the United States was prepared to use a powerful new weapon unless they *surrendered*. When no word came from the Japanese, Truman ordered the atomic bomb to be used. Bombs fell on Hiroshima and Nagasaki three days apart, killing and injuring thousands and causing misery beyond belief. Finally, Japan surrendered.

Though thousands of people had died or were terribly injured in battle, Nevadans at home had good reason to celebrate as World War II ended.

Chapter **9** Review

What Do You Remember?

1. What were the national goals of the New Deal?
2. Why did Nevada receive so much federal money during the New Deal?
3. How did the New Deal affect Nevada?
4. What was the new state slogan used to attract the wealthy from other places?
5. What methods did Nevada use to attract people to live in and visit the state? How successful were these efforts?
6. How did early casino operators Harold Smith and William Harrah help business in Reno?
7. Name some things that helped downtown Las Vegas grow.
8. How did the Las Vegas Strip begin? How was it different at the time than it is today?
9. Which two men are credited for Las Vegas being called "Sin City"? Tell something about each man.
10. What were some of the events that led to World War II?
11. How did the war change Nevada's economy?
12. How did Basic Magnesium help the country and Nevada?
13. How did the war affect racial minorities in Nevada?
14. What events finally ended World War II?

Geography Tie-In

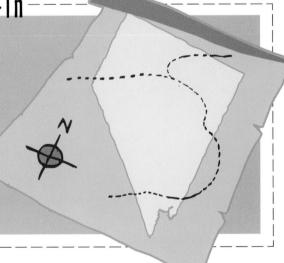

1. Obtain a list of the CCC camps in Nevada and find where each of them would be on a Nevada map. Can you locate other information about the camps? Where would you look for information?

2. Using a map of the West, find the roads connecting parts of Nevada to parts of California. Draw a conclusion as to how isolated Las Vegas was. Was the Reno area just as isolated from the rest of the country?

3. Find the military installations built in Nevada during World War II and place them on a map. What sources did you use?

Timeline of Events

1949
The Freeport Law means goods can be stored in Nevada warehouses without paying property tax.

1950–1953
Korean War

1960
Moulin Rouge Agreement. Las Vegas casinos begin allowing African American customers.

1945   1950   1955   1960

1958
The population of Las Vegas passes that of Reno.

1945
World War II ends. The Cold War begins. Nevada passes its first tax on gaming revenue.

1951
Above ground nuclear testing begins in Nevada.

1960
Squaw Valley hosts the winter Olympics.

Modern Nevada

WORDS TO UNDERSTAND
anonymous
arboretum
atrium
bootlegging
capitalism
census
charity
communism
conspiracy
corruption
detonate
franchise
gazebo
illusionist
legitimate
nuclear arms
radiation
rival
suburban
suppress

A nuclear test package is lowered into the ground for underground testing at Yucca Flats, about 70 miles north of Las Vegas, 1981.

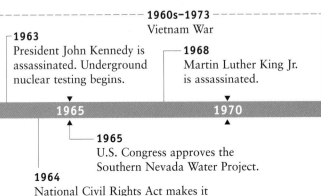

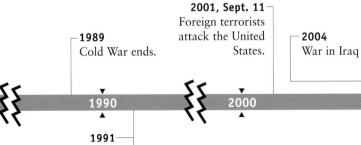

◄ - - - - - - - **1960s–1973** - - - - - - - ┐
Vietnam War

1963
President John Kennedy is
assassinated. Underground
nuclear testing begins.

1968
Martin Luther King Jr.
is assassinated.

1989
Cold War ends.

2001, Sept. 11
Foreign terrorists
attack the United
States.

2004
War in Iraq

1965   1970   1990   2000

1965
U.S. Congress approves the
Southern Nevada Water Project.

1991
Persian Gulf War

1964
National Civil Rights Act makes it
illegal to discriminate because of race.

1991
Reno opens the
Truckee River Walk.

179

From Hot to Cold

World War II changed the western United States. The great need for trained soldiers, weapons, and other supplies led to many military bases and defense projects and helped attract workers to the Southwest.

World peace after the war was short-lived. Soon the United States and Soviet Union were involved in a "cold war." It was called the Cold War because the countries never fought each other with guns.

The United States and the Soviet Union had been allies during World War II. They fought together to defeat Germany. But when the war was over, they became enemies. Each tried to be the first to explore space. Each tried to be the strongest country in the world.

The Cold War prompted Americans to take steps to protect themselves. Some people built bomb shelters in their basements. School children had bomb drills where they sat under their desks or in the hall until the drill was over.

Activity

Capitalism or Communism?

There are many forms of government and economic rule in the world. In the United States of America, we enjoy the benefits of democracy and *capitalism*. We can live, study, work, buy, and sell where and how we wish, as long as we obey the law.

Some nations of the world live under *communism*, where the government has more control of people, property, and the economy.

Capitalism: Private (individual or company) ownership of land, property, and business, with government regulation over some kinds of businesses

Communism: Government ownership of all land, property, and business. The government controls where and how people live, study, work, buy, and sell.

Research and learn more about these forms of governing the world. Talk with your class about countries that live under these two forms of government and economics. Weigh the benefits of each system. Then draw conclusions as to which system has proven more beneficial for people, and why.

Both countries built more and more weapons. They wanted to protect themselves in case of an attack. The government spent more money on the military, which helped Nevada's economy.

Cold War fears included worrying that members of the Communist Party might take over the U.S. government. People suspected of being communists were fired from jobs as teachers or government workers. They were rarely given a chance to defend themselves.

American leaders began to limit free speech. President Harry Truman required "loyalty oaths" of federal employees. The term "McCarthyism" was coined when Senator Joseph McCarthy of Wisconsin began accusing people of communist leanings. Many people in Nevada agreed with McCarthy, but many others did not, as this quote shows:

> McCarthy has contributed absolutely nothing to checking the communist *conspiracy* in this country. He has, however, . . . spread suspicion and fear among the people and by these very acts has weakened our defenses against the dangers of communism. . . . [He is] the most immoral, indecent, . . . scoundrel ever to sit in the United States Senate.
>
> —Hank Greenspun

Nevada in the Cold War

As the nation entered the Cold War in the late 1940s, Nevada politicians fought their own war against communism. At the heart of it was Senator Pat McCarran. In Washington, D.C., he warned about the Soviet menace and questioned the patriotism of various federal officials. McCarran also introduced bills in Congress to limit immigration from Eastern Europe and force Americans to answer questions about their political views. Both bills were designed to keep communists out of the United States.

Newspapers Fight Communism

Donald Reynolds, who owned several newspapers and later owned radio and television stations in Las Vegas and Reno, bought control of the *Las Vegas Review-Journal*. Then some of his employees left the paper and started a *rival* newspaper. They sold it to Hank Greenspun, who turned it into the *Las Vegas Sun*.

Greenspun gave the public a choice in newspapers, which was good business. But he had other reasons to oppose the *Review-Journal*. Both papers were anti-communist, but Greenspun, unlike his competitor, believed that accusing others of disloyalty was un-American, and he said so in his newspaper.

What do you think?

Is it good for the public when businesses, including newspapers, compete with each other? How might it help or hurt the public?

The Cold War Benefits Nevada

Governor Charles Russell took office as the Cold War heated up Nevada's economy. The mining industry grew from the needs of national defense. Copper was the most important ore. The need for gold and silver also grew, but lead, zinc, oil, manganese, and mercury brought more money into the state.

After World War II, the Las Vegas Army Air Corps Gunnery School reopened as Nellis Air Force Base. The federal government sold Basic Magnesium to the state, which sold it to chemical companies. Research and production at the plant increased as the need for better weapons and technology grew.

The *Ely Daily Times* welcomed the news of more copper mining in White Pine County. "Confidence in the future of this district is manifest everywhere," reported the paper.

Space Race

In 1957, a little over a decade after the end of World War II, Americans were shocked to learn the Soviet Union had launched the world's first satellite. Called *Sputnik*, it made Americans aware that they were no longer leading the way in space.

In America's schools, more science and math courses were required. American students were to be the nation's "secret weapon." Within a few years, however, the U.S. space program had caught up and surpassed the Soviets. We had satellites gathering photos and information in space. The United States even sent astronauts to walk on the moon.

Nevada has played only a small part in the Space Race. Nellis Air Force Base and the Nevada Test Site at Yucca Mountain have been sites for research.

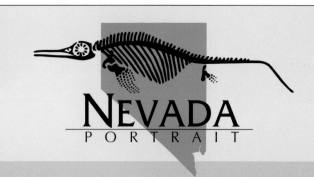

NEVADA
PORTRAIT

Hank Greenspun
1909–1989

Herman Milton "Hank" Greenspun was born in Brooklyn, New York. He grew up and went to law school. Then he was drafted into the army during World War II. He wrote for a military newspaper, was made a captain, and was put in charge of maintaining weapons. He met his wife while serving in Ireland.

When Hank returned home after the war, a friend talked him into driving together to Las Vegas, and he loved the lively city. He started an entertainment magazine, then handled publicity for the Flamingo. He also invested in building the Desert Inn. While it was being built, a cousin approached Greenspun about aiding Israel in its war against the Arab nations. Greenspun helped Israel obtain guns and ammunition, which was against the law.

Greenspun began publishing the *Las Vegas Sun*, and wrote articles attacking Senators McCarran and McCarthy. He charged that their anti-communist witch-hunt violated the right of free speech. He also fought against local *corruption*, especially involving McCarran's friends. One morning in 1952, almost every casino canceled its advertising in the *Sun*. Greenspun learned that a phone call from McCarran's office to a hotel owner had started the whole thing. Greenspun refused to back down. He was here to stay.

Greenspun began buying land that his family later developed into a *suburban* community called Green Valley. Then he won the contract for the local cable television *franchise*. Cable TV boomed, and his son later sold the company for more than $1 billion.

After Greenspun died, his family continued his legacy of *charitable* giving. They gave land and money to the University of Nevada, Las Vegas (UNLV) and other causes.

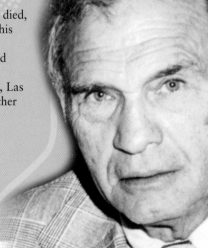

Bombs in the Backyard

The quest for a strong defense prompted Nevada's most controversial act during the **nuclear arms** race. After dropping atomic bombs on Japan, the United States tested the bombs again in the South Pacific. But federal officials wanted to test in the United States. The costs would be lower and the security greater.

President Truman signed the order that created the Atomic Proving Ground—the Nevada Test Site, less than 100 miles from Las Vegas.

Important research in above-ground testing went on at the test site. Scientists spent many years studying uses of nuclear power and what to do with the waste it left behind. The government paid Nevada's universities to assist in experiments.

The tests became part of daily life. Many southern Nevadans would listen to the countdown, usually early in the morning, and watch their ceiling lights sway. For those on the upper floors of tall buildings, the shaking was even greater.

One of the stranger experiments at the Test Site was known as the "Charge of the Swine Brigade." To learn how atomic tests affected different fabrics, the army dressed pigs in army uniforms and regular clothes and put them near the test site. Some were put a few feet away, others a few hundred feet, and others still farther away. Since pigs will be pigs, they gained weight and had to be refitted with new clothes. Did the pigs survive the test? No!

Marketing the Mushroom Cloud

Pictures and drawings of mushroom clouds appeared in advertisements, on postcards, and on book and magazine covers. One beauty shop showed an "atomic hairdo," in the form of a mushroom cloud. One motel called itself the Atomic View Motel, and one business sold pieces of a window broken during a test as "atomic glass."

A Las Vegas furniture store advertised a "Great Atomic Bomb Sale," saying, "We've blown our top, too." A car dealer claimed, "Atom Drops on High Prices."

> It's exciting to think that the . . . proving ground is . . . helping national defense. We had long ago written off that terrain as wasteland, and today it's blooming with atoms.
> —Governor Charles Russell, 1952

One explosion displaced 12 million tons of earth and formed this crater 320 feet deep and 1,280 feet in diameter.

Nevada
Test Site

The Unhappy Truth

Nevadans had nothing to fear from the atomic tests, or so they thought. First, these were American bombs, not those of the enemy. Besides, the federal government assured everyone that the nuclear *radiation* was safe.

Sadly, the government failed to tell the truth. In some cases, the men in charge were unsure of the effects of radiation but never said so. In other cases, they knew but said otherwise.

One newspaper author said, "The truth is, there isn't the slightest proof of any kind that the . . . tests in Nevada have ever affected any human being anywhere outside the testing ground itself."

Suspicions grew as strange things took place when the winds shifted—thousands of sheep died near St. George, Utah, when an atomic cloud flew over. In the southern Utah desert, the actors and crew filming *The Conqueror* with John Wayne wound up suffering from cancer and other illnesses related to radiation.

Those who suffered most were workers at the test site and "downwinders" who lived near the sites. They were exposed to high levels of radiation, and many became

"The Story of the Nevada Test Site"

The Atomic Energy Commission published "The Story of the Nevada Test Site" to teach children about atomic testing. Among the statements in the pamphlet are these:

> There is only one known instance in which testing resulted in injury to anyone. . . . An elderly man at Hiko, Nevada, . . . was startled by the blast . . . while shaving and reacted so sharply that he strained his neck.

The book also said:

> Some turkeys in eastern California . . . stampeded into a corner of their pen and many smothered after they were startled by the effects of a [test bomb].

ill. Today, the federal government pays some of the families of people who died from cancer as a result of the testing. But the cause of illness is hard to prove many years later, and most of the claims have been denied.

In Congress, the Subcommittee on Oversight and Investigations stated in 1980:

> All evidence suggesting that radiation was having harmful effects, be it on the sheep or the people, was not only disregarded but actually *suppressed*.

Members of the Northern Nevada Development Authority toured the Yucca Mountain Project.

The U.S. government plans to create the world's first high-level radioactive waste dump at the site.

Most tests have been conducted in this valley at Yucca Flat. The entrance to the test site is about 65 miles north of Las Vegas.

The End of Testing

The first aboveground test was *detonated* in 1951. About 120 tests followed until the United States and the Soviet Union finally signed a treaty in 1963 that ended the tests.

After that, more than 400 tests were made below the ground. Finally, in 1992, testing was stopped.

What do you think?

Why would the government deny any health dangers from the testing? Could it have been lack of knowledge? Lack of real evidence?

Could the goal of being a world leader, which included having atomic bombs, have been more important than possible harm to American citizens? Would a similar situation be allowed today?

Nuclear Waste

When the U.S. stopped testing atomic bombs in 1992, Nevadans were glad the federal government continued several research programs at the site.

But other nuclear issues proved less welcome. In the 1980s Congress began the process of trying to find a place to store high-level nuclear waste. In 1987 it passed a

Activity

Yucca Mountain

Find reports and articles on the Internet, in newspapers, and in library books on Yucca Mountain. After reading about the situation, take a stand on whether or not you agree or disagree that Nevada should hold the nuclear waste for the country. With your classmates, present your point of view in a skit, song, poster, or debate.

law designed to make Yucca Mountain, on the Nevada Test Site, the place to be considered. Nevada leaders have fought this ever since. They have argued that it is unfair for Nevada to serve as the nation's nuclear waste dump. They have also pointed out the possible dangers to the cities and countryside through which the waste would be transported on its way to Nevada. Scientists have countered that the waste will be stored and protected, making it perfectly safe when it is on the road or in the ground.

In 2002, the U.S. secretary of energy announced that Yucca Mountain would be the site of the repository, prompting more outcries and court cases. Led by U.S. Senator Harry Reid, Nevada's congressional delegation fought to stop or slow down the process. In 2007, when Reid became majority leader—the highest-ranking position in his party in the Senate—the dump's fate looked gloomier than it had in many years.

Wars in Asia

"I Hate War"

The quote "I hate war" is from President Franklin Roosevelt and is inscribed in stone on the monument to him in Washington, D.C. Roosevelt was president during most of World War II, though he died several months before the end of the war. Most people in the world also hate the terror, destruction, and loss of life associated with war. Despite the horrors of war, however, soldiers from Nevada fought along with other Americans to preserve freedom in different parts of the world.

The Korean War

In 1950, only five years after the end of World War II, the United States found itself at war once more, this time in Korea. Soldiers from North Korea invaded South Korea in an effort to take over the country and put it under the control of a communist government. The North Koreans used Soviet tanks and planes. President Harry S. Truman and leaders of 15 other nations sent troops to help the South Koreans defend themselves and keep communism from spreading.

At first, Americans did not pay much attention to the war. Everyone felt the war would end quickly, but it lasted three years. Of the 33,686 American soldiers who lost their lives in the war, 34 were from Nevada. Today, thousands of soldiers from both North and South Korea still guard the border between the two countries.

The most prominent Nevadan involved in the war was Mike O'Callaghan, who later become governor. He suffered through the amputation of most of one of his legs. He moved to our state after his military service.

Alvin Anderson was part of an all-African American unit in the U.S. Army. Chinese troops captured him in 1950, and he spent the rest of the war in a prison camp. His one daily meal was cabbage soup, maybe with some potatoes in it. "I realized from the beginning that you've got to eat to live," he said. "Some guys tried to pass on it, thinking the next time the food would be better, and they got weaker and weaker."

Tony Cotignola retired to Nevada from New York. He said, "When you are 18, you think you're going to live forever until you see somebody dead and realize it could happen to you."

The Vietnam War

During the 1960s the United States sent troops to Vietnam, a faraway country in Southeast Asia. The South Vietnamese were defending their country against the communist soldiers from North Vietnam. Much like in Korea, the North Vietnamese wanted to unite the country under one communist government.

The Vietnam War was the longest war in American history, starting in the early 1960s. The United States was sharply divided between those who felt the war could be won and those who wanted our troops to be sent home. Many people believed we had no reason to be involved. Others thought it was important to help fight communism everywhere in the world, especially since millions of innocent civilians were being killed in Vietnam.

People held protest marches and demonstrations against the war. Ralph Denton ran for the House of Representatives in 1966, and recalled:

Nevada: A Journey of Discovery

Vietnam was a big issue, and I struggled trying to decide what our position should be. When I did become opposed to the war, it had serious effects on personal relationships. My neighbor's son in Vietnam, a young marine, was killed. His father thought I was a traitor. I don't know how long it's going to take this country to get over the tragedies of Vietnam. I don't think we're over it yet.

The death toll in Vietnam rose. Suffering of soldiers and civilians there was tremendous. Newspapers reported hundreds of men as POWs, or "prisoners of war," and others as MIAs, or "missing in action." Finally, in 1973, a peace agreement was signed, and U.S. troops came home. When it was finally over, 2–3 million Vietnamese had died. More than 58,000 Americans had also died, including 151 from Nevada.

Continuing into the 21st century, Nevadans and other Americans were involved in other foreign wars. You will read about these conflicts later in this book.

Vietnam is a hot, humid country. Native animals include elephants, monkeys, and snakes. At the time of the war, the people—mostly rice farmers—lived in houses made of reeds that kept out the rain.

At the historic meeting at the Moulin Rouge, Dr. James McMillan is at the head of the table. To his left is Las Vegas mayor Oran Gragson, and to his right is Hank Greenspun. The photo was taken in 1960. Photo courtesy of Marie McMillan.

Civil Rights and Wrongs

Throughout Nevada, African Americans and open-minded whites worked to change laws that discriminated against blacks. The problem became especially clear when Squaw Valley, California, close to Lake Tahoe, was scheduled to host the 1960 Winter Olympics, and athletes from some African nations would be barred from hotels because of their skin color. Members of the Reno community, white and black, became involved.

Civil rights became a much more important issue in Las Vegas, because its larger black population was segregated west of the railroad tracks. More black professionals moved in—the town's first black doctor, Charles West; its first black dentist, James McMillan; and Bob Bailey, an entertainer. They joined other black residents like businesspeople Woodrow Wilson and Lubertha Johnson, teacher Mabel Hoggard, and many ministers.

Then the Moulin Rouge Hotel, called "the nation's first major interracial hotel," opened in 1955. Before the hotel was built, black entertainers performing in Las Vegas were forced to seek overnight rooms in all-black boarding houses. Black tourism was non-existent.

Opening night was hosted by boxing champion Joe Louis and featured performances by the Platters and flashy chorus-line routines. Within the next few months Louis Armstrong, George Burns,

NEVADA PORTRAIT

Dr. James McMillan
1917–1999

Dr. James McMillan was one of several prominent African Americans who changed Nevada. He was the public face of Nevada's civil rights movement. His demand for action in 1960 led to the end of official discrimination against black customers in Las Vegas casinos.

McMillan was born in Mississippi. His father died before James' second birthday, and when he was five, he saw the Ku Klux Klan whip his mother. His family eventually settled near Detroit, Michigan. He went to the University of Detroit, where he was a star athlete, then earned a degree in dentistry. He served in the U.S. Army during World War II and then in the Korean War. "I was back in the army. Apparently they had decided they could use a dentist with flat feet and a bad shoulder," said Dr. McMillan.

McMillan moved to Las Vegas and joined others in organizing protests to gain more jobs and better treatment for African Americans. He said, "By the time I got to Las Vegas, it was rigidly segregated. You couldn't get into any of the places downtown to eat. You could go into the stores, but if you tried on clothing you couldn't put it back on the rack; you had to buy it, . . . and you couldn't live anywhere other than in the West Las Vegas area."

McMillan and another man started publishing a community newspaper. Today, it is the *Sentinel-Voice*. McMillan and his friends built a housing project for seniors and formed the Nevada Black Chamber of Commerce to promote African American-owned businesses. Later, as a member of the school board, McMillan pushed for new schools to be built in West Las Vegas. He also served three terms as president of the local chapter of the National Association for the Advancement of Colored People (NAACP).

Nat King Cole, Jack Benny, Frank Sinatra, and Sammy Davis Jr. performed at the hotel.

When civil rights activists scheduled a march in 1960 to protest racial discrimination in Las Vegas resorts, hotel owners and Governor Grant Sawyer hurriedly set up a meeting with NAACP president Dr. James McMillan and other leaders at the Moulin Rouge. Most of the hotel owners agreed to open their hotels to blacks and eventually to hire them for more than just cleaning, dishwashing, and other low-paying jobs.

The Civil Rights Act of 1964 did away with the kind of legal discrimination that Nevada's African Americans had been fighting. The new law resulted from the protests and pressure from a national movement led by the Rev. Dr. Martin Luther King Jr. But changing people's minds was another matter, as was the fight to make up for centuries of racial discrimination.

The Women's Movement

Black Nevadans were not alone in demanding fair treatment. Women also fought for better treatment and equality. After working in factories and other traditionally male jobs during World War II, women had quit their jobs and returned home when the war was over. Some women, however, liked working outside the home. Even though women nearly always made less money than men for the same jobs, and even though many jobs were not even available to women, they liked the income and independence that came from working. They also found that new inventions such as better washing machines and clothes dryers enabled them to do household chores more quickly. They had time on their hands.

In Nevada, some women tried to get jobs in casinos. Reno and Lake Tahoe resorts had long employed female dealers, but Las Vegas city officials recommended against hiring them, and North Las Vegas leaders banned them entirely. They were worried that female dealers would work for

We Shall Overcome

Whenever civil rights protesters gathered, people held hands, swayed side to side, and sang "We Shall Overcome." It was the theme song of the March on Washington the day Martin Luther King Jr. gave his famous "I Have a Dream" speech in 1963.

We shall overcome,
We shall overcome,
We shall overcome,
Someday
Oh, deep in my heart,
I do believe, that
We shall overcome
Someday.

We'll walk hand in hand,
We'll walk hand in hand,
We'll walk hand in hand,
Someday.
Oh, deep in my heart,
I do believe, that
We shall overcome
Someday.

African Americans and others held signs in Carson City in 1969. They were protesting the exclusion of blacks from casinos.

less pay than male dealers, and so casinos might replace the men with women. The men, they said, needed the jobs to support their families.

Yet women made advances in Nevada in the two decades after the war. Sarann Knight-Preddy became the first African American and the first woman to hold a gaming license for her casino in Hawthorne. More women were being elected to the legislature in the 1950s: former Las Vegas school superintendent Maude Frazier, Lincoln County school teacher Hazel Denton, Las Vegas realtor Helen Herr, and Washoe County's Mabel Isbell all served. Mildred Bray was state superintendent of education.

Reno—The Biggest Little City in the World

During the 1950s and early 1960s, Nevada depended upon more than atomic clouds and mining to build its economy. Federal defense spending shot up. Federal support for better highways and better airplanes made travel easier. This meant that the West attracted more visitors, and more people moved to Nevada.

Nevada took advantage of all of these factors with the passage of a Freeport Law. Both the government and private businesses needed space to store extra materials. The state legislature passed a law allowing goods "in transit" through the state to be warehoused without being subject to property taxes. This means that a company could store goods they were going to ship later, and the goods would not be taxed as if they were "owned."

It worked. Within two years, Reno had several warehouse and manufacturing companies that provided jobs. Nevada voters amended the state constitution to make the Freeport Law permanent. Reno's central geographic location among population centers of the West made it an ideal place for warehousing and shipping.

The postwar period brought other changes to the city. The local government limited where casinos could be built, putting them mainly in the Virginia Street area, away from homes and other businesses.

A new hotel, the Mapes, was named for and owned by a Reno family who had helped promote the city's annual rodeo. At 12 stories, the Mapes was the first high-rise built in the United States after World War II. It proved to be a great success. Once again, the jobs needed to run a casino, as well as the money tourists spent on having a good time, helped the economy.

The River Walk

Many American cities suffer from a declining downtown. Usually, it is the oldest part of a city, so it becomes rundown as people and businesses move to newer, more modern homes and buildings in other parts of town or in the suburbs.

As early as the 1960s, Reno officials discussed trying to turn downtown into a plaza where people could walk, meet, and relax. Finally, in 1991, the Raymond I. Smith Truckee River Walk, named for the man who built Harolds Club, was completed. Pedestrians could stroll past and admire fountains and sculptures while vendors sold goods and entertainers performed.

The River Walk is a classic example of the old and new Nevada. It attracts tourists who walk among the casinos to take a break from gambling and sit on benches in *gazebos*. But local residents enjoy it too. Businessmen and casino workers often take brown bags and books for a pleasant lunch by the river.

Bill Raggio, a Washoe County legislator, loves his native city. He said, "Reno is a well-kept secret. We have the four seasons, but we don't have really severe weather. We have quick access to Lake Tahoe and the mountains, and you can get to your office in 10 minutes."

Tourists and local people enjoy the River Walk.

Visitors and Growth

Reno kept growing. The 1,720-room Silver Legacy opened in 1995. The Peppermill and Clarion expanded. The Reno Hilton was off the beaten path of Virginia Street, closer to the airport. The Nugget in Sparks and the Boomtown near Verdi also expanded and prospered.

The construction was not limited to casinos. Reno opened the National Bowling Stadium in 1995. It included not only bowling lanes, but also sculpture, an *atrium*, and high-tech video displays. The *Los Angeles Times* called the Bowling Stadium "the Taj Mahal of tenpins."

The Nevada Museum of Art, opened in 2003, was the culmination of a 70-year effort to showcase the arts. Not only did the museum bring in major exhibits, but its architecture, inspired by the nearby Black Rock Desert, won national attention. Meanwhile, the University of Nevada, Reno, continued to host major concerts and events at the Lawlor Events Center.

Reno kept growing and prospering. The warehousing law passed years ago continued to bolster the economy. So did thriving retail and construction trades. The Biggest Little City in the World kept getting bigger as the 21st century began.

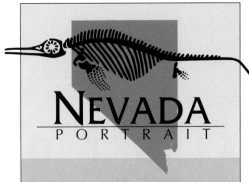

Sue Wagner

Sue Wagner moved to Reno in 1969 with her husband and infant son. She quickly became active in the community.

In 1974, Wagner won the first of her three terms in the Assembly. Then she ran for the state Senate. She won, but with a heavy heart; her husband, a researcher at the Desert Research Institute, died in a plane crash while working on weather experiments. Left with two children, Wagner kept working on issues important to women, but also on such subjects as campaign financing and ethics. The *Reno Gazette-Journal* called Sue Wagner a "one-woman whirlwind."

After a decade in the Senate, Sue Wagner ran for lieutenant governor. During the campaign, tragedy struck again. A small plane on which she was flying crashed not long after taking off from the Fallon airport. Her fellow candidate, state treasurer Bob Seale, was injured, and his wife was killed. Wagner suffered serious injuries.

Wagner may have been down, but she wasn't out. She won the election, becoming the first woman ever elected lieutenant governor in Nevada. Then she went to work for the University of Nevada, Reno, and was a member of the Nevada Gaming Commission. By 2004, Sue Wagner had spent three decades in public service, helping to build a better Nevada while overcoming personal troubles.

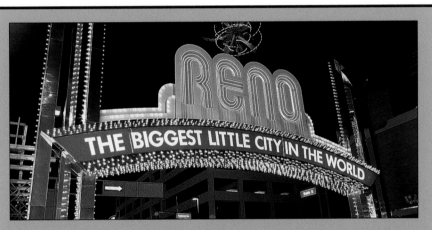

▶ Photo by Jeff Gnass

The Arch

One landmark in the heart of Reno really began in the late 1800s when soldiers returned from the Spanish-American War and marched down Virginia Street. An arched sign above the street said, "Welcome Home."

A decade later, Reno hosted a world heavyweight championship fight that attracted many reporters from other cities. Some of them liked Reno and suggested a slogan: "The Biggest Little City in the World."

In 1920, the Reno Roundup Association put up a new arch to advertise a rodeo and show. Later, city officials put up a newer arch. The arch looked barren with only the word "RENO" at the center, so they held a contest for a slogan. The winner was the phrase "Biggest Little City in the World," remembered from an earlier time.

By the mid-1980s, however, the arch had seen better days. A new arch, unveiled in 1987, still welcomes tourists to Reno.

HISTORY
OF *Some*
LAS VEGAS
CASINOS

The big economic boom in southern Nevada was also due to the rise of the casino industry. More than a dozen major hotels opened on the Las Vegas Strip, across town from the downtown region. The owners came mainly from cities such as New York City, Detroit, Cleveland, and Chicago, where they had operated casinos illegally. Many of these men were the children of immigrants who had come from Eastern Europe, fleeing persecution because they were Jewish.

Las Vegas Boulevard, called "the Strip," changed quickly. The Thunderbird, Desert Inn, Sahara, Sands, Riviera, and Tropicana opened on one side of the street. The New Frontier, Dunes, Hacienda, and Stardust opened on the other. A few years later, Caesars Palace opened. The casinos were supposed to be luxury resorts. They hardly compare to today's standards, but they were a lot different from the original low-rise, western-style hotels.

Mirage in the Desert

Hotel-casinos on the strip got larger and more grand. After the MGM Grand (now Bally's) opened in 1973, several smaller hotel-casinos opened, and existing hotels expanded. Then Steve Wynn changed the face of the strip with the opening of The Mirage in 1989. The show at the Mirage featured *illusionists* Siegfried and Roy with their white tigers. Outside, surrounded by an artificial lake, a volcano went off at regular intervals. It was the most elaborate hotel built on the Strip and attracted tourists in large numbers.

The Mirage started a building boom. Wynn added the Treasure Island next door to the Mirage. He offered great outdoor entertainment there as well. College students got jobs as pirates who jumped off a sinking pirate ship to a background of cannon fire. In 1998, Wynn opened the Bellagio, the most luxurious hotel Las Vegas had seen, with fountains set to music, an *arboretum* with a variety of plants, and an art gallery where Wynn displayed his own collection.

The Lion Roars

On three different occasions, Kirk Kerkorian has built Las Vegas's largest hotel-casino—indeed, the largest in the world. Twice, it has been an MGM Grand. The second, even grander, one opened in 1993 with more than 5,000 rooms, a lion facing the street, and a theme park that reflected increased efforts in Las Vegas to cater to families. It has been replaced by a

conference center and, soon, new condominiums.

Kerkorian built New York, New York, modeled on the city and complete with the Statue of Liberty and a roller coaster. The next step was to take over another casino company. In 2000, he offered a deal to stockholders in Wynn's Mirage Resorts.

A Bigger Top

Under the leadership of William Bennett and William Pennington, Circus Circus became hugely successful. The men invited middle-class gamblers and their families to enter the big top on the Strip, and their efforts paid off handsomely. They built resorts in Reno and Laughlin, and soon looked farther down the Strip.

First came the Excalibur, modeled on a Medieval castle, complete with jousting and other examples from King Arthur and the Knights of the Round Table. Next door the company built the Luxor, which resembled an Egyptian pyramid. Then came Mandalay Bay, with a shark reef.

Keeping Up

For older hotels, all of this construction and expansion forced them to keep up so they could compete. They had another option too; they could try to benefit from all that was going on. Caesars Palace responded to the changes. Its owners built The Forum Shoppes, complete with shows featuring animated Roman characters and a fiery Atlantis spectacular. They also built a huge new theater for entertainment diva Celine Dion.

Smaller, older casinos survived and often prospered. Hotels toward the north end of the Strip like the Stardust, the Riviera, the Frontier, and the Sahara survived by providing rooms and gambling for tourists with less money than those who came to the newer, more expensive resorts. Farther north, the Stratosphere provided dining about 1,000 feet above Las Vegas with great views and both a roller coaster and a thrill ride.

Steve Wynn

Steve Wynn fell in love with Las Vegas at the age of 10. His father, who ran bingo games back east, brought him along on a visit to the city. After his father died, and Wynn graduated from the University of Pennsylvania, he returned to Las Vegas with his wife, Elaine. He was involved in the New Frontier Hotel and a couple of businesses.

Wynn invested in a small downtown casino, the Golden Nugget. He quickly turned it into an attractive resort, adding a hotel tower. Then he invested in gambling in New Jersey, which became the second state to make gambling legal in 1976.

Wynn had always thought big. He signed Frank Sinatra, an entertainer popular on the Strip, to an exclusive contract to play downtown. Then he thought bigger. With help from investors, he financed the building of the Mirage at high risk. When the Mirage opened, the rumor was that it would take a daily profit of $1 million to pay off the debt for its construction, but the resort proved so profitable that the debt was paid in six months.

But Wynn has done much more than create some of the most beautiful hotels in the world. He built his own golf course, where he played rounds with everyone from President Bill Clinton to basketball star Michael Jordan. He became an expert in art, buying works that he displayed in a gallery. He was active in politics, setting up his own polling and telephoning operations and hiring lobbyists to work on his behalf. He changed the city he loves.

Steve Wynn often says that Jay Sarno, builder of Caesars Palace and Circus Circus, greatly influenced him. He tells of showing Sarno a new sign he put up in front of the Golden Nugget. "Jay looked at me and sighed. He said, "Steve, Steve, ya gotta nice sign, but Steve, Steve, Steve, ya gotta do something with water."
And he did.

Modern Nevada

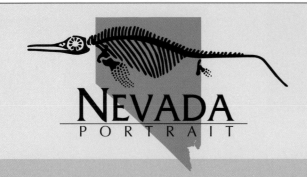

NEVADA
P O R T R A I T

Moe Dalitz
1899–1989

While many casino operators kept their illegal connections, they also tried to become more **legitimate**. Moe Dalitz was one of these men who had to keep one foot planted on each side of the line.

Dalitz was raised in Michigan. His father was in the laundry business, and Dalitz also ran laundries at first. But, like many other young males in large cities during Prohibition, Dalitz saw other ways to make money. He became involved in **bootlegging** and running illegal casinos. He shipped boatloads of illegal alcohol across the Great Lakes from Canada to the United States. He later said, "How was I to know those gambling joints were illegal? There were so many judges and politicians in them, I figured they had to be all right." He added, "If you people wouldn't have drunk it, I wouldn't have bootlegged it."

Later, Dalitz moved to Las Vegas to take over construction of a hotel-casino. Dalitz and his partners showed great ability at running casinos. The Desert Inn, with its championship golf course, proved highly profitable. The men went on to operate the casino at the Showboat, and they took over the Stardust while it was under construction.

But Dalitz did more than build and run hotels and casinos. He and others built several housing subdivisions, the Boulevard Mall, Commercial Center, Sunrise Hospital, and other landmarks.

Dalitz also gave away a lot of money to good causes—and his charity was usually **anonymous**. No one knew who had given the money. He bought the furniture for the first building at UNLV and donated millions to community organizations.

Dalitz had another side. While still tied to organized crime, he and his partners gave huge sums of money to men running for office. Dalitz spent a lot to keep some politicians from winning elections, especially those who might threaten the power of casino operators.

Dalitz died shortly before his 90th birthday. He was famous for his business sense and gifts to his community, but he was still a mystery to many.

Battle for Downtown

Like Reno, Las Vegans faced the problem of how to revitalize downtown, away from the glittering Strip. Las Vegas as a city lacks the financial support of the largest hotel-casinos because the Strip is part of the county. The development of Summerlin, the master-planned community near the old downtown area, has attracted large numbers of residents and businesses.

One way city residents changed downtown was to vote in new leadership. In 1991, voters voted in as mayor Jan Jones, a businesswoman better known for her television commercials. Her big project to change downtown was the Fremont Street Experience.

The next mayor, Oscar Goodman, continued support for Neonopolis, an entertainment complex boasting a video and skill paradise, with skeeball, air hockey, and the latest ride simulators and video games. Classy, affordable eating places keep the neon theme. On the second floor, visitors bowl and view the giant video walls. There are theaters and a collection of antique neon signs that light up the night.

Goodman also worked on attracting a major league sports franchise, and helped land the 2007 NBA All-Star Game for southern Nevada. He sought to develop 61 acres of vacant downtown land with shopping, a performing arts center, condominiums, and a treatment center for those with Alzheimer's Disease.

WATER FOR LAS VEGAS

One of the key reasons for the growth of Las Vegas was the Southern Nevada Water Project. Nevada wanted to use water from the Colorado River, but the question was how to pump it into the city and surrounding valley. After many years, the final project included six pumping plants, a reservoir, a 4-mile tunnel, and 31 miles of pipeline to bring water from Lake Mead to Las Vegas.

The first stage of the project opened in 1971, and the second began 10 years later. As a result, Las Vegas received its Colorado River water. It was possible for Las Vegas to support more people than it ever had before.

Underground water pipe is being buried during construction.

Governor Mike O'Callaghan and others watch the first water flowing from Lake Mead, 1971.

Modern Immigrants

Nearly 600,000 Nevadans are immigrants or the children of immigrants. This is about 30 percent of the state's population.

What is it like to move to the U.S. from elsewhere and live in Nevada? What is it like to be part of an ethnic group? Here are some stories about those who took the risk to start over in a new country.

Europeans

Battista Locatelli, a teenager at the time, and his sister, brother, and two cousins came from Italy in 1949. His only money came from serving passengers on the boat when he crossed the Atlantic. The family then crossed the United States by train. Locatelli became a waiter at fine California restaurants.

> When I went to interview for a job, I dressed my best—nice clothing, hair nailed down. They even looked under your fingernails. . . . It's all about the service. Everything I did, I did with tender loving care. The secret to success is simple—work, work, and more work.

Locatelli worked in a restaurant. He also drove a truck, and his singing in traffic caught other people's attention. He moved to Las Vegas to sing in a show, but the show never opened, so he went back to waiting tables and singing. Then he decided to open his own restaurant near the Las Vegas Strip. Today, Battista's Hole in the

Wall is a favorite in Las Vegas. Until they sold Battista's recently, his family helped run the restaurant so he could run marathons and bicycle up to 30 miles a day, even though he is in his 70s.

Hispanics

The majority of Nevada's Hispanic citizens were born in the United States, but nearly a fourth are from other countries. Why do so many Hispanics move to Nevada? For the most part, they come for the following reasons:

- They have friends and relatives here.
- There is affordable housing.
- There is a good supply of service jobs that don't require a mastery of English.

Newsweek magazine projects that by 2025, Nevada will be the fourth-largest Hispanic state in the country, only behind California, Texas, and New Mexico. Why?

Bernice Soltelo and her husband and children moved to Las Vegas from California and earned enough to own a home and a new car. She said, "It just proves that if you work hard here you can make it. We are a success story. You won't believe the things we can afford now."

Asian

James Yu, president of the Asian Chamber of Commerce in Las Vegas, immigrated from South Korea. He graduated from UNLV's College of Hotel Administration and returned home to Korea to work at a hotel. But, he said:

> The moment I got back home I started missing the things I enjoyed in America. In Korea, you don't have air conditioning and heating in houses. Over there, even if you have a car, there is no place to park. It sounds really petty, but, in real life, it has a lot of meaning.

Another family, the Chanderrajes, are natives of India. Raj Chanderraj is a leading cardiologist (heart doctor) who is active in numerous professional and civic groups. His wife, Radha, is an accountant and attorney who serves on the Nevada Gaming Commission. Asked about her appointment, she said, "We've always wanted to give back to the community, which has been so good to us."

Battista Locatelli welcomes patrons at the Hole in the Wall.

Who Are We Now?

Nevada has been the most rapidly growing state for every decade since 1960. We began the year 2004 with a population of more than 2 million. Of that number, about 70 percent lived in southern Nevada.

Senior citizens are a growing group. Many retired people have moved into one of the three Sun City communities in southern Nevada.

Today, in the population race, Las Vegas and Henderson are first and second, Reno is third, and North Las Vegas is quickly catching up. This is a change from 2000, when Reno had the largest population.

You Hold the History of the Future

You have been reading the history of others, but this century will be yours. The future belongs to you. Whatever you choose to do with it will influence those who live after you. What things could you work to change? What part of living in Nevada do you want to keep? What heroes in Nevada history could influence your decisions?

Activity

The 2000 U.S. Census

The U.S. Constitution requires that each state conduct a *census* every 10 years to find out how many people are living there. The government uses this information to determine how many members of the U.S. House of Representatives a state can have.

Study this chart of our state's population. What problems might occur when a person tries to determine his or her race of origin?

Group	Percent
White, not of Hispanic/Latino origin	65.2
Hispanic or Latino	19.7
Black (African American)	6.6
Asian	4.4
American Indian	.1
Other, 2 or more races	4

Source: 2000 U.S. Census Report

To learn more about our population, including statistics on gender (male or female), age, income, and nation of birth, go to this website: www.census.gov. Find the box on the right side of the screen that says "State and County Quick Facts" and find Nevada.

According to the information given on the website:

- What was our total population in 2000?
- What percent of our state's people were born in a foreign country? How many people is that?
- What percent are 18 years of age or younger? How many people are in that age range?
- What percent are high-school graduates?
- What percent of the people in the state live in a home where a language other than English is spoken?

On a separate piece of paper, use some of the information to create a pie chart. Draw a picture of yourself near the piece of the pie that most reflects you and your family.

1960 Winter Olympics

In February, 1960, under stormy skies, the greatest winter athletes in the world gathered in Squaw Valley, California, near Lake Tahoe. Both California and Nevada residents prepared for the event. As the sun broke through the clouds, two thousand pigeons were released into the air, a sign of peace between nations. Spectators stood quietly as the Olympic Torch completed its journey from Europe. Following the Olympic Oath and the "Star-Spangled Banner," the games were declared open while the sky erupted with fireworks and balloons.

Squaw Valley had 20 feet of snow prior to the Games, but a massive rain washed most of it away. However, in the nick of time, 12 new feet of snow fell.

The games included many "firsts." They were the first to be nationally televised and the first to use artificial ice for speed skating events. Computers were first used to tally results of races. The Opening and Closing Ceremonies were directed by Walt Disney and included 5,000 performers from California and Nevada. Daily admission, which allowed a person to see five major events, cost $7.50.

You can read more about the Olympic Games of 1960 and see photos of the games by going to www.tahoecountry.com/oldtimetahoe/oly mpics.html

From left to right: *Capt. David M. Brown, Col. Rick D. Husband, Dr. Laurel Salton-Clark, Dr. Kalpana Chawla, Lt. Col. Michael P. Anderson, Cmdr. William C. McCool, Col. Ilan Ramon*

The Space Race Revisited

Nevada has played only a small role in the space race. Nellis Air Force Base and the Nevada Test Site have been sites for research, but the state has a connection to recent, sadder developments.

On February 1, 2003, the space shuttle *Columbia* disintegrated as it re-entered the earth's atmosphere. All seven crewmembers died, including Captain William McCool. His parents, Audrey and Barry McCool, both teach at UNLV.

At the time of the shuttle disaster, students and teachers at Frank Lamping Elementary School in Henderson were putting together a science and space program. When they learned that the McCools lived in Las Vegas, they asked them to become involved. Barry McCool came to the school and talked to students. He said, "There are students out here this morning who will have the opportunity to contribute to mankind's exploration of space."

In the school courtyard, students have put a mural of the crew and a garden with seven rose bushes—one for each astronaut. A granite bench is inscribed with the names of the crew and the date of the disaster.

Chapter 10 Review

What Do You Remember?

1. Why was the Cold War called by that term?
2. What country was the rival of the United States during the Cold War?
3. Describe two differences between capitalism and communism.
4. How did the Cold War benefit Nevada business?
5. Chose one of these people and tell something about their contribution to Nevada: Moe Dalitz, Hank Greenspun, Steve Wynn, Sue Wagner, Dr. James McMillan.
6. How did the nuclear arms race affect the land and people in Southern Nevada?
7. Describe the use of Yucca Mountain by the U.S. government in the 21st century.
8. What two wars after World War II involved Nevada soldiers?
9. Describe some of the events of the civil rights struggle in Nevada.
10. How were some of the discrimination problems solved legally?
11. What new law helped Reno grow?
12. Why is Reno called "The Biggest Little City in the World"?
13. How has the Las Vegas Strip changed? Who was responsible for changing it?
14. How was downtown Las Vegas improved?
15. How did the Southern Nevada Water Project help Southern Nevada?
16. What were some of the "firsts" of the Winter Olympics in Squaw Valley?

Geography Tie-In

1. Find the Truckee River on a state road atlas. Now find a map of Reno and follow how the river goes through the city. Find the National Bowling Stadium and the Nevada Museum of Art, and see what other local landmarks you can find. Check other Nevada rivers to see if they flow through the middle of towns.
2. Find Yucca Mountain on a map and find the cities closest to the Nevada Test Site. How might activities at the Site affect people in these cities?

Activity

1. Write a play about living in your town in Nevada when you are 50 years old. How will Nevada be different? What will probably stay the same?
2. Research one of the topics in this chapter to learn more about something important to your life or about a subject that interests you. Give a report to the class alone, with a friend, or with a small group.

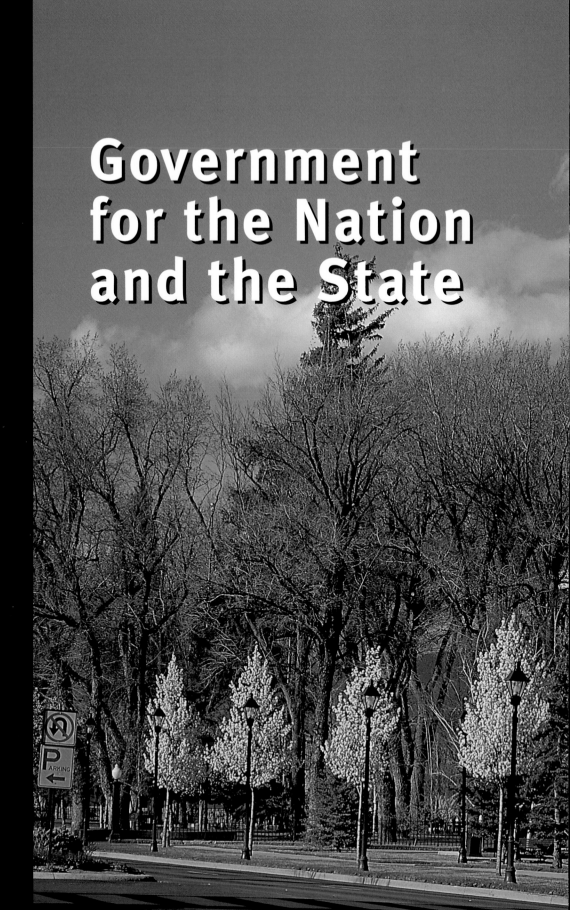

Government for the Nation and the State

Our state government meets in the beautiful Nevada State

After 17 weeks of debate and compromise, the delegates signed our Constitution. In the foreground we see Alexander Hamilton whispering to Benjamin Franklin (with cane), while George Washington presides over the signing. James Madison, the main author of the document, is sitting across the table from Franklin.

Governing the United States

Back in 1776, the year Fathers Garces and Escalante were exploring parts of the West, the Second Continental Congress met at Independence Hall in Philadelphia, Pennsylvania, and approved the Declaration of Independence. The men wanted a country where they could elect representatives to make the laws. The American colonies at the time had no say in British rule.

About 11 years later, in 1787, the American Revolution was over, and 55 men met in the same building to write what became the Constitution of the United States of America.

James Madison, from Virginia, came to be known as the Father of the Constitution because he had studied ancient governments of the world and designed most of the plan for the government of the new *republic*. Other famous men at the convention were George Washington and Benjamin Franklin.

The Constitution was written to limit the powers of government so the people would never have to live under the kinds of *tyranny* they had seen in European countries. The Constitution is still, after over 200 years, the foundation of our democratic government.

We, the People

We, the people of the United States, in order to form a more perfect Union, establish justice, insure domestic tranquility, provide for the common defense, promote the general welfare, and secure the blessings of liberty to ourselves and our posterity, do ordain and establish this Constitution for the United States of America.

–Preamble to the Constitution, 1787

When the Constitution was written, most American men were farmers or merchants. Most women worked at home and on the family farms. Few men or women had much education.

Today, over 200 years later, most Americans live in urban areas, work at thousands of kinds of jobs that nearly always include computers, and are educated in public and private schools. In spite of the many changes in the country, the Constitution remains a source of pride and the basis of a government for a free people.

The Bill of Rights

About three years after the Constitution was written, Congress added 10 important *amendments* called the Bill of Rights. The men remembered the words of the Declaration of Independence:

We hold these truths to be self-evident—That all men are created equal; that they are endowed by their Creator with certain unalienable rights; that among these are life, liberty, and the pursuit of happiness.

The men wanted a guarantee that their new government could never take away their rights.

Amendments 1-10. The Bill of Rights (1791)

These amendments include freedom of

religion, speech, and the press. Other freedoms are the right to assemble, to bear arms, to have a speedy public trial, and to have a trial by jury. These amendments are very important to our way of life.

The Tenth Amendment is very important. It states that the government has only the specific powers given to it by the Constitution. All other powers remain with the states or the people.

Over the years, people have sometimes tried to pass laws that would take away the freedoms protected by the Bill of Rights. The judges of state courts and the U.S. Supreme Court interpret laws. If a law is declared unconstitutional, that law cannot stand.

People Need Rules and Laws

Whenever people live in groups, they need rules or laws. Families have rules about honesty, respect, housework, homework, and when to be home at night. Rules help things go smoothly, and laws protect people and their rights. Rules and laws reflect what matters to people in a community.

In Nevada and in all other states, there are several levels of government. The federal government makes laws that apply to everyone in the country. Other laws are made at the state level. Rules called ordinances are made at the local county and city levels.

We must live by the laws of all levels of government, but we can challenge some laws through courts or work to pass amendments to laws. When you are old enough, you can vote for the leaders who will help make the laws.

What do you think?

In the United States we are ruled by laws, not by the whims or desires of **monarchs** or **dictators**. Both our state and federal constitutions give directions on how laws are made by elected representatives of the people. Which way do you think is best for Americans?

Our Rights and Obligations Are Set by the U.S. and Nevada Constitutions

Rights	Obligations
Free speech and press	Respect the opinions of others
Assembly and petition	Pay taxes
Freedom to vote in free elections	Vote and help choose good leaders
Freedom of religion	Be tolerant of other religious beliefs
Fair trial by jury	Serve on juries when called
Freedom from: • Excessive bail • Excessive fines • Cruel punishment	Support law and order
Due process of law	Give evidence in court
Habeas corpus (the right to go before a court or judge before being sent to prison)	Assist in preventing crimes and detection of criminals
Just payment for private property taken for public use	Abide by decisions of the majority
Freedom from slavery	Respect rights of the minority
Freedom from unreasonable search and seizure	Respect public and private property
Freedom to bear arms	Live peaceably
Other rights are given to the people.	Meet financial obligations
	Respect the flag and serve the nation when required

Activity

Government Glossary

There are words you need to understand before you can understand the many ideas of government. Some of these words have to do with our democratic government. Other words have more to do with forms of government in other countries. Work with a group to learn the definitions of each term, and then have a contest with another group to see which group can define the most words.

Capitalism: An economic system in which all or most of the means of production, distribution, and exchange are privately owned and operated for profit

Citizen: One who owes allegiance to a nation and is entitled to its protection

Communism: An economic and political system in which property and goods are owned by the government and products are shared by all

Concurrent powers: Any powers that may be exercised by both the federal government and state governments

Constitution: Body of fundamental law, setting out the basic principles, structures, processes, and functions of a government, and placing limits upon its actions

Delegated powers: Those powers the Constitution grants or delegates to the national government, such as expressed powers, implied powers, and inherent powers

Democracy: A form of government in which political control is exercised by all the people, either directly or through their elected representatives

Enumerated: Those powers specifically stated in the U.S. Constitution

Federalism: (or federal system) A form of political organization in which governmental power is divided between a central government and state governments

Foreign policy: The actions and positions that a nation takes in every aspect of its relationships in world affairs

Implied powers: Those powers of the government 'necessary and proper' to carry out the expressed powers

Interest groups: Organized bodies of individuals who share some goals and try to influence public policy to meet those goals

Local government: A county and/or city government

Monarchy: A government where a king, queen, or emperor exercises supreme powers

Nation-state: A political community that occupies a definite region and has an organized government with the power to make and enforce laws

Natural rights: Belief that individuals are naturally endowed with basic human rights as opposed to rights conferred by law

Parliamentary system: A form of government that gives governmental authority to a legislature that selects the executive from its own members

Popular sovereignty: When the vote of the citizens is considered the final authority

Presidential system: A government where voters elect the president, or chief executive, for a fixed term of office. Voters also elect members of the legislative branch

Public policy: All decisions and actions of government

Representative government: A form of government in which power is held by the people and exercised indirectly through elected representatives who make decisions and vote for laws

Republic: A government where citizens elect representatives to make laws

Reserved powers: The powers not delegated to the national government by the Constitution, nor prohibited to the states, are reserved to the states, or the people

Rule of law: The principle that every member of a society, even a ruler, must follow the law

Rule of man: The ability of government officials and others to govern by their personal whim or desire

Social contract: Agreement of all the people in a society to give up part of their freedom to a government in return for protection of their natural rights

Socialism: An economic system in which the government owns the basic means of production, determines the use of resources, distributes products and wages, and provides social services such as education, health care, and welfare

Supremacy Clause: Article VI, Section 2 of the Constitution, which states that the Constitution, laws passed by Congress, and the treaties of the United States "shall be the supreme law of the land and binding on the states"

Totalitarianism: (or dictatorship) A system of government in which a single leader or group has complete authority to rule

Tribal government: (or tribe) A political entity with the right to self-government

(Source: Nevada Social Studies Standards, Nevada Dept. of Education)

Political Parties

In the United States, adults elect representatives to vote for them in the U.S. Congress. They also elect a state governor, state senators and assemblymen or assemblywomen, a mayor, and many other people. To elect people who think more like they do, voters often choose candidates who belong to a certain political party.

A political party is a large group of people who have a lot of the same ideas about government. Political parties raise money and work hard to get members of their party elected to office.

Most people in Nevada and the rest of the United States belong to either the Democratic Party or the Republican Party. There are also third parties, such as the Socialist Party, Libertarian Party, Green Party, and so on. Some citizens run for office or vote as Independents. They do not belong to any party.

The following guidelines are some beliefs of the two main parties.
Remember that there are always many different beliefs within a party.

Democrats

- Government should be wisely used to improve life for all.
- Public education is a high priority and should be fully funded.
- Civil rights should be protected regardless of color, gender, or sexual orientation.
- Pro Choice (the mother should be able to choose whether or not to have an abortion).
- The environment is fragile and should be protected.
- Unions have the right to strike.
- The state has a responsibility to assist the poor, children, and the elderly.
- Health care should be available to everyone regardless of income.

Republicans

- Government has grown too large and should be downsized.
- Public education is a priority, but private and home schools also have a role.
- Government should not legislate personal responsibility.
- Pro Life (no abortions except in certain cases regarding health of the mother).
- Environmental decisions should be balanced against economic impact.
- Strong businesses provide good jobs, so businesses should be protected.
- The wealthy should not be penalized for making good choices and making money.
- Health care should be available, but it is not a right and is best handled by the private sector.

What do you think?

- Can a political party whose members share many of the same ideas be more effective than individuals working alone?
- Do you think it is a good idea to vote for a party, or to find out about candidates on an individual basis?

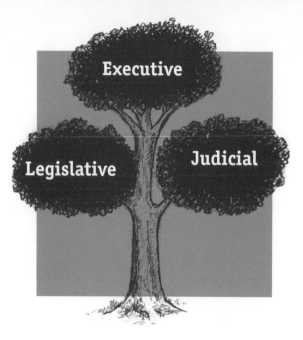

Executive

Legislative   Judicial

Executive Branch: Carries out the laws

The governor is the head of this branch and works with many departments and agencies. The governor signs bills that then become laws, or vetoes bills passed by the legislative branch.

Judicial Branch: Interprets the laws

The courts decide if a law is in keeping with the constitutions of the state and the country. Courts protect the rights of everyone.

The Legislative Branch

The state *legislature* is the branch of government that makes laws for the state of Nevada. It consists of an upper house, or Senate, and a lower house, or Assembly. Voters in the state elect members to both houses.

Voting Districts

Adult citizens of the state are divided into districts of roughly even populations. Voters in each district then vote for senators and assemblymen to represent the wishes of their district. Because Nevada is so large, and so much of the population is concentrated in the urban areas of Las Vegas and Reno, the majority of legislators live in or near these cities. Others represent seven counties and a vast amount of territory.

How Long Do Legislators Meet?

The legislature meets once every two years for 120 days (about four months) in Carson City. Because lawmakers only meet during this time, or during additional special sessions, they are called citizen legislators and have other jobs. Their jobs range from doctor to rancher, lawyer to lineman. Legislators are paid for the time they meet.

Amending the Constitution

Like the U.S. Constitution, our state constitution can be changed by amendments. An amendment must be passed by a vote of at least two-thirds of each house of the state legislature. If it

State Government

The Nevada Constitution organizes government in much the same way as the U.S. Constitution. Both our federal and our state governments have three branches of government—executive, legislative, and judicial. The duties of each branch are spelled out in the constitutions.

Branches of Government

Each branch of government has its own power. Each branch also limits the power of the other two branches. The duties of government are divided so no single branch can become too powerful.

This balance of power is a system of *checks and balances*. It helps protect our rights because no one person or even one group of people can make laws or take all of the power. Each branch checks what the other branches do.

Here is a summary of how the checks and balances system works in our state government:

Legislative Branch: Makes the laws

State legislators belong to either the state Assembly or the Senate. Their *bills* (proposed laws) become laws only after a signature by the governor. Even years later, their laws may be thrown out if the judicial branch finds them unconstitutional.

passes there, it is placed on the ballot in November for a public vote.

An Amendment and Taxes

In 2003, the legislature was unable to finish its business in the 120 days. The problem was a disagreement over taxes. Governor Kenny Guinn supported a tax increase of more than $800 million. A group of 15 assemblymen led an effort to block that increase, saying it was too large.

Several years earlier, in 1994 and 1996, voters had amended the state constitution to require a two-thirds vote of each house to approve tax raises. Without the 15 assemblymen, the raise was stalled in the Assembly, and the Senate was also divided on the issue.

Two special sessions of the legislature were called, and in a unique case, the executive branch sued the legislative branch, and the Nevada Supreme Court heard their arguments. The court ruled that, in this case, the two-thirds requirement was less important than the section of the constitution that emphasized the importance of education. And, since education would be harmed without more tax funding, the court threw out the two-thirds provision, but only for that session and for that issue. The tax raise was finally approved.

Teenagers in the Legislature

Each year, Boys State and Girls State meet near Carson City, often around the end of the legislative session. The groups of Nevada high school students form their own legislative bodies and hear from various state officials about government. It is a great opportunity for young men and women to learn something about how government works.

You can find out more about this program from your local high school.

Nevada's State Legislature

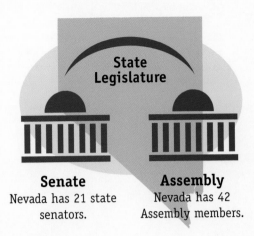

Senate
Nevada has 21 state senators.

Assembly
Nevada has 42 Assembly members.

National Congress

Nevada voters also elect representatives and senators to represent the state in the United States Congress in Washington, D.C. The representatives and senators work with representatives of all the other states to make laws for the nation.

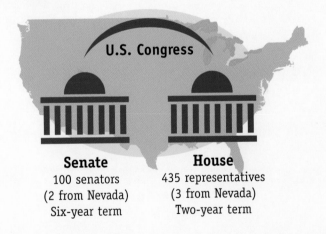

Senate
100 senators
(2 from Nevada)
Six-year term

House
435 representatives
(3 from Nevada)
Two-year term

Even though together the Senate and House are called Congress, representatives to the House are usually called congressmen and congresswomen. Members of the Senate are called senators.

1. How many senators represent the people of Nevada?
2. How many representatives (congressmen or congresswomen) represent the people of Nevada?

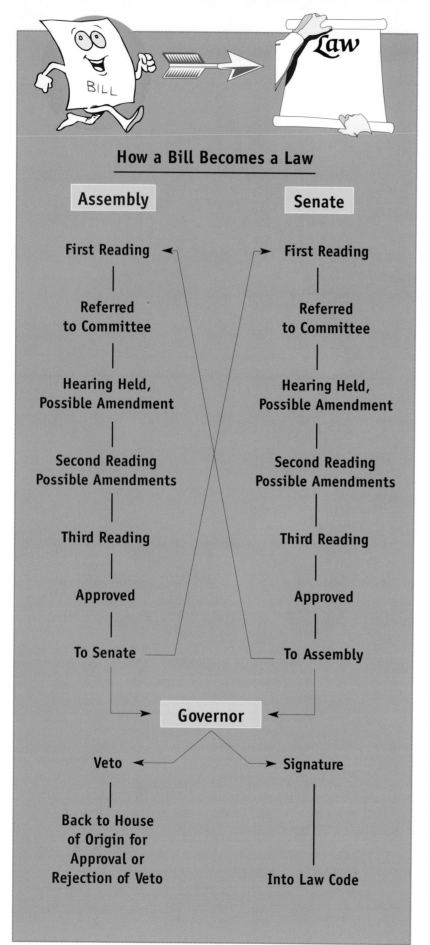

How a Bill Becomes a Law

Assembly

First Reading
|
Referred
to Committee
|
Hearing Held,
Possible Amendment
|
Second Reading
Possible Amendments
|
Third Reading
|
Approved
|
To Senate

Senate

First Reading
|
Referred
to Committee
|
Hearing Held,
Possible Amendment
|
Second Reading
Possible Amendments
|
Third Reading
|
Approved
|
To Assembly

Governor

Veto
|
Back to House
of Origin for
Approval or
Rejection of Veto

Signature
|
Into Law Code

How a Bill Becomes a Law

Passing a bill is a way to establish new laws and programs, allow the state to spend money on important projects, and change or repeal existing laws. In Nevada, anyone—an individual, a special-interest group, a public official, and even the governor—can suggest a new bill.

To see how it works, let's follow a bill as it becomes a law. Suppose you and your classmates want to propose a new law to preserve the forests in the state. You could contact any of your state legislators. A bill can originate in either the Senate or the Assembly. Let's say you decide to write a letter to your state senator, Marion Dogood. If Senator Dogood likes your idea, she will have it drafted, or put into written form. Then she is the sponsor of the bill.

Now the bill is ready to be introduced to the Senate when it is in session. The Senate secretary will read the bill aloud. It is given a title and a number, and Senator Dogood's name is included as the sponsor. This is called a "first reading."

From here, the bill goes to a committee for review. If the committee wants to speedily move the bill along, it can simply send the bill on to the next step. Usually, however, the committee carefully studies the bill and listens to interested people at a public meeting called a hearing. For example, with Senator Dogood's open land bill, environmental groups, builders, or other citizens may come to Carson City to give their opinions about the bill. After listening to the public, the committee may decide the bill needs to be amended.

After the committee amends the bill, it goes back to the Senate. It is read aloud, which is called a "second reading." At this point, it can be further amended by the senators. The President of the Senate will schedule a third reading, and your bill is now ready for a vote! If a majority of the senators vote yes, the bill is sent to the Assembly for a vote and the whole process is repeated there. If the senators vote no, the bill can be sent back to the committee for changes that might help it pass.

Once both houses of the legislature pass the bill, it is sent to the governor. He or she may sign it, and the bill becomes a law. However, the governor may "conditionally veto" the bill (which means it will be returned to the legislature for changes), or simply *veto* it. A veto means that the governor does not approve.

The story does not end there. If the governor vetoes a bill, the legislature can attempt to "override" the veto with a two-thirds vote of both houses.

There is another way for your bill to pass without the governor's signature. If the governor does not sign or veto the bill within 45 days, it becomes law.

What Can Citizens Do?

A lot! Citizens can:
- Give ideas for laws to their legislators. Many ideas for bills start this way.
- Attend a public hearing on the day the bill is debated, or "heard." It is a good idea to bring as many people as possible to the meeting. They may get to talk to legislators about their experiences.
- Call or e-mail the governor's office to give an opinion on bills.

Alan Bible
1909–1988

Few have served their native state with more distinction than Alan Bible. And few have done so more quietly. Alan Harvey Bible was born in Lovelock and was raised there and in Fallon. He attended the University of Nevada in Reno, and he wanted to go to law school after graduating. First he went to Washington, D.C., in search of a job on Capitol Hill. There U.S. Senator Pat McCarran offered the one position he had—an elevator operator.

Bible took the job and learned all he could about government. He finally graduated from law school and returned to Reno with a job as an attorney in McCarran's law office. Then he was elected to various political offices. After McCarran died, Bible completed McCarran's term in Washington. Then Bible planned to leave the Senate because he missed living in Nevada, but pressure from Democrats at home and in Washington persuaded him to stay in the Senate. He won reelection and then two more terms before retiring.

As a senator, Bible affected the whole country. He played an important role in winning Senate support for many of the national parks and monuments you may have visited. His only failure was his inability to win approval for a national park in Nevada. Not until after Bible left the Senate would Nevada become the last state in the U.S. to boast of a national park.

Bible worked hard at representing mining, ranching, tourism, and other Nevada industries. He was responsible for the Washoe Project, which helped bring more water to Reno. He also worked to protect the beauty of Lake Tahoe while aiding its important tourist industry.

He was, I believe, the consummate senator. Dignified and efficient, with a lively sense of humor, he worked without seeking public recognition. Alan was attentive to his **constituents,** *but never forgot the needs of our nation as a whole.*

—Ted Stevens, Senator

The only advice we can give to those who would seek a career in public life is to pattern their character after Alan Bible. If they do they will become, as he did, a public official in whom trust was not betrayed.

—Hank Greenspun

NEVADA
PORTRAIT

Jim Gibbons

In 1997, Jim Gibbons became one of Nevada's three U.S. Congressmen. He represented most of the State of Nevada, spanning from Reno to Elko and including the growing suburbs of Las Vegas. He earned a bachelor's and then a master's degree in geology from the University of Nevada, Reno. He also obtained a law degree.

Gibbons also has a distinguished military career. A former combat pilot and decorated veteran of both the Vietnam and Persian Gulf Wars, Congressman Gibbons served in the United States Air Force from 1967 to 1971. Attaining the rank of Colonel, he joined the Nevada Air Guard in 1975.

Gibbons served three terms in the Nevada State Assembly. In 1991, he received the call to report for active combat duty in the Persian Gulf War and joined more than 800 Nevadans from the Nevada Air National Guard in the conflict. He returned home, later ran for Congress, and, in 2006, was elected governor—making him the first member of Congress to be elected to the highest office in the State of Nevada.

"I have always felt a sense of honor in serving my country... be it in the military or in Congress. It is a privilege for me to continue to serve the people of Nevada, a state that I am proud to call home."

The Executive Branch

The executive branch enforces laws made by the legislature. To perform these duties, there are elected officials, numerous agencies, and thousands of state employees. They collect taxes, build highways, and maintain prisons. They give state aid to schools and perform many other necessary tasks.

This branch is headed by the governor, who is elected by the people of the state. The duties of the governor include:

- Submitting a budget on how state tax money will be spent
- Working with the state legislature to get laws passed. He signs bills into law or vetoes bills he disagrees with.
- Appointing hundreds of people to agencies, boards, and commissions
- Supervising the day-to-day work of agencies
- Representing the state in all kinds of ceremonies
- Serving as commander of the Nevada State National Guard
- Granting a pardon to legally release a person from jail

Women in Politics

Women play an important role in Nevada politics. Beginning in the 1980s, a woman has held one of Nevada's seats in the U.S. Congress. Barbara Vucanovich, the first woman elected to Congress from Nevada, served for seven terms before retiring in 1996. In 1998, Shelley Berkley was elected to represent Nevada in the U.S. House of Representatives.

Women also won important statewide offices. In 1990, Sue Wagner became the first woman elected lieutenant governor and later became a member of the powerful Gaming Commission. In 1998, Lorraine Hunt, a former Clark County commissioner, restaurant owner, and singer, was elected lieutenant governor. Frankie Sue Del Papa served three terms as attorney general.

Women also rose to leadership positions in the state legislature. Dina Titus, a political science professor at UNLV, has spent more than a decade as the Democratic leader of the state Senate, while attorney Barbara Buckley became Nevada's first female speaker of the Assembly in 2007.

Ethnic Groups in Government

In addition to serving eight terms in the Senate, Joe Neal became the first African American to run for governor in the general election. Perhaps reflecting the growth of Nevada's Latino population, Bob Coffin and Dario Herrera both ran for congressional seats, while African American and Hispanic men and women worked in other government jobs.

Brian Sandoval

Brian Sandoval was the first Latino to serve as Nevada's attorney general. But being first is nothing new for Sandoval. He practiced law, then won a reputation for hard work in the state legislature. He was a leader of the Gaming Commission. Before his term as attorney general was complete, Nevada's U.S. Senators Harry Reid and John Ensign nominated him to be a U.S. District Judge.

Harry Reid

Harry Reid was born in Searchlight, an old mining camp south of Las Vegas. His father worked in the mines. One of his earliest memories is of his mother picking rocks out of his father's back after a hard day at work.

After finishing middle school, Reid had to leave Searchlight to go to high school. He stayed with a Henderson family during the week and attended Basic High School. It was here that Reid got his start in politics. He was elected as student body president. One of his history teachers, Mike O'Callaghan, would also change Reid's life. O'Callaghan helped set up a scholarship for Reid to attend Utah State University, where Reid majored in history and political science. O'Callaghan also helped Reid get a job on Capitol Hill so he could attend law school in Washington, D.C.

After graduating, Reid practiced law in Henderson, served as city attorney and was elected to the local hospital board. He was elected to the Assembly in 1968, before his twenty-ninth birthday. Two years later, he became Nevada's youngest lieutenant governor. The governor he reported to was his old history teacher, Mike O'Callaghan.

Reid faced adversity during the 1970s. He lost two major elections. His political career seemed over. Then O'Callaghan appointed him chairman of the Nevada Gaming Commission. In that job, Reid had to deal with the state's biggest industry and some of Nevada's biggest problems. Gangsters from other cities had taken over several hotel-casinos on the Las Vegas Strip and were stealing money for their friends back home. Reid helped run several of them out of state, and his political career was revived. In 1982, he won election as a congressman. In 1986, he won the first of his four terms—so far—in the U.S. Senate. He showed his colleagues that he was willing to work hard and earn their trust. He did it so well that they started electing him to leadership positions. Twenty years after entering the U.S. Senate, Reid was chosen to be the majority leader.

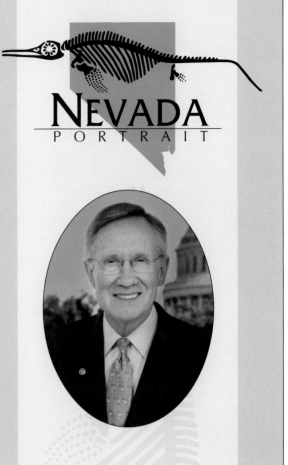

NEVADA
P O R T R A I T

Activity

Government Department Websites

State government affects our lives from the cradle to the grave. When a baby is born, the birth must be recorded at the county courthouse. The doctor and hospital each have a state license. When a person dies, even the undertaker has to have a license.

The state pays part of the cost of educating young people in public schools. The teacher has a state license. Catching a fish, driving a car, and even getting married are licensed by the government.

You can find government department websites by going to the Nevada State Home Page and clicking on the link that says "departments/agencies" [www.state.nv.gov/Agencies.html]. Choose one agency that interests you and click on the agency to learn about it. Choose a way to report what you find. You can write, draw, act out, make a tape recording, or even make a model.

Here are a few of the many departments and agencies in the executive branch:

- Agriculture
- Business and Industry
- Conservation
- Corrections
- Economic Development
- Education
- Employment
- Gaming Control
- Human Resources
- Military
- Minerals
- Motor Vehicles
- Public Safety
- Taxation
- Tourism
- Transportation
- Wildlife

NEVADA
P O R T R A I T

Grant Sawyer
1918–1996

The University of Nevada's Oral History Program published *Hang Tough! Grant Sawyer: An Activist in the Governor's Mansion.* Here are some excerpts from this story of a former governor:

I was born in Twin Falls [Idaho], the youngest of three boys. Our parents divorced when I was three years old. We boys had chores. . . . [W]e milked the cows and we had other assignments—slopping the pigs and that sort of thing—which we did after we came home from school each day. In the summers we would work out in the fields, haying and with the beets and the potatoes. . . . Farm life was pretty bleak, and I didn't care for it at all.

I was no genius, I'll tell you that—but in high school I was interested in drama and I kept my grades up high enough to be eligible to perform in nearly all of the plays.

My brothers and I worked every summer at something. . . . After transferring to the University of Nevada I worked for the highway department one summer with my older brother; another summer, I worked in a mine.

My mother was always involved in taking care of the poor . . . . During the Depression she ran a service that cooked meals for homeless people.

As poor as we were, there was never any question from the day we were born that we brothers were going to go to college. . . . Nobody knew how, but we were going to go!

My whole experience at the University of Nevada [Reno] was wonderful. Relationships that developed while I was there, the whole atmosphere . . . they were two of the best years of my life.

After graduation, Sawyer spent a year in law school, then entered the U.S. Army during World War II. After law school, he moved to Elko and soon was elected district attorney. Later, he filed for governor on the last day he could run.

I had been elected governor of Nevada. My elation was short-lived. My first year in office was stormy, and I never want to go through another year like it.

After a while it began to get to me. You consider yourself an honorable person surrounded by honorable people, and to be constantly accused of being something less gets to be very annoying. I developed the attitude, "I will show these people that Nevadans are like everybody else, maybe better than some other people. We are not the riffraff that they make us out to be!"

Governor Sawyer took several steps designed to change Nevada. Many of his policies resembled those sought by the President of the United States, John F. Kennedy.

- He pushed the legislature to pass civil rights laws.

- He won legislative approval of a Gaming Commission to regulate casinos.

- He created the List of Excluded Persons, called the "Black Book" because it was kept in a black notebook. It listed those people who had links to organized crime, violent criminals, cheaters, and anyone else the state wanted to be kept out of casinos.

The Judicial Branch

There are several basic types of courts in the state. Each type has a different number of courts and judges. In some courts, a judge or judges make a decision of *innocence* or guilt. In other courts, a jury does this.

Municipal Courts

It is through the *municipal* (city) courts that most people come in contact with the legal system. Municipal cases involve *misdemeanor* offenses such as simple *assault* and shoplifting. Motor vehicle violations such as illegal parking, speeding, and driving while intoxicated with alcohol or drugs are also handled by these courts.

Municipal courts are operated by the city or town where they are located.

Justice Courts

The justice courts handle *felony*, gross misdemeanor crime, traffic matters, small claims disputes, *evictions* from rental apartments when people don't pay their rent, and other matters involving less than $7,500. The courts issue protective orders and warrants.

These courts also conduct preliminary hearings to determine if there is enough evidence to hold criminals for trial at district courts.

District (Trial) Courts

These courts preside over cases of felony, gross misdemeanor crimes, civil matters above $7,500, and family law issues, including juvenile crimes, abuse, and neglect. Each court has judges who listen to the *accused* and his or her attorney. The courts conduct jury and non-jury trials.

The judges also hear appeals from lower courts. Nevada has eight district courts, and they vary in size from Clark County, which has 37 judges, to a rural district in which one judge is responsible for all of Humboldt, Lander, and Pershing Counties.

State Supreme Court

The highest court is the State Supreme Court. The seven justices in this court review the decisions and appeals from district trial courts. They must interpret laws that are unclear or that conflict with other laws. The court also supervises the entire judicial system of the state.

Nevada Supreme Court

District (Trial) Courts

Justice Courts

Municipal Courts

Civil and Criminal Cases

In a *civil case*, a person claims to have been injured by the actions of another person. By "injury" the court means any harm done to a person's body, property, reputation, or rights. For example, civil cases involve car accidents, discrimination, or defective products. The injured person is seeking *damages*, usually in the form of money, to pay for his or her loss or injury.

In a *criminal case*, a person is accused of committing a serious crime such as robbery, murder, or drug possession. The person accused of a crime is called a *defendant*. The defendant has a defense attorney who represents him or her in court.

A *prosecutor* is an attorney who represents the State of Nevada. He or she tries to prove that the defendant committed the crime.

A judge oversees the trial and makes sure the rules of the court are followed. The verdict of guilty or not guilty is usually decided by a jury. The jury is made up of citizens who live in the community where the crime took place.

Levels of Government

In Nevada and all other states, there are several levels of government. The **national** government, often called the **federal** government, makes laws that apply to everyone in the country. Other laws are made at the **state** level. Rules called ordinances are made locally at the **county** and **city** levels. We must live by the rules and laws of all the levels of government.

Each level of government has elected men and women who make laws. Each level collects taxes. Each level uses tax money to provide services to the people.

County Government

The county form of government was brought to America from England. A county is simply a smaller region of a state. A county has government leaders and laws, often called "ordinances," though people living in the county still have to obey the rules and laws of the state and federal governments.

Nevada is divided into 17 counties. One county, Ormsby, was consolidated with its major city, Carson City. So, Carson City is its own county.

Each county is run by a small group of county commissioners.

One town in each of the counties is the county seat where the county government is located. You can get a passport, a copy of your birth certificate, or view public documents such as voting lists, tax records, and real estate records at the county courthouse.

County government is responsible for county courts and law enforcement. If you are speeding on the highways, you may get pulled over by the flashing lights of a county police car. Counties often run health clinics, build roads, parks, and libraries, and provide other services for the people.

City Government

Local municipal (city or town) government is even closer to home than county government. A city is managed by one of the following:

- mayor and city council
- city manager and city council
- commissioners

How these groups function depends on the location. In Boulder City, for example, council members used to choose the mayor, but now he is elected separately. Las Vegas has seven city council members, with the mayor presiding over meetings.

Like counties, cities and towns build and maintain roads, have a police and fire department, and run parks and recreation programs. They make laws for traffic, zoning, and other matters. Cities provide programs like fireworks on the Fourth of July and other special holiday celebrations.

Government Services

Today, national, state, and local governments do more than make laws and enforce them. They do more than tax people. Governments have established many agencies that regulate

Nevada Counties and County Seats

HUMBOLDT
Winnemucca

ELKO
• Elko

PERSHING
• Lovelock

Battle Mountain

WASHOE
Reno

CHURCHILL

LANDER   EUREKA
Eureka •

WHITE PINE
• Ely

LYON
• Yerington

• Fallon

Minden
DOUGLAS

MINERAL
• Hawthorne

NYE
• Tonopah

Carson City

STOREY
Virginia City

ESMERALDA
Goldfield •

Pioche •

LINCOLN

CLARK

Las Vegas

N
W   E
S

Nevada: A Journey of Discovery

many activities of the citizens and provide services.

State and local governments collect taxes to establish and pay for public education, roads, police and fire protection, libraries, public health services, job services, welfare support, and many other services.

Nevada helps the unemployed, disadvantaged children, the elderly, disabled people, and the mentally ill get cash for food, clothing, and shelter.

The Employment Department helps all people get job training and find jobs. The office matches workers and employers. It also provides money to help workers who have been laid off to cover expenses until they find a new job.

Taxes pay for programs that protect our land and water from pollution. Taxes pay for the protection of animals.

Firefighters are paid with tax dollars. In 2002, hundreds of firefighters battled over 10,000 acres of Sierra fires. The fires had whirlwinds of flames that forced evacuation and sent crews scrambling to safety.

Education

Public schools are also a government service. Tax dollars are used to pay for school buildings, teachers' salaries, and textbooks. If you attend a private school, your parents pay a fee for your education.

Since state and local tax money is used to pay for public education, the state legislature can require school districts to do certain things. Students must attend 180 days of classes each year. They must meet standards in core subjects—reading, writing, science, social studies, communication, mathematics, health, and fitness.

Local School Districts

The voters of each school district elect members of the school board. The boards adopt policies to fit local needs, make decisions about teachers and school staff, set learning standards, and help choose teaching materials.

Each county has a school district. Some, like Clark County, are so large it is hard for educators to keep up with all the new schools needed each year in Las Vegas and surrounding communities.

Activity

Higher Education

Nevada students can study a wide variety of subjects after high school graduation. The state has two universities, the University of Nevada, Las Vegas (UNLV), and the University of Nevada, Reno. There are also two four-year colleges and three community colleges, in addition to an institute that conducts research on the desert and a medical school linked to both universities. UNLV has the state's only law school.

Because Nevada is so large, most of the schools offer distance education classes. Students hundreds of miles away from campuses can use the Internet and watch videos, take exams, engage in discussions on-line with classmates, and do many of the things that students on campus can do.

Nevada's large size means that its community colleges serve large areas. The Community College of Southern Nevada serves Clark, Lincoln, Nye, and Esmeralda Counties. Great Basin College serves Elko, Eureka, Humboldt, Lander, and White Pine Counties, and offers a few four-year degrees because it is about 240 miles from any other four-year school. Western Nevada Community College offers classes in Carson City, Douglas County, and Churchill County. Truckee Meadows Community College is in Washoe County.

Which college would you like to attend? Contact a few of these schools and compare their admissions requirements, courses, tuition costs, and class size.

Doing Your Part

Citizenship means membership in a nation, including all rights, duties, and responsibilities that go with it. As a citizen of the United States, you can expect government to protect your rights to life, liberty, and property.

You have the right to free speech, but you also have the responsibility to speak respectfully and kindly to others, and to listen to their points of view.

You have the right to freedom of religion, so you have the responsibility to respect the right of others to belong to a different religion, or to no religion at all.

"Musts" of Citizenship

Certain duties are "musts" of citizenship. You must attend school for a required number of years. You must obey the laws. You must pay taxes. You have the right to a jury in court, so you must do jury duty if summoned. Today we have a volunteer military, but you must serve in the armed forces if called. You must respect the rights of others.

"Shoulds" of Citizenship

American citizens also have responsibilities that they "should" do. These "shoulds" are not required by law, but they are important if democracy is to work. At age 18 you gain the privilege to vote. You should vote if you are eligible, and you should encourage others to vote. You should become informed and understand the problems facing our local, state, and national governments.

You should support the political party of your choice and other groups working to improve government.

Volunteer

You should volunteer to work without pay when something needs to be done in your community. You can pick up trash in public places and never litter. You can volunteer to work during city clean-up days. You can help younger children read or do math. You can help older people or people with disabilities with yard work, housework, or transportation.

Find a way you can volunteer to make your community better.

Activity

Be a Person of Character

Can you imagine a place where no one is ever hurt by another person? Where crime does not exist? Where educated people work together to make things better for everyone? A country and a state are only as strong as the character of the people who live there. The higher the level of honesty, morality, and fairness in a community, the better the place will be for everyone.

Do your part! You should always:

- Choose your actions wisely.
- Tell the truth.
- Be kind and helpful to others.
- Respect the ideas of others. Never ridicule or "put down" other people.
- Obey rules.
- Be polite.
- Learn to work and do a good job.
- Respect parents, teachers, and leaders.
- Take care of property—never break or destroy it.
- Help keep your home, yard, and classroom clean.
- Get an education—work hard on all your school-work.
- Ask for help when you need it.

Adult leaders have the job of solving problems in their cities or towns. Some of the things adult leaders do are:

- Take care of children.
- Help people get a job, food, and a place to live.
- Protect the environment.
- Help businesses so people will have jobs.
- Provide schools for children and adults.
- Help their community grow.
- Vote and elect good leaders.

How else can teens and adults help provide a good life in our country? Choose one of the items on the lists above, or think of other items, and write or tell about an experience you have had that shows or does not show that kind of character.

Voting: A Citizen's Responsibility

Unlike people in many parts of the world, citizens of New Jersey and all states in the United States have the right to vote for the people they would like to have represent them. Every American citizen over the age of 18 has the right to vote unless he or she is in jail for committing a crime.

Unfortunately, many people choose not to participate in elections. In 2000, only 51% of Americans participated in the presidential election, the closest election in history. And votes do count. In 1914, Francis Newlands won a term in the Senate by 40 votes. In 1998, Harry Reid beat John Ensign by only 428 votes.

Registering to Vote

To vote, a person must be registered with the county. This is done at shopping centers, homes, and other places. Many people choose to register to vote when getting or renewing a driver's license. There is no charge for registering.

Most people register as either Democrats or Republicans, or they choose to be a member of another smaller party. Some people belong to no party and register as Independents.

Vote for Me!

Part of our democratic form of government is voting for good leaders and telling them what we want them to do.

It is the responsibility of the citizens to vote for leaders who will be fair to all groups of people, be reliable (do what they promise), and make wise decisions. Voters should choose leaders who have the courage to stand up for what they believe is right.

What do you think?

- Why do so few Americans participate in the election process?
- What can be done to encourage people to use their important right to vote?

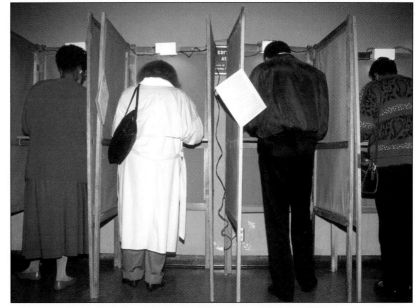

Voters are a vital part of a democratic government.

Activity

Combating Prejudice

Probably no other problem in the world has caused as much pain and suffering as prejudice. You know that prejudice is when a person is treated with indifference or ridicule on the basis of his or her "group." That group could be a race, gender, religion, or economic class.

Remember the time before the Civil War when slavery caused terrible suffering? Men and women brought from Africa against their will were judged, solely on their race, as being less intelligent than white people. It was also widely believed that black people were not entitled to proper food, clothes, shelter, education, or family ties. At the time, there were no laws to protect the rights of people of color, whether slave or free.

Remember times in history when whole groups of people were barred from jobs, jailed, and killed because of their religion? Though rarely part of religious doctrine, the belief that "It's our way or no way," can be a form of prejudice.

Today we have laws that protect people against some kinds of prejudice. It is against the law to bar a person from voting, moving into a neighborhood, or going to a public school on the basis of gender or race. In the hearts of people, however, many kinds of prejudice still exist.

Analyze a time in history or in modern times when prejudice caused suffering. It could be prejudice against an entire race of people, or prejudice against the poor or people with disabilities. It could be prejudice that you have seen or felt. Share your thoughts in writing, art, drama, or music.

Chapter 11 Review

What Do You Remember?

1. Where and when was the United States Constitution written?

2. "We, the people of the United States . . ." is the beginning of what important government document?

3. Congress added 10 important amendments, called the _____ ____ ____, to the U.S. Constitution. What are some of these rights?

4. Define "Rule of Law" and tell how it is important to our country and our state.

5. What are the two main political parties of the United States?

6. What are the three branches of government, and what does each do?

7. How many senators does each state send to the U.S. Senate in Washington, D.C? How many representatives does Nevada send to the U.S. Congress?

8. Describe some ways citizens can influence the laws that are made.

9. Who is our current governor, and what are some of his/her duties?

10. If you must go to court for shoplifting, what kind of court would hear your case? What kinds of cases go before the State Supreme Court?

11. Describe the purpose of four levels of government. List at least five public services that are paid for with tax money.

Activity

Balance Individual Rights and Public Needs

Both lawmakers and the judicial system try to balance the rights of individuals with the needs and rights of the public.

Mr. Smith, for example, has the right to drive his car whenever he wishes. The rest of the people in his town, however, want clean air, and cars pollute the air and use valuable fuel resources.

Joe Meeker, a ninth-grader, wants to skateboard through the neighborhood park and jump off the stair railings going down to a picnic area. People walking on the sidewalks, however, don't want to worry about being in the way of a skateboarder. They are worried that Joe might get hurt on the stair railing, and that the railing will break. They don't want to eat lunch near noisy skateboarders.

Mrs. Jeffries wants to walk her dog in the same park, and she doesn't think people mind if her frisky dog runs over and jumps up on a group of children playing on the grass. She knows the dog is harmless. Some children love the dog, but others don't like dogs with dirty paws jumping on them.

- What rules and laws can assure that both the rights of individuals and the needs of the public are met?
- What other situations can you think of where rights and needs seem to conflict with each other?

Activity

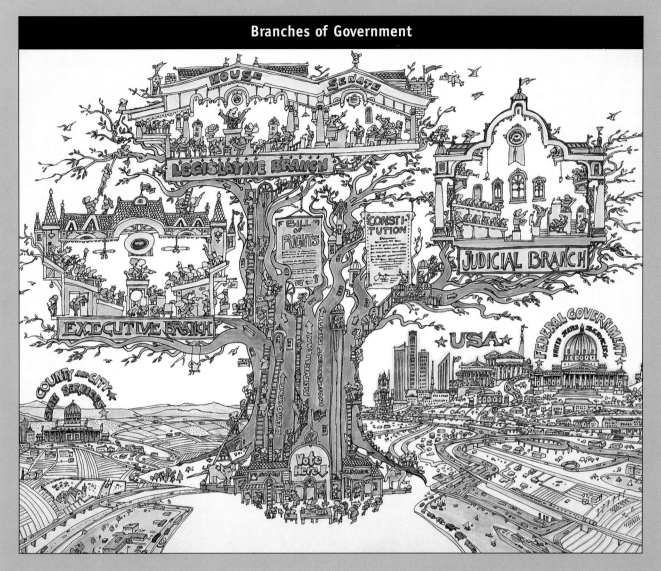

It's Your Government!

Remember, all levels of government—national, state, and local—have three branches of government—legislative, executive, and judicial.

This means that laws are made in the legislatures of both Nevada and Washington, D.C. It means that a president is head of the executive branch of the United States, and a governor is head of the executive branch of a state. There are courts at all levels.

Look at the drawing above of the United States government.

1. Find the two documents that are the basis for our government today.
2. Find the symbols of the political parties.
3. Find the people voting for representatives who will vote in the legislature.
4. Find the two houses in the legislative branch. Remember, both houses must pass all bills. Who must sign them before they become law?
5. Find the jury and the judge in the judicial branch.
6. Find the federal, state, county, and city services provided by government.

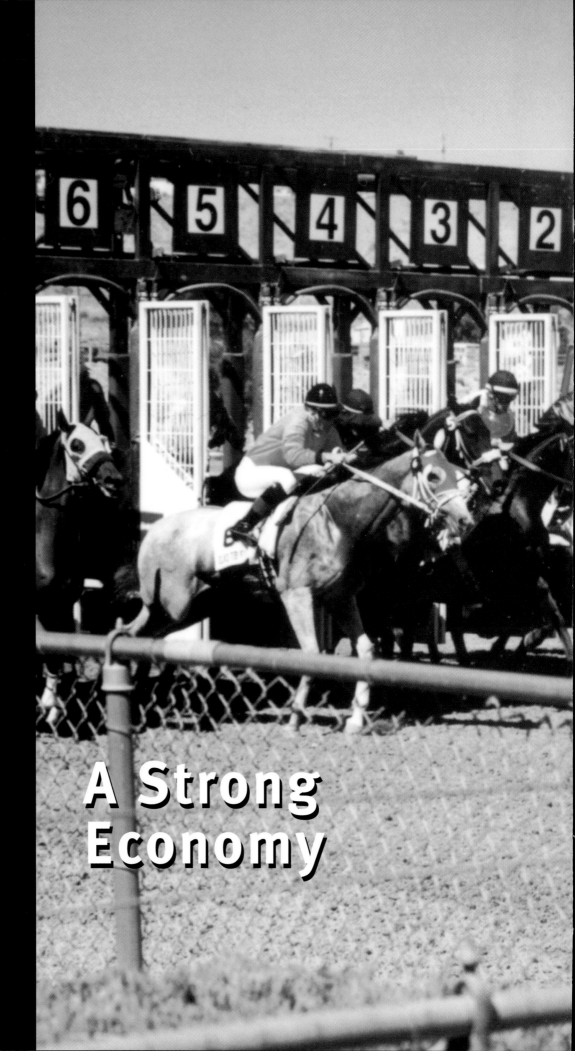

A Strong Economy

Chapter **12**

Tourists and local people come to Elko to cheer on their favorite horse.

Photo by Travis Miller

Economic Systems

*E*conomics is the study of production, distribution, and consumption of *goods* and *services*. In other words, it is people and machines making, shipping, selling, and buying.

Economics affects all of us. In a strong economy, adults have a job, earn money, save for the future, and buy goods and services they need. In a poor economy, many people are out of work or earn such a low wage they cannot afford the basic things that make life enjoyable.

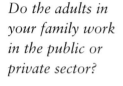

Do the adults in your family work in the public or private sector?

Our Free Market System

In the United States we have a *free market system*, also called *capitalism*. Anyone is free to start a business and make or sell goods. The owner can keep the business for years or sell it. The owner chooses whom to hire and decides how much to pay them. All businesses have to follow government regulations, and almost all businesses pay taxes, but the government does not own or run most businesses.

How does this work? Each day, millions of men and women in the United States work in factories, offices, and on farms. The government does not tell the people where to work. It does not decide where most of the businesses should be built. It does not set prices for most goods and services. Yet the work is done, prices are set, businesses and workers earn money, and most Americans are able to buy the products they need.

How does the economy work with so little planning? The desire of most people to improve their own lives makes it work. People make decisions to get an education and job training and to find a job that gives them satisfaction and income. They are free to find jobs in any city.

The government takes part in many economic activities, but individuals and private businesses are the backbone of the American economy.

Public and Private Sectors

Even though we have a free market system, where businesses are privately owned, the government also hires many people to work in its many departments and agencies.

Government jobs are part of the *public sector* because the workers work for the public. They might be teachers, post office workers, park rangers, or judges. There are hundreds of government jobs in the public sector.

All other jobs are part of the *private sector* because the businesses are privately owned. Men and women in the private sector work in stores, hotels, factories, farms, research plants, and banks. They work in businesses of all kinds that are not owned or run by the government.

Economic Systems in the World

Capital is the tools, machines, and other items used to make new products to be sold. Capital is also money used to start and run a business. Different economic systems use capital in different ways.

Here is a list of some of the world's economic systems:

- **Tribal:** People live near each other in a community and work together to produce food and goods. The group trades with other groups. There might be private ownership, but the whole group shares the use of land and many goods.

- **Capitalism (Free Market):** The majority of capital and business is privately owned and run by citizens. There are, however, government regulations and rules, and the government hires people to work in public service jobs.

- **Socialism:** There are various forms of ownership and control by the government.

- **Fascism:** All capital is privately owned, but it is tightly controlled by the government.

- **Communism:** All capital and means of production are owned and controlled by the government.

Government and the Economy

National, state, and local governments have major roles in our free market system.

GOVERNMENT ROLES	EXAMPLES
Establish and enforce laws that affect economic activity. The Federal Trade Commission investigates business activities.	Laws try to: • Prevent companies from taking unfair advantage of each other • Ban misleading advertising • Set safety standards for workplaces • Set minimum wages • Prohibit businesses from discriminating on the basis of race, sex, or age • Protect the environment • Permit businesses to operate only in specific zones (areas of town)
Provide goods and services for the public.	Governments on all levels provide many services at little or no direct cost to the users, including police and fire protection, roads, parks, job training and placement, and schools. The national government also runs the military and a postal service. Tax money supplies the government with funds to provide services. Some people receive financial aid in the form of welfare, social security, unemployment, and medical plans. This money also comes from taxes.
Regulate public utilities.	Utilities include electricity, gas, water, sewers, and local telephone service. The government grants special status to utility companies so they may operate without competition, but rates are regulated.
Work for economic stability. All national banks belong to the Federal Reserve System.	There are ways the U.S. government tries to boost the economy. One way is to provide jobs. Workers might build new buildings or highways. The government may also cut taxes so people have more money to spend. Then businesses will produce and sell more goods, which provides more jobs. Controlling interest rates helps stabilize the economy. Interest rates are set by the Federal Reserve System and affect the amount of money that will be loaned. Lower interest rates encourage borrowing and spending, which helps the economy.
Protect the works of authors and inventors. The U.S. Patent and Trademark Office awards patents for new machines, methods, and manufactured products. The Copyright Office of the Library of Congress in Washington, D.C., issues copyrights.	An inventor may keep the patent, sell the patent, or license the rights to a manufacturer. Licensing gives the inventor a fee every time the invention is made and sold. If someone else wants to use copyrighted material, he or she must get permission and pay any required usage fees.

When there is a large supply of something, the cost is lower. When there is a small supply of something, the cost is higher. For example, if a store has too many basketballs, the balls might go on sale.

water pipes, and scientists develop medicines. People pay other people for these services and many more.

Supply, Demand, and Price

The quantity of goods and services available affects how much things cost. We call this *supply and demand*.

Supply and demand influences the price of goods and services. When there is a *shortage* of something many people want and need, the price often goes up because people are willing to pay more to get it. Of course, if people cannot afford an item, they cannot buy it no matter how much they want to. What do you want to buy that you cannot afford right now?

Companies who produce goods have to try to balance the supply they produce with the demand. Supply is also affected by the *competition* among sellers. If three companies produce DVD players, there will be a greater supply than if only two companies produce all of the DVD players, and the price may go down because each company wants to offer the lowest price.

However, competition among *consumers* can also affect a price. It works kind of like an auction, where so many people want the same thing that they will pay more to get it. If a famous performer

Goods and Services

Our economy is based on producing, selling, and buying goods and services. Everyone needs basic things to survive—food, clothing, and shelter. Other things—such as books, computers, certain brands of clothes, your favorite food, sports equipment, CD players, musical instruments, and automobiles—are probably also important to your lifestyle. All these items are goods.

You also need services from other people. Nurses and doctors help people who are sick or injured. Teachers educate students, pilots fly business people or tourists to other places, plumbers install

Do the adults in your family work to provide goods, services, or both? What jobs do they do?

The quantity supplied is the amount of goods that producers plan to sell during a given period at a given price. If other things remain the same, the quantity supplied increases as price increases. Why is this so?

What if You Are Selling?

The amount of goods or services producers plan to sell depends on many factors. The main ones are:
- The selling price of the goods or services
- The cost of resources used to produce the goods
- Technology (New technologies create new products and lower the costs of producing existing products.)
- The number of other suppliers (competition)
- Expected future prices (Will people wait until the price goes down or buy now before the price goes up?)

What if You Are Buying?

The goods or services consumers plan to buy depends on many factors. The main ones are:
- The price of the goods
- The prices of related goods (Is another product about as good?)
- Income (Can people afford it now, or later?)
- Population (How many people want the same thing?)
- Preferences (Will people prefer a product over another product?)
- Expected future prices

comes to town to put on a concert, and there are only a limited amount of seats in the concert hall, the price for tickets could be very high. However, if a performer sings outdoors at a fairground and thousands of people can attend, the cost of tickets will probably be lower.

Supply and demand also influences production of goods and services. Businesses want to produce what the people will buy.

Substitution

In many cases, people will pay a high price for an item if they really want it and have enough money to pay for it. In other cases, people may substitute one item for a less expensive one. If a student wants an expensive brand of clothes but has little money, the student will have to buy other clothes that don't cost so much. Traveling across the country? If you can afford it, you will buy a plane ticket, but if you can't, you might buy a bus ticket that costs less.

The Supply of Natural Resources

Water is a vital resource supplied by nature. People who use the water must find ways to keep their demand in line with the supply. A long period of drought in the West is currently affecting the water level of the Colorado River and Lake Mead. People in Las Vegas have been given limits on watering their lawns and washing their cars, and the cost of water is rising.

Workers Are Part of Supply and Demand

If hundreds of teenagers want to cut lawns during summer vacation, they will probably all earn low wages. However, if most teenagers wanted to sell clothes in stores, the few teens who were willing to cut lawns could earn a lot of money. Why? Their services would be more in demand.

Opportunity Costs, Tradeoffs, and Choices

Every working day in mines, factories, shops, and offices and on farms and construction sites across our country, millions of people produce a vast amount of goods and services valued in the billions of dollars. The quantities of goods and services that can be produced are limited by the:

- Available resources (including goods, natural resources, and educated human beings)
- Technology (including the expertise to make and use electronics and machines)

At any given time, we have a fixed amount of resources to produce goods and services. We cannot make, buy, or use everything. We have to make choices that involve *tradeoffs*—we must give up something to get something else. When land developers take farmland and divide it up for homes, they are making a tradeoff.

All the things we do and buy are part of an opportunity. Every opportunity has a cost in time and money. This is called an *opportunity cost*. With every choice, we try to get the highest value.

Perhaps you have $25 to spend. You could spend it over a week on fast food, or you could spend it all today on a pair of jeans that you could wear for a long time. You could get an expensive haircut or a cheaper one, buy a concert ticket, or save your money for college tuition.

How will price affect what you buy? What choices will give you the most value for your money? What choices might be the most valuable for your community?

Make a list of the things you spent money on during the last week or the last month. What tradeoffs did you have to consider? What value did you receive? Could you have made better decisions?

Supply and Demand in the Mines and on the Farms

The laws of supply and demand also shape mining and the farming and ranching industries. When the booms in Virginia City, Tonopah, and Goldfield ended, the problem was that the ore had been dug out. But today, when more gold is on the market, the price often falls. You learned in an earlier chapter how the need for silver coins in history affected its price and production.

Economic Growth

Many things must come together for a nation to produce and sell goods and services. The better a nation can do this, the more economic growth it will have. Until resources are used to produce and sell goods, the people of a country may always be economically poor. A state and a nation must have:

- **Natural resources:** land, minerals, trees, sunshine, and water
- **Capital:** items such as tools, supplies, and equipment needed to produce other items; the money needed to buy these items
- **Labor:** people who work or are seeking work, and their education and skills. Also the people who run their own businesses (entrepreneurs)
- **Technology:** scientific and business research and inventions

Trade and Specialization

As in the earlier periods of history, people can produce for themselves all the goods they consume, or they can concentrate on producing one or a few goods and then trade (buy and sell) with others. Producing only one good or service is called *specialization*.

In almost all human activities, what one person does easily is very hard for another person to do well. The same applies to land and resources. One plot of land is fertile but has no mineral deposits; another plot of land has a great view but is not good for growing crops.

Trading our specialized skills for those of others is the foundation of our strong economy. We trade with the local farmer, with businesses in other states and other nations of the world. Without trade, we would have no bananas, coffee, foreign cars, or the inexpensive clothes we wear.

Look at the labels in your closet, kitchen, and garage to see how this principle works in your life.

▶ Drawing by Jon Burton

A Bicycle Factory

A bicycle is a simple example of producing goods by using natural resources, capital, labor, and technology.

Study this artwork of a bicycle factory.

- What natural resources are being used?
- What capital is needed?
- What training and education might the labor force have?
- What examples of technology do you see?
- What kinds of job specialization do you see?

Measuring the Economy

Government and business leaders want to know how the economy is doing so they can keep the economy strong. Economists measure production, costs of living, and employment and report it in these ways:

- **Gross Domestic Product (GDP):** the value of all goods and services produced in a country during a year

- **Consumer Price Index (CPI):** prices paid by urban consumers for a representative sample of goods and services including food, housing, clothes, and transportation

  Compare the buying power of the U.S. dollar in one year with its buying power in another year at http://stats.bls.gov.cpi

- **Unemployment Rate:** the percentage of the labor force that is unemployed

A person is counted as unemployed if he or she is over age 16 and is actively looking for a job but cannot find one. (Students, those who choose not to work, and retirees are not counted in the unemployment rate.)

In a healthy nation and state, most of the people who want a job would have one.

In April 2004 the national unemployment rate was 5.6%. Nevada's unemployment rate at the same time was 6.4%. That means that for every 100 people who were either working or looking for work, 6 people in Nevada could not find a job.

To check the current national and state unemployment rates, see the website of the U.S. Department of Labor at: http://stats.bls.gov

Activity

U.S. Unemployment Rate Since 1990

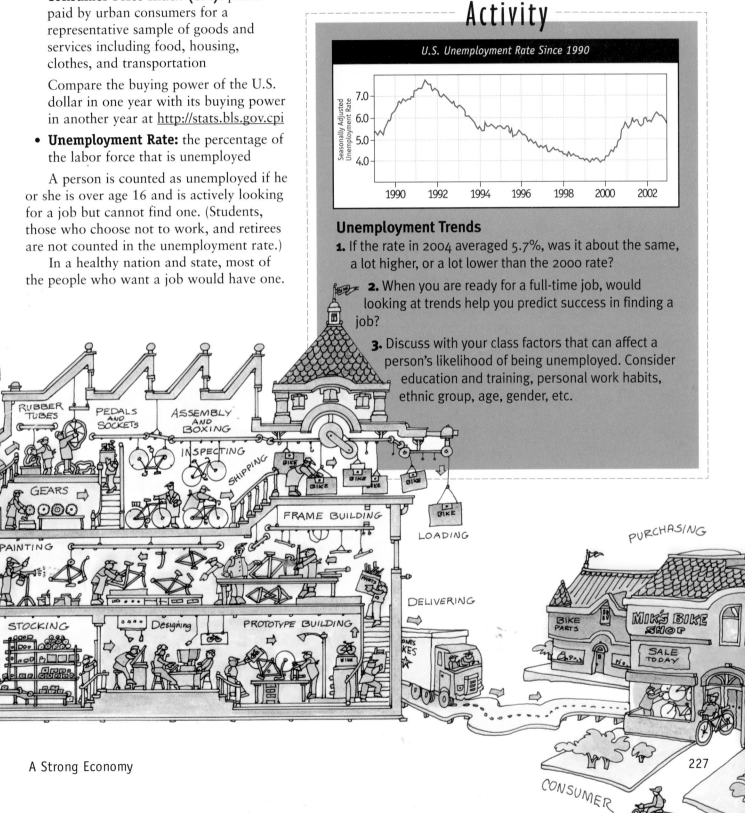

Unemployment Trends

1. If the rate in 2004 averaged 5.7%, was it about the same, a lot higher, or a lot lower than the 2000 rate?

2. When you are ready for a full-time job, would looking at trends help you predict success in finding a job?

3. Discuss with your class factors that can affect a person's likelihood of being unemployed. Consider education and training, personal work habits, ethnic group, age, gender, etc.

Did you know that without mining, you could not have a computer, telephone, or television? What metals are used in this equipment?

Mining gold and silver are important to the state's economy. This worker is pouring liquid gold.

Produced in Nevada

Nevada never has been known as a manufacturing state, at least not in the way that you might think of the steel mills of Pittsburgh or automobiles of Detroit. But Nevada produces a lot of important goods and services.

Mining

Nevada is still among the biggest mineral producers in the United States—indeed, in the world. "The Silver State" remains Nevada's nickname, but in recent years mining has involved much more than the precious metal that attracted would-be millionaires to the Comstock Lode. Nevada continued to produce large quantities of gold throughout the 1990s and into the 2000s.

Gold production has been crucial in an area referred to as the Carlin Trend. In some years, the Carlin Trend has been responsible for about half of all of the gold produced in the U.S.

The geothermal and oil industries have contributed to a national quest for energy sources. Other minerals you may not think of remain very important. They include coal, gypsum, iron, lead, lime, manganese, mercury, molybdenum, oil, opals, salt, talc, tungsten, turquoise, uranium, and zinc.

Mining continues to produce hundreds of millions of dollars in profits and payroll for Nevada. It is still one of the state's most important industries.

Tourism

Nevada is known throughout the world as a tourist mecca. Las Vegas is the most famous part of the state—the subject of major sporting events, the home of celebrity performers like Celine Dion and Rita Rudner, the site of big concerts by everyone from Britney Spears to Luciano Pavarotti, and fabulous casino-hotels.

Las Vegas even has its own popular network television series like "Las Vegas," about security in a casino, and "CSI: Las Vegas," about crime scene investigators.

Photo by Madelyn Suttles ◄

Photo by Kerrick James ◄

Tourists and locals cycle at Red Rock Canyon. How might this help our economy?

Photo by Travis Miller ▶

The Basques were sheepherders who first came to Elko County from Europe in large numbers between 1860 and the 1920s. For over 40 years their descendants have held the Basque Festival in Elko. The festival brings tourists from around the country.

Photo by Travis Miller ▶

Anthony Zuiker, who created the show, grew up in Nevada and attended UNLV. He learned what he needed to know to write the show by riding with policemen to crime scenes.

Las Vegas also boasts nationally important sporting events. The National Finals Rodeo, NASCAR stock car races, and championship boxing matches have a long history there.

But Nevada is more than Las Vegas. Tourists come to the casinos and natural beauty of Reno and Lake Tahoe, the starkly beautiful Pyramid Lake, Great Basin National Park near Ely, Lehman Caves, Red Rock Canyon, the casinos of Laughlin, Mesquite, Elko, and West Wendover, and the Black Rock Desert. Every hotel in town is sold out for Elko's Cowboy Poetry Festival in January. And residents go to the places the tourists frequent and to numerous local and state parks, cultural events, and museums.

Patricia Marchese, an administrator in the Clark County Parks and Recreation Department, explains the value of building up the arts and culture:

> Not everyone is interested in sports or is good at them, and there is a lot of research concluding that the arts and dance are just as good at keeping people on the straight and narrow. . . . You have top Broadway shows here, Cezannes here, Russian jewels here, all in casinos. I would hope this would turn into an enlightenment that will lead people to greater support of the local arts.

Agriculture

Because Nevada has so little water, it might seem unlikely that farming remains an important part of the economy. To the contrary, the state boasts a lot of livestock and crops. Farmers and ranchers raise cattle, chickens, hogs, horses, and sheep. Farmers raise alfalfa, barley, corn, oats, potatoes, and wheat.

Retail Sales and Warehousing

Just like in the rest of the country, people in Nevada make a living selling goods to tourists and residents. People from all over the world shop in the unique stores of our casinos and downtown areas. In Reno, retail and warehousing employ more people than hotels and casinos. Goods from many places are stored tax-free in Reno warehouses, waiting to be shipped across the country.

This boy and his sheep are competing in the Elko County Fair.

Workers Earn Money

Most businesses hire employees and pay them either an hourly wage or a yearly salary.

The federal government sets a *minimum wage* that applies to all workers 18 years of age or older. States may also set their own minimum wage as long as it does not go below the federal wage. Employers cannot pay less than the minimum wage for most jobs, but they can pay higher.

The minimum wage applies to all workers in the state, but the number of employees earning tips beyond their base wage is well above the national average. These workers include not just waiters and waitresses, but also casino dealers. Their tips are not part of their salary, but they help explain why dealers and valet parking attendants often make only minimum wages, or close to it.

Nevada follows the federal minimum wage rate. It was $5.15 per hour in 2004.

Right-to-work

Nevada is a right-to-work and fire-at-will state. Employers can dismiss employees at any time and without any stated reason, but they cannot discriminate against anyone on the basis of gender, race, color, national origin, age, religion, or disability.

Training Now to Make Money Later

Sometimes jobs that need the most workers do not pay the highest salaries. While there are lots of jobs for *retail* salespeople (people who work in stores), and waitresses and waiters, the wages are low because these jobs do not require much training or education.

Are you willing to sacrifice time and money now to get an education and earn more money later?

Jobs that pay the highest salaries often require the most education. But education, especially after high school, is expensive in time, effort, and money. Economists use terms like "opportunity costs and benefits" to describe the trade-off between effort, sacrifice, and reward on the job.

This is something students should consider carefully when they think about training for certain kinds of work. Are the students willing to study at a university for many years? Are they willing to pay the cost of all the training?

A Great Job

What do workers want from a job?
- ✔ Steady work without layoffs
- ✔ Fair wages
- ✔ Health insurance
- ✔ Paid sick days, vacations, and holidays
- ✔ Safety in the workplace
- ✔ Appreciation for good work

What do employers want from workers? They want employees who:
- ✔ Are trained to do the job
- ✔ Are careful and accurate
- ✔ Work without wasting time
- ✔ Get along with other workers
- ✔ Come to work on time each day
- ✔ Keep customers satisfied

Other questions are harder to answer. Are there any guarantees a person will like the work once he or she gets into a profession? Will he or she be able to earn a good living?

Some people work at jobs that take a lot of training but don't pay as much money as other jobs. Teaching and social work are often in this category. Many workers are willing to give up some "opportunity benefits" for the satisfaction they hope to feel on the job and the help they hope to give to others.

Wages and Productivity

The hourly wage or yearly salary a person earns is sometimes affected by his or her *productivity* and by the market value of the goods or services he or she produces. A car salesman often earns a high sales commission because of the high cost of cars. A student who serves fast food gets paid less because the food is a low-cost item. What jobs pay workers according to how much they produce?

The median (middle) household income in Nevada in 2004 was $57,600.

The per capita (per person, or per worker) wage was $16.24 per hour.

The median household income includes all working adults who live in the home. Why is household income larger than per capita income?

Activity

Working in Nevada

As in all states, there are many kinds of jobs in Nevada, all requiring different amounts of skill, education, and training. Our state is different from all others in that our largest employers are casino-hotels. It takes a huge staff to clean thousands of rooms, prepare and serve food, run the games, and manage the business. What employer hires the second largest number of workers?

Study the information on these charts to compare the largest number of available jobs to the salaries earned at these jobs. What jobs are not on the charts at all? Do more research on these jobs to see what career you might want when you get older. Talk to workers to find out the best and worst things about their jobs.

The figures in these charts are for December, 2003.

The Industries That Employ the Largest Numbers of Workers

Industry	Persons Employed	% of the Workforce
Leisure and Hospitality	298,860	28.2%
Trade, Transportation, and Utilities	193,810	18.3%
Education and Health Services	136,050	12.8%
Professional and Business Services	116,330	11.0%

The Largest Employers

Bellagio, LLC
MGM Grand Hotel/Casino
Gold Coast Hotel & Casino
Clark County School District
Mandalay Bay Resort and Casino

The Highest-Paying Industries

Industry	Persons Employed	Mean Wage Per Hour
Natural Resources and Mining	8,820	$23.12
Public Administration	67,720	$21.79
Education and Health Services	136,050	$21.42
Construction	95,200	$20.44

Source: Current employment statistics, Nevada Dept. of Employment, in cooperation with the Bureau of Labor Statistics, U.S. Dept. of Labor

The Global Market

During the end of the 20th century, a global market became a reality. Almost every commodity, product, and service is now produced and sold around the world. Computers and the Internet have linked the entire globe in a web of information, trade, and finance.

Today, California is the nation's bridge to the Pacific Rim (countries that border the Pacific Ocean), especially Asia and Canada. Nevada's goods are moved by train and truck to the seaports of California. From there they are shipped across the Pacific Ocean to people in faraway places.

Even though Nevada was only 44th in the 50 states in exports in 2000, workers made money by making and selling goods. Exporting goods still provides jobs. In 2000, it took the work of over 6,000 people to organize, store, and ship goods to other states and countries.

A commodity is any useful thing that is bought or sold. Products of agriculture, mining, or manufacturing are commodities.

Nevada's Exports

Top Export Markets:
(in order of total sales)

Canada
Japan
Mexico
European nations
South/Central America
The Caribbean
China

Top Export Products:
(in order of total sales, for a total of $1.2 billion)

Transportation equipment
Electronic and electric equipment
Manufacturing products
Industrial machinery and computers
Scientific and measuring instruments

(Source: U.S. Commerce Department and the U.S. Agriculture Department, 2000)

World Trade Terms

When you listen to the news, you will often hear the words below. Discuss with your class what the words mean. Were the bananas you ate this week imported? Was there a tariff added onto the cost, or were the bananas part of a free trade agreement between countries? Who made money growing, selling, and shipping the bananas? Who benefited from bringing them into the country? What other goods would you not have if countries did not trade with each other? How does trade affect the standard of living for the world's people?

Rows of shipping containers are filled with all kinds of goods that are shipped overseas and sold to customers.

Import: to bring goods into the country

Export: to ship goods out of the country

Quota: a limit on quantities of goods shipped in or out of the country

Embargo: a government order prohibiting the departure of ships carrying certain goods; an order prohibiting transportation of certain goods by any method

Tariff: a tax on imports or exports. Tariffs raise the price of goods from other countries so consumers will buy less expensive local goods. High tariffs are used to protect the industries of a country and the jobs in those industries.

Free trade: to trade freely between countries without tariffs and other trade barriers. The North American Free Trade Agreement (NAFTA) went into effect in 1994. How does it affect trade?

The Mighty Dollar

Today, we use money to buy what we need, but it wasn't always so. American Indians used the barter system to exchange items they had for those they wanted. Fur traders sometimes used gold or silver coins from their native country. Once towns and cities were established, banks printed paper money called bank notes. The holder of a note could come in and exchange it for silver or gold or use it as money to buy things.

After a time, state governments printed money, but people in other states sometimes did not trust its worth. Later, the federal government printed paper money and made coins that could be used across the country.

Saving, Loaning, and Interest

Saving money is almost as important as earning it. In the early days, people saved money in fruit jars, under the mattress, or in a hole out in the yard. Today, banks and credit unions are convenient and safe places to keep savings. Savings up to $100,000 are insured by the federal government. That means if the bank fails, the federal government will give you back your savings.

Interest

Banks and credit unions pay you a small amount of money, called *interest*, on the money you put into a savings account. Banks can also sell you a certificate of deposit, called a CD, that will earn interest at a higher rate. If you purchase a CD, however, you agree to keep the money in the bank for a certain number years.

When you put money into a savings account, a CD, or a checking account, the money doesn't just stay there in a box with your name on it. The bank uses your money to make loans to other people. The bank charges the borrower a much higher interest rate than the bank pays you on your savings. This is one of the ways banks make money.

Each depositor insured to $100,000

FDIC
FEDERAL DEPOSIT INSURANCE CORPORATION

Save or Spend?

Save for larger items. Abby earns money babysitting and mowing lawns. She spends her money quickly on CDs, fast food, and jewelry. Abby's friend Sarah earns money at a hamburger stand. She spends half of her money and puts the other half in the bank. She is saving for a car.

Save to avoid paying interest. When Sarah first started saving at the bank, she was disappointed in the low amount of interest her money earned. Sarah's parents, however, showed her how much money she would save by not having to borrow money for a car.

Interest Earned and Paid

YOU EARN	
Savings Accounts at a Bank	.75% to 1%
CD Certificates at a Bank	1% to 3%

YOU PAY	
Credit Cards	8% to 23%
Bank or Credit Union Auto Loans	4% to 6%

How Does It Grow?

Account starting with $1,000 at 2.6% Interest (Multiply times 5 if you need $5000 in five years)

	Ending Balance
1 year	$1,026.25
2 years	$1,053.20
3 years	$1,080.85
4 years	$1,109.23
5 years	$1,138.35

Debt of $5,000 at 18% Interest

Length of Loan	Interest Paid	Principal Paid
1 year	$845.89	$677.75
2 years	$713.31	$810.33
3 years	$554.80	$968.84
4 years	$365.28	$1,158.36
5 years	$138.66	$1,384.72
Total paid:	**$2,617.94**	**$5,000.00**

Why Save?

You may have money today, but what about tomorrow? It's good to have some money saved. You can also use your savings as a down payment for expensive items like cars. If you save enough money to pay half the cost of a car before you buy it, you will only have to borrow enough money to pay for half of the cost. You will save thousands of dollars in interest.

Compound Interest

When financial institutions loan money, they charge **compound interest**. It adds up much faster than a one-time percentage of the total called "simple interest." How does compound interest work?

On a set schedule—once a day, week, or month—interest is figured as a percentage of the remaining balance (the amount still owed). This interest is then added to the balance, which makes it higher. The next time interest is figured, it is figured on the higher amount. Compound interest grows rapidly if the percentage of interest is high enough and if it is added often.

Compound interest works against you if you are the one paying off credit card debt or a car loan. By law, financial institutions have to tell you how much total interest you will end up paying on a loan if you make the lowest payment required each month.

If you take a long time to repay the loan, or keep charging on a credit card, you could end up paying more interest than you borrowed in the first place.

Higher-Risk, Higher Interest

If you are borrowing for a home or a car, the interest rate will be lower, because if you don't pay back the loan, the bank can take your car or your home. Loans for other purposes such as travel, to buy furniture, or other things, are riskier for the bank, and so they will charge a higher interest rate.

Cash, Checks, Cards

Today, personal checks, backed up by money deposited in a bank or credit union, are an easy way to pay for things. **Debit cards** can also be used to make purchases with money you already have in your checking account. **Credit cards**, on the other hand, are a way to postpone paying for things you buy. Each month, you can either pay the entire balance owed, or part of it. Credit card companies charge for the service of lending you money by adding interest to each month's bill.

Inflation

It doesn't take a financial expert to know that the prices of many things have gone up over the years. Inflation is the rate at which prices for everything, from a loaf of bread to a new car, increase over time.

For most of this century, the rate of inflation averaged about 3% per year. There are some exceptions. Electronic items such as calculators, televisions, DVD players, and laptop computers have gone way down in price because manufacturers have learned better ways to make them.

Chapter 12 Review

What Do You Remember?

1. Describe our free market economic system.
2. Give examples of jobs in the public sector and the private sector.
3. List three examples of the role of government in our free market system.
4. List three examples of goods and three examples of services.
5. When there is a lot of something, the price usually goes _____. When there is not enough of something people want, the price usually goes _____. This is called _____ _____ _____.
6. Describe three ways the government measures the economy.
7. List three of the most important industries in Nevada and give an example of each.
8. What industries in the state hire the most workers? What industry pays the highest wages?
9. What are the top three foreign countries that buy Nevada products?
10. What are some advantages of saving money?
11. What is the difference between a debit card and a credit card?
12. What is interest? How can you decrease the amount of interest you pay?

Activity

It's Your Economy

Copy the diagram on a piece of paper and work with a partner or a team to give at least two examples of these components of our economy.

Then choose one of these subjects and do more research on it. Present what you learned in an oral, written, dramatized, or illustrated form.

Money

Free Market Economy

Goods and Services

Economic Growth

Glossary

The definitions for words are as they are used in the chapters of this textbook.

A-B

accused: one charged with an offense; the defendant

adapt: to adjust or change to fit new circumstances

Allies: countries that fought on the side of the United States during World Wars I and II

amendment: a change or addition to a constitution

amenities: extras that give comfort, convenience, or enjoyment

annex: to take and incorporate a territory within the domain of an existing state

anonymous: not named or identified

appease: to bring to a state of peace

arbitrator: one who listens to both sides in a dispute and then makes a decision

arboretum: a place in which trees are grown for scientific and educational purposes

archaeologist: a scientist who studies artifacts and ruins

arid: dry

assault: a violent attack

assay: to analyze ore and judge the worth of it

atlatl: a spear thrower

atrium: an open patio or court inside a building

bankrupt: a state of financial ruin

bill: a proposal for a law

bootlegging: making, transporting, or selling alcoholic beverages

C

capital: items needed to produce other items; the money needed to buy resources and run a business

capital: the money needed to run a business

capitalism: a free market economic system where the majority of capital and business is privately owned and run by citizens, not the government

capitalism: private ownership of land, property, and business

census: a government count of the population

charity: the giving of money

checks and balances: a system that limits the power of any one branch of government

circulation: movement from person to person or place to place

civil case: a case involving personal, not criminal, issues

civilian: one who is not part of the military

commodity: any useful thing that is bought or sold

communism: government ownership of all land, property, and business

communist: one who believes in government ownership of all property, goods, and means of production, as opposed to a democratic government and capitalism

competition: others who produce and sell about the same item

compound interest: interest figured on the sum of the loan plus accrued interest on a regular basis

concentration camp: during World War II, a place where Jews and other prisoners were kept and murdered

conclude: to reach an agreement by reason or on the basis of evidence

conquistador: one who conquers; a leader in the Spanish conquest of America

conservationist: a person who advocates planned management of natural resources

conspiracy: unlawful acts of a group as the result of secret agreements

constituents: voters

consumer: one who buys goods and services

continental drift: the theory that the earth's continents were one land mass that drifted apart

controversial: relating to the expression of opposing views

controversy: a discussion or quarrel marked by expression of opposing views

convert: to change from one belief to another

credit card: a card that authorizes purchases on credit with added interest costs

creditor: a person or business to whom money is owed

criminal case: a case involving a serious crime such as robbery, murder, rape, or drug possession

currency: coins or paper money used as a medium of exchange

D

damages: money paid for personal loss or injury

debit card: a card that authorizes the cost of purchases to be subtracted from a bank balance

decade: a period of 10 years

decay: to undergo decomposition

defendant: the person accused of a crime

delegate: someone chosen to speak or act for a group

deport: to legally send out of the country

depression: a time when there are fewer jobs and means of production

destination: a place to which one is traveling

detonate: to explode with sudden violence

dialect: a regional variety of language

dictator: one with absolute rule

dictatorship: a form of government in which absolute power is concentrated in one leader or in a small close-knit group

dispute: to call into question

distinct: distinguishable from others

draft: a system of selecting people for compulsory military service

drought: a long period of dry weather

E

economic downturn: a time of declining production, jobs, and income

economics: the study of the production, distribution, and consumption of goods and services

elevation: the height above the level of the sea

endangered: in danger of disappearing from the earth altogether

envision: to see in the mind

ethnocentricity: believing your culture is superior

eventually: at an unspecified later time

evict: to force a renter out by legal process

F

fault line: a break in the earth's crust

felony: a grave crime declared by law

figurine: a small carved or molded figure

fluctuation: a shifting back and forth

fluted: having grooves

franchise: a business granted the right to market a company's goods or services

free market system: an economic system where anyone is free to start and run a business

G

gazebo: an open, free-standing roofed structure

gender: male or female

geography: the study of places and their physical and human characteristics and locations

geology: the study of rock and land formations to learn the physical history of the earth

glut: an excessive amount

goods: items that are made, bought, and sold

grist mill: a structure where grain is ground into flour

H-I

high grading: a practice of workers stealing ore from mines

Holocaust: a time during World War II when millions of Jews and others were taken from their homes and murdered

igneous rock: hardened magma that comes from inside the earth

illegal: against the law

illicit: unlawful; not permitted

illusionist: a slight-of-hand performer; a magician

imperial: relating to an empire

industrialist: one who owns or manages an industry

inflate: to enlarge or raise higher

influx: a coming in

initiative: a way for voters to propose their own laws to the legislature

innocent: free from legal guilt or fault

inquiry: a request for information

interchangeable: able to be used for many purposes

interest: a charge based on a percentage of the amount borrowed

interference: concern or opposition from others

interlocking: locked together or interconnected

internment camp: a place where some Japanese Americans were forced to live during World War II

intimidate: to make timid or fearful

intolerance: the quality of being unwilling to give or share social, political, or religious rights

invertebrate: an animal that lacks a spinal column

investor: one who commits money in order to receive financial gain

irrigation: the process of using canals to bring water to crops

isolationist: one who sees no need for government to be involved beyond its borders

L

lamentable: to be regretted or grieved for

lavish: marked by profusion or excess

legislature: a body of lawmakers consisting of two houses

legitimate: having legal status

luxury: a condition of abundance, great ease, and comfort

M

magnate: a person or rank, power, and influence

mar: to detract from wholeness or perfection

mass production: producing goods in quantity, usually by machine

medicinal: used to cure disease or relieve pain

memorable: worth remembering

metamorphic rock: rock that was deeply buried and greatly changed by pressure and heat

minimum wage: by law, the lowest amount a business can pay an employee

misdemeanor: a crime less serious than a felony

monarch: one who reigns over a kingdom and has superior rank and power

monopoly: when one company is the sole provider or producer a certain product

moral: having to do with high principles of human behavior

municipal: relating to a city

N-O

native: natural to a certain place

necessity: something that is necessary or indispensable

nuclear arms: atomic weapons of mass destruction

opportunist: one who takes advantage of opportunities with little regard for principles

opportunity cost: the cost of choices in time and money

P

pacifist: one who wants peace and is against war

per capita: per person

petition: a written request for action or change

petroglyph: Native American art carved into rock

pictograph: Native American art painted or drawn on rock

plate tectonics: the study of how the earth's crust moves

platform: a declaration of principles on which a person or group stands

plummet: to fall sharply and abruptly

popular sovereignty: a doctrine that government is created by and subject to the will of the people

posthumous: after death

preferential vote: a vote used only to show preference, or choice, of candidates

primary source: an original record made at the time

private sector: jobs for private businesses, not the government

productivity: ability to produce: output per man-hour

Progressive Era: a time of great reform and change during the first 20 years of the twentieth century

prophecy: a prediction of things to come

propose: to put forward a plan or idea

prosecutor: an attorney who tries to prove that the accused person committed a crime

prosperous: the state of having more than enough

public sector: jobs for the government

R

radiation: the process of emitting radiant energy in the form of waves or particles

radical: tending to make extreme changes in views and policies

radioactive: having nuclear properties

radiocarbon dating: dating old material by the amount of remaining carbon

ration: a share of food that is distributed evenly to all

recall: a vote to keep or remove an elected official from office

reclamation: reclaiming the land for productive use

referendum: a provision that allows voters to request that a current law be put on the ballot for public vote

refine: to separate minerals from ore

regulate: to govern or direct according to rule

reign: to rule; to be predominant

rendezvous: a gathering where fur trappers and Indians traded furs and supplies

renowned: celebrated; famous

republic: a government where citizens elect representatives to make laws

reputation: overall character as seen and judged by people

resemblance: the quality of being almost alike or similar

residency: an official place (town or country) of residence

retail: selling small quantities of goods to the final consumer; selling in stores

retaliation: returning like for like; revenge

rival: competing; each striving to equal or excel

roulette: a gambling game in which players bet on which compartment of a revolving wheel a small ball will come to rest in

S

sagacity: great wisdom

satire: a literary work holding up human vices and follies to ridicule

scholar: one who studies under a teacher; a learned person

scrip: paper certificates paid to workers to be used as money

secede: to leave one country in order to form another country

secondary source: something written or produced by someone who was not there at the time

sediment: loose sand, pebbles, and tiny shells of sea animals

sedimentary rock: rock that was formed by compaction of sediment such as sand or shells

seedy: shabby or run-down

services: in economics, services done for payment

shortage: when there is not enough of an item for all who want to buy it

shrewd: given to artful ways of dealing and clever awareness

sink: a depression in the land surface that has no outlet for the flow of water

skirmish: a minor fight in war

socialism: a form of collective ownership and distribution of goods instead of private ownership of property and goods.

specialization: concentrating one's efforts on a specific skill, product, or practice; producing only one kind of product or service

specimen: a portion of material to be tested

stabilize: to make more secure and avoid fluctuations

stalactite: a mineral formation that hangs from the ceiling of a cave

stalagmite: a mineral formation that forms upwards as water drips from above

stock: a financial share in a business

strike: a protest where workers stop work until new agreements are made

stringent: marked by strictness and severity

subsidy: a grant or gift of money

subtle: not obvious

suburban: having to do with the residential communities on the outskirts of a larger city

supernatural: relating to conditions beyond the visible universe; relating to a god or spirit

supply and demand: relating to how the amount of goods and services available and the demand for them affects production and price

suppress: to put down by authority or force

surplus: left over after needs are met

surrender: to give up and stop fighting during war

suspected: to be imagined guilty without proof or evidence

suspicious: tending to arouse suspicion and distrust

T-Z

technology: the practical application of knowledge, often using tools, machines, or electronics

temperance: the avoidance of alcoholic drink

toll road: a road that requires a fee for use

tradeoff: relating to making a choice by giving up something in order to get something else

transcontinental: spanning a continent

treacherous: hazardous; dangerous

tyranny: oppressive power exerted by government

vaudeville: a light comic theatrical performance including dialogue, dancing, and song

vicinity: nearby

workmen's compensation: money workers get when they are sick or injured on the job

Index

Credits

AP/Wide World Photos 184
Battista's Hole in the Wall 196
Boulder City Museum
    and Historical Association 155
Carolyn Fox 2, 3, 200-201
Chuck Place 34
Courtesy of Bureau of Reclamation 195
Courtesy of Congressman Jim Gibbons 210
Courtesy of Governor Kenny Guinn 211
Courtesy of Marie McMillan 188
Courtesy of Mrs. John F. Clymer
    and The Clymer Museum of Art 46-47
Courtesy of Sue Wagner 191(bottom right)
Gary Rasmussen vi-vii, 5, 6 (top), 11, 14, 25, 26
    (bottom), 27 (bottom), 30 (bottom), 51
Jeff Gnass 66-67, 191 (middle)
photo by Jim Stimson 6-7, 8, 16, 17
© 2004 John Dittli 40
John Burton 219, 226-227
Keith Eddington 50
Kerrick James 228 (bottom)
LDS Historical Department, Archives 37
Larry Angier 28
Larry Prossor 12, 15, 158

Las Vegas News Bureau 192 (bottom left),
    193 (center)
Library of Congress 68 (top), 71, 76 (top), 87
    (bottom), 89, 91, 95, 99, 123 (bottom right),
    126, 146, 149, 164, 167 (top), 169, 172,
    174 (top)
Madelyn Suttles 228 (top)
MGM Grand Hotel and Casino 192 (center)
NASA 198
National Archives 79, 81, 176
National Nuclear Security Administration
    178-179, 182, 183
Nevada Commission of Tourism 20
Nevada Historical Society 55 (middle), 68
    (bottom), 80, 103, 106-107, 108, 109, 110
    (bottom), 111, 113, 114, 116, 118-119, 120,
    122, 123, 125,128-129, 131, 132, 134-135,
    136 (top), 138 (bottom), 139, 160, 162-163,
    165, 167 (bottom), 189
Nevada State Museum 24
North Wind Picture Archives 41
Personal Collection of John Peterson,
    Brandon, Vermont 137
Phil Schofield cover, 13

Reno Sparks Convention
    and Visitors Authority 190
Sahara Hotel and Casino 192-193 (center)
Scottsbluff National Monument, paintings
    by William Henry Jackson 52, 62, 160
Susan Myers 187 (right)
The Bancroft Library,
    University of California, Berkeley 53, 93
The Beinecke Rare Book
    & Manuscript Library, Yale University 101
Tom Gamache 9
Tom Till 29
Travis Miller 142-143, 221, 229 (both)
UNLV Library, Special Collections 22-23, 31,
    33, 38, 39, 42, 43(bottom), 75, 76,
    (bottom), 78, 97, 100, 112, 130, 138 (top),
    145, 147, 149 (bottom right), 150, 151,
    153, 154, 156, 157, 159, 166, 168, 170,
    171, 174 (bottom), 175, 181, 194, 209, 212
United States Department of Energy 18
United States Capitol Historical Society 202
Utah Historical Society 58, 70 (top)